Cop

SECOND EDITION

D1065770

The Librarian's Copyright Companion

SECOND EDITION

by

James S. Heller

Paul Hellyer

Benjamin J. Keele

William S. Hein & Co., Inc.
Buffalo, New York
2012

Publisher's Cataloging in Publication

Heller, James S.

The librarian's copyright companion / by James S. Heller, Paul Hellyer,
Benjamin J. Keele. — 2nd ed. — Buffalo, NY : William S. Hein, 2012.

p. ; cm.

ISBN: 978-0-8377-3872-7 (print)

Revision of the 2004 edition by James S. Heller.

Includes bibliographical references and index.

Summary: The transition from print to digital continues. The Copyright Act
has changed a little, but not for the better. This book begins with the premise that
copyright exists to promote the dissemination of information, and while creators
have certain rights, so do users. This new edition updates every chapter and adds
a new chapter on the library as a publisher. Also included is information on recent
developments such as Creative Common licenses and the use of digital video (e.g.
YouTube) in the classroom.—Publisher.

Contents: General principles — Restrictions on the use of copyrighted materials
— Liability for infringement — Fair use (Section 107) — The library exemption
(Section 108) — Digital information and software — Licensing — Audiovisual
works and non-print media — The library as publisher — Conclusion —
Appendixes (resources, texts, guidelines, samples, model policies).

1. Copyright—United States—Handbooks, manuals, etc. 2. Librarians—United
States—Handbooks, manuals, etc. 3. Copyright infringement—United States.
4. Fair use (Copyright)—United States—Handbooks, manuals, etc. 5. Library
copyright policies—United States—Handbooks, manuals, etc. 6. Copyright and
electronic data processing—United States—Handbooks, manuals, etc. 7. Copyright
licenses—United States—Handbooks, manuals, etc. 8. Libraries—Special
collections—Nonbook materials—United States—Handbooks, manuals, etc.
9. Libraries—Publishing—United States—Handbooks, manuals, etc. I. Hellyer,
Paul (Paul Alan) II. Keele, Benjamin J. III. Title.

KF2995 .H45 2012   2012950442
346.7304/82—dc23   1211

Printed in the United States of America

This volume is printed on acid-free paper.

DEDICATION

ೞಀೞ

The Librarian's Copyright Companion, Second Edition, is dedicated to the staff of the College of William & Mary's Wolf Law Library.

TABLE OF CONTENTS

ಬಿಂಕ

Table of Contents

PREFACE

🏵🏵

A lot has happened since the first edition of *The Librarian's Copyright Companion* was published in 2004, and a lot hasn't changed.

As for what's new, it's more evolution than revolution. The transition from print to digital continues apace: digital format is the default version for periodicals and journals in many libraries, and YouTube and other digital media are now commonly used in teachers' classrooms.[1] In academia, many libraries have created digital archives or scholarly repositories, and have themselves become publishers. Print reserves have pretty much given way to e-reserves and commercial products like Blackboard. In a decision reached just as this book was going to press, a U.S. District Court in Georgia clarified the meaning of fair use for materials placed in e-reserves. The decision has been viewed as a win for libraries, but may be appealed.

The Copyright Act has changed a little, but not for the better. Efforts to amend the library exemption by the Section 108 Study Group went nowhere after three years of hard work. The fair use (section 107) and the public performance and display exemptions (section 110, which includes the TEACH Act) also remain unchanged. The U.S. Supreme Court continues to affirm anything Congress does that expands the term of copyright (*Eldred v. Ashcroft* in 2003 and *Golan v. Holder* in 2012).

What also hasn't changed is the fact that the publishing/copyright owner industry still promotes its views loudly and clearly. A great example is the October 2011 issue of *Information Today: The Newspaper for Users and Producers of Digital Information Services*, which had as its lead article "Armstrong: the Voice of Copyright." Tracey Armstrong, President and CEO of the Copyright Clearance Center (CCC), is not the voice of

---

[1] YouTube even has its own "copyright center" for owners, users, and educators: http://www.YouTube.com/t/copyright_center.

copyright. Ms. Armstrong may be a voice of copyright representing and advocating for copyright owners, publishers, and other producers of intellectual property, but she is definitely not the voice of copyright.

Here are some excerpts from the *Information Today* article, followed by our comments:

> Armstrong: "We are looking at licenses that can be used on mobile devices, on laptops, on PC's, wherever you are in your enterprise or outside, when you're visiting clients on the road or studying abroad, whatever you're doing."

Us: It's nice to be able to get information anywhere and everywhere. But are you ready to pay for content every time you use it? What about fair use?

> Armstrong: "[The CCC is] about access and ease of use and using licensing to help enable that. . . . We're not about locking up content; we're about creating access. Think of us as the keys to creating access to that content through licensing."

Us: Let's call a spade a spade. The Copyright Clearance Center knows that in a digital world you can't keep content behind a locked door. But they would like you to believe that there is a door, that it is locked, and that you need to pay them for the key. The CCC continues to "educate" users about the risk of infringement, and they are effective. Many in the private sector have simply abandoned fair use and just pay royalties through the CCC. They now have their eyes on academic libraries, and you can bet that public libraries are next.

Our book is another voice of copyright, written by three lawyer librarians. We understand that interpreting copyright can be tricky. There's some black, some white, and a lot of gray. When we are confronted with a copyright question we approach it as a lawyer does: (1) what are the facts; (2) what does the Copyright Act say; and (3) are there court decisions addressing facts like these?

The Association of American Publishers, the Copyright Clearance Center, and other rights organizations such as Attributor begin with the premise that if you want to use something, you have to pay for it. We begin with a different premise: copyright exists to promote the dissemination of information, and while creators have certain rights, so do users. There are many situations where users do need permission or pay royalties.

But there also are many situations where users do not need to ask for permission because the use is permitted under the Copyright Act.

The 2012 edition updates every chapter from the first edition of *The Librarian's Copyright Companion*, and we add a new chapter on the library as a publisher. You will find information on recent developments such as Creative Commons licenses and the use of digital video (e.g., YouTube) in the classroom. And we continue to believe there is a need to counter the self-serving voices of publishers and copyright owners, and those who do their bidding.

Chapter One
GENERAL PRINCIPLES
𝕰𝕺𝕮𝕾

The Bureau of National Affairs (BNA), a major legal publisher, puts this warning in many of their publications:

> Photocopying any portion of this publication is strictly prohibited unless express written authorization is first obtained from BNA Books . . . . Authorization to photocopy items for internal or personal use, or the internal or personal use of specific clients, is granted by BNA Books for libraries and other users registered with the Copyright Clearance Center (CCC) . . . provided that $1.00 per page is paid directly to CCC . . . .

We didn't ask BNA for permission to reprint their copyright statement, nor did we pay anything for it. But we're not worried about being sued. Under the fair use doctrine, copyright law allows authors to quote each other for purposes of criticism.[1] So here's our criticism of BNA's warning: although it may be an accurate statement of BNA's wishes, it's not an accurate statement of the law. Users are often allowed to copy portions of copyrighted material without permission; our use of BNA's copyright statement is just one example. And if you don't need permission, you don't need to pay $1.00, or *any* amount, to the Copyright Clearance Center.

Statements like BNA's are not uncommon. Publishers and pro-publisher organizations routinely make overreaching statements about copyright law. As you may have already guessed, our book is not written from the publishers' perspective. It's written by librarians, for librarians.

If you believe that access to information and creative works ought to be a privilege rather than a right, you probably wouldn't have picked up this book. Librarians like to share intellectual property. That's our job.

---

[1] We discuss fair use in Chapter Four.

This creates some tension between copyright law and the work that librarians do. We should stay within the law, but that doesn't mean surrendering to publisher scare tactics. In this book, we'll show you how to do your job while staying within the boundaries of copyright law.

Copyright Defined

> ### 1.1. Copyright
> - Exclusive Rights
> - Original Work
> - Specified Time

First things first. The Copyright Act begins with definitions of about fifty words and phrases, but not the word "copyright."[2] Subject to some limitations, a copyright is the exclusive ownership of and right to make use of an original literary, musical, or artistic work for a specified period of time.

Copyright is one part of what is called "intellectual property", which also includes patents, trademarks, and trade secrets. Like copyrighted materials, patents and trademarks are protected by federal law. Patents apply to useful inventions (such as drugs or computer chips), while trademarks are names or logos used to market goods or services (such as Coca-Cola or Kleenex). State and federal laws protect a company's trade secrets (such as Coca-Cola's formula for Coke). Because patents, trademarks, and trade secrets have little impact on librarians' work, the subject of our book is limited to copyrights.

---

[2] 17 U.S.C. § 101 (2006).

The Copyright Act

1.2. U.S. Constitution, Article I, Section 8, Clause 8

Congress may "promote the progress of science and the useful arts by securing for a limited time to authors and inventors the exclusive right to their writings and discoveries."

Copyright protection does not just "happen." The U.S. Constitution authorizes Congress to pass copyright legislation,[3] and Congress has enacted legislation pursuant to that authorization. The Copyright Act of 1976[4]—the legislation now in force in the United States—was the first complete revision of our federal copyright statute since 1909.

Congress recognized as early as the 1950s that the 1909 Act was outdated. But Congress, as we know, usually moves more at the speed of the tortoise than the hare. The 1976 Act, which took more than twenty years to pass, was only the fourth major revision of our federal copyright statute since the first such Act was passed in 1790,[5] the others occurring in 1831,[6] 1870,[7] and 1909.[8]

In drafting the 1976 Act, Congress tried to balance the often competing interests of copyright owners and those who use copyrighted works. Input from creators, publishers, educators, librarians, and other interested parties resulted in an Act one commentator called "a body of detailed rules reminiscent of the Internal Revenue Code."[9]

But we are not given detailed rules for everything. Occasionally Congress gave us guidelines, such as those for classroom copying and off-air taping, rather than legislation. Although not part of the Act, some guide-

---

[3] U.S. CONST. art. I, § 8, cl. 8.
[4] Pub. L. No. 94-553, 90 Stat. 2541 (1976).
[5] Act of May 31, 1790, ch. 15, 1 Stat. 124 (1790).
[6] Act of Feb. 3, 1831, ch. 16, 4 Stat. 436 (1831).
[7] Act of July 8, 1870, ch. 230, 16 Stat. 198 (1870).
[8] Act of March 4, 1909, ch. 230, 35 Stat. 1075 (1909).
[9] 1 MELVILLE NIMMER, NIMMER ON COPYRIGHT, Preface to the 1978 Comprehensive Treatise Revision.

lines were included in its legislative history and have been cited by courts attempting to interpret Congressional intent. Additionally, some provisions of the Act were intentionally left ambiguous to allow for later interpretation by the courts.

Congress recognized the needs of educators, scholars, and librarians in the 1976 Act, although not always to their satisfaction. Teaching, scholarship, and research are specifically mentioned in section 107, the fair use provision. Library copying is addressed in section 108. Certain public performances for instructional purposes are permitted under section 110, which was amended to address distance education in the 2002 TEACH Act. Each of those sections is discussed in greater detail later in this book.

The 1976 Act also created a single structure of copyright, one which is governed by federal law. This means that if you research a copyright question, you need only use federal sources of law such as the United States Code and decisions from federal courts.

Copyright does *not* place an author's work in a lockbox. The primary purpose of copyright is *not* to compensate creators. The U.S. Supreme Court has stated, many times, that copyright is a means to a greater societal end: the dissemination and promotion of knowledge.[10] As librarians, we promote the dissemination of knowledge. With this in mind, when there is a close call whether a certain use is or is not allowed, we tend to resolve the answer in favor of the library or the user, rather than the copyright owner.

Organizations that represent publishers and other copyright owners, such as the CCC and the Association of American Publishers (AAP), take a more restrictive view of user rights. When you read statements from organizations representing publishers and copyright owners about permissible uses of copyrighted works, remember whence they came.

---

[10] "The sole interest of the United States and the primary object in conferring the monopoly [i.e., copyright protection] lie in the general benefits derived by the public from the labors of authors." Fox Films Corp. v. Doyal, 286 U.S. 123, 127 (1932). "[T]he ultimate aim is, by this incentive, to stimulate artistic creativity for the general public good." Twentieth Century Music Corp. v. Aiken, 422 U.S. 151, 156 (1975). *See also* United States v. Paramount Pictures, 334 U.S. 131, 158 (1948) ("[C]opyright law . . . makes reward to the owner a secondary consideration"); Feist Publ'ns v. Rural Tel. Serv., 499 U.S. 340, 349 (1991). Congress has made similar statements. Working on the Berne Convention Implementation Act of 1988, the House Judiciary Committee wrote, "The primary objective of our copyright laws is not to reward the author, but rather to secure for the public the benefits from the creations of authors." H.R. REP. NO. 100-609, at 22 (1988).

Copyrightable Works

1.3. Section 102
Copyrightable Works

- Literary works
- Musical works
- Dramatic works
- Pantomimes and choreographic works
- Pictorial, graphic, and sculptural works
- Motion pictures and other audiovisual works
- Sound recordings
- Architectural works

If the work is original, and fixed in any tangible medium of expression

But not ideas, procedures, processes, systems, concepts . . .

Copyright protection is very broad. The Copyright Act provides that a wide array of works may be copyrighted, as long as they are "original" and "fixed in any tangible medium of expression."[11] "Original" means that the work was independently created by the author (not copied from another source) and has at least a minimal level of creativity.[12] Only the parts of a work that are original are subject to copyright protection.[13]

There must also be an *expression* for copyright to attach. This is often called the idea/expression dichotomy: Only the expression of an idea is protected by copyright, not the idea by itself.[14] For example, you cannot copyright the idea of a romance between a northern gunrunner and a southern belle in the post–Civil War South, but Margaret Mitchell could copyright the *expression* of that idea in her novel *Gone With The Wind*.

---

[11] 17 U.S.C. § 102(a) (2006).
[12] Feist Publ'ns v. Rural Tel. Serv., 499 U.S. 340, 345 (1991) ("The requisite level of creativity is extremely low; even a slight amount will suffice.").
[13] *Id.* at 348.
[14] 17 U.S.C. § 102(b) (2006); SunTrust Bank v. Houghton Mifflin Co., 268 F.3d 1257, 1263–64 (11th Cir. 2001); Ho v. Taflove, 648 F.3d 489, 497–98 (7th Cir. 2011).

Because procedures or methods of operation are not subject to copyright protection, something like a simple recipe cannot be copyrighted.[15] A Julia Child cookbook that includes recipes, descriptive text, and illustrations (and presumably many calories), however, is copyrightable. If you doubt whether a computer program is an unprotected method of operation or instead protected expression, remove the doubt: Computer programs *may* be protected by copyright.[16]

Copyright is available only for works "fixed in a tangible medium of expression."[17] Fixation occurs when the embodiment of the work "is sufficiently permanent or stable to permit it to be perceived, reproduced, or otherwise communicated for a period of more than transitory duration."[18] Fixation is easily accomplished. The legislative history to the 1976 Act notes the breadth of Congress's intent:

> Under the bill it makes no difference what the form, manner, or medium of fixation may be—whether it is in words, numbers, notes, sounds, pictures, or any other graphic or symbolic indicia, whether embodied in a physical object in written, printed, photographic, sculptural, punched, magnetic, or any other stable form, and whether it is capable of perception directly or by means of any machine or device 'now known or later developed.'[19]

In other words, text, images, and graphics—essentially anything we can see in print, on a television screen, on an iPad, or in some other medium—are sufficiently "fixed" to be copyrighted.

A helpful guide from the U.S. Copyright Office lists several categories of works generally *not* eligible for federal copyright protection for the reasons outlined above:

- Titles, names, short phrases, and slogans; familiar symbols or designs; mere variations of typographic ornamentation, lettering, or coloring; mere listings of ingredients or contents;
- Ideas, procedures, methods, systems, processes, concepts, principles, discoveries, or devices, as distinguished from a description, explanation, or illustration; and

---

[15] 17 U.S.C. § 102(b) (2006).
[16] Computer Mgmt. Assistance Co. v. Robert F. DeCastro, Inc., 220 F.3d 396, 400 (5th Cir. 2000); Atari Games Corp. v. Nintendo of Am., Inc., 975 F.2d 832, 838 (Fed. Cir. 1992).
[17] 17 U.S.C. § 102(a) (2006).
[18] *Id.* § 101.
[19] H.R. REP. NO. 94-1476, at 52 (1976).

- Works consisting entirely of information that is common property and containing no original authorship (for example: standard calendars, height and weight charts, tape measures and rulers, and lists or tables taken from public documents or other common sources).[20]

One other category that should be added is impromptu speeches or presentations. The written version of a speech will be protected because it meets the fixation requirement, but the speech itself will not be protected under the Copyright Act unless it was taped or otherwise "fixed" by the speaker or someone authorized by the speaker.[21]

Although the works mentioned above are not copyrightable, they may be subject to other types of legal protection, such as patent, trademark, trade secret, or unfair competition law.

Copyright Notice

A copyright notice is not necessary for a work to be copyrighted.[22] Copyright attaches automatically when an original work is created. A work is created "when it is fixed in a copy or phonorecord for the first time."[23]

There *are* advantages to including a copyright notice. First, the notice identifies the copyright owner and indicates the date the work was published. Second, it informs the public that the work is protected. Third, the notice makes it difficult for a defendant in an infringement suit to claim that he or she was an innocent infringer—someone who was not aware and had no reason to believe that his or her acts were infringing. This is important for copyright owners, for a court may reduce statutory damages if the infringer was an "innocent" infringer.[24]

---

[20] U.S. COPYRIGHT OFFICE, CIRCULAR 1: COPYRIGHT BASICS (revised Aug. 2010).

[21] 17 U.S.C. §§ 101, 102 (2006).

[22] *Id.* §§ 401–405.

[23] The U.S. Copyright Office writes:

> "Copies" are material objects from which a work can be read or visually perceived either directly or with the aid of a machine or device, such as books, manuscripts, sheet music, film, videotape, or microfilm. "Phonorecords" are material objects embodying fixations of sounds (excluding, by statutory definition, motion picture soundtracks), such as cassette tapes, CDs, or vinyl disks. Thus, for example, a song (the "work") can be fixed in sheet music ("copies") or in phonograph disks ("phonorecords"), or both.

U.S. COPYRIGHT OFFICE, CIRCULAR 1: COPYRIGHT BASICS (revised Aug. 2010).

[24] 17 U.S.C. § 504(c)(2) (2006).

The Copyright Act specifies the form and position of the copyright notice for "visually perceptible copies," which are those that can be seen or read. The notice must be "affixed to the copies in such a manner and location as to give reasonable notice of the claim of copyright,"[25] and should include the following elements:

- the symbol © or the word "Copyright," or the abbreviation "Copr.";
- the year of first publication of the work; and
- the name of the copyright owner.[26]

Although copyright notices provide important information, watch out for notices that try to tell you what you cannot do, like the notice from BNA that we printed at the beginning of this chapter. Here's another one that appears on the verso of the title page of Haynes Johnson's *The Best of Times: American in the Clinton Years*:

> All rights reserved. No part of this publication may be reproduced or transmitted in any form or by any means, electronic or mechanical including photocopy, recording, or any information storage and retrieval system, without permission in writing from the publisher.

This notice suggests that you cannot copy anything from this book. That is not true. A simple copyright notice cannot dilute your rights. You do not agree to be bound by a copyright notice simply by buying a book. You *will* honor binding contracts—usually for digital products—to which you have agreed. But just because a copyright notice says "you cannot do this" does not mean that you can't.

On the other hand, some publications expressly permit certain copying without payment of fees. Most scholarly journals published by U.S. law schools have a notice similar to the one you find in the *William and Mary Law Review*:

> Copyright © 2012 by the *William and Mary Law Review*. Except as otherwise provided, the author of each article in this issue has granted permission for copies of that article to be made available for classroom use, provided that (1) the copies are distributed at or below cost, (2) the author and the *William and Mary Law Review* are identified, (3) proper notice of copyright is affixed to each copy and (4) the *William and Mary Law Review* is notified of the use.

---

[25] *Id.* § 401(c).
[26] *Id.* § 401(b).

Broader and more specific is the notice in *The Journal of Economic Literature* and the publications of the American Economic Association:

> Permission to make digital or hard copies of part or all of this work for personal or classroom use is granted without fee provided that copies are not distributed for profit or direct commercial advantage and that copies show this notice on the first page or initial screen of a display along with the full citation, including the name of the author. Copyrights for components of this work owned by others than AEA must be honored. Abstracting with credit is permitted. The author has the right to republish, post on servers, redistribute to lists and use any component of this work in other works. For others to do so requires prior specific permission and/or a fee.

The Bottom Line: First, assume that a work is protected by copyright—even if it does not include a copyright notice—unless you know it's in the public domain. Second, copyright notices that purport to tell you what you may or may not do can't limit your fair use rights or other rights under the Copyright Act, but they may allow you to do more than the law would otherwise permit. Third, if you agree by contract not to use a work in a particular way, you will abide by the contract.

Works in the Public Domain

1.4. Works in the Public Domain
- Materials never were copyrighted
- Copyright has expired
- Works of the U.S. government
- Laws of state and local governments

Works in the public domain are not protected by copyright. When a work is in the public domain—or if it *is* protected by copyright but the use is allowed under the Copyright Act—you do not have to receive permission, or pay royalties, to use it. Works in the public domain include those that never were copyrighted, works in which copyright has expired, and works of the United States government.

Under the Act, works of the U.S. government—any work prepared by an officer or employee of the federal government as part of his or her official duties—may not be copyrighted.[27] Although this appears straightforward, there are some possible twists, such as works prepared for the government under contract, and copyrighted works included in government publications.

Whether a work prepared by an independent contractor under a federal contract or grant is copyrightable generally depends on the terms of the contract between the government and the contractor. The status also may be governed by legislation or agency regulations.[28] Therefore, even though a work prepared by the RAND Corporation under a government contract may have been funded with taxpayer dollars (which one might think should place it in the public domain), it may be protected by copyright if the contract or a federal statute or regulation so provides.

A copyrighted work does not lose its copyright status just because it is included in a work of the U.S. government. For example, a senator wants to include in the *Congressional Record* a copyrighted poem written by one of his constituents. As a work of the federal government, the *Record* is not protected by copyright. However, the poem does not lose its copyright protection because it is reprinted in the *Record.*

Conversely, a non-copyrightable governmental work that is reprinted by a private publisher, or a portion of a governmental work included in a privately created work, does not lose its public domain status.[29] For example,

- A publisher who reprints all of the federal statutes dealing with public education cannot claim copyright in the text of the laws.
- A publisher who reprints a report by the U.S. Surgeon General cannot claim copyright in the text of the report.
- A publisher who includes in its newsletter proposed and enacted federal regulations from the Federal Register and the Code of Federal Regulations cannot claim copyright in the text of the regulations.

---

[27] 17 U.S.C. § 105 (2006).
[28] H.R. REP. NO. 94-1476, at 59.
[29] *See* Building Officials & Code Adm'rs, Inc. v. Code Tech, Inc., 628 F.2d 730 (1st Cir. 1980).

Some materials published by state or local governments—unlike works of the federal government—may be copyrighted.[30] This means that a report published by a state department of transportation *may* be protected. As more and more states place more and more information on their websites, states are publicizing their perceived intellectual property rights. For example, here is what the state of Florida writes about its "MyFlorida" website:

> MyFlorida.com is owned and operated by THE STATE OF FLORIDA, DEPARTMENT OF MANAGEMENT SERVICES (referred to as "DMS" herein). No material from MyFlorida.com or any Web site owned, operated, licensed or controlled by THE STATE OF FLORIDA or DMS may be copied, reproduced, republished, uploaded, posted, transmitted, or distributed in any way. Materials may be downloaded on any single personal computer, for non-commercial use only providing all copyright and other proprietary notices are kept intact. Modification of the materials or use of the materials for any other purpose is a violation of THE STATE OF FLORIDA and DMS's copyright and other proprietary rights. For purposes of this Agreement, the use of any such material on any other Web site or networked computer environment is prohibited. All trademarks, service marks, and trade names are proprietary to THE STATE OF FLORIDA and DMS.[31]

Who are these Cocoanuts? The State of Florida claims copyright not only in its website as a compilation (discussed below), but in *all* of the materials in the website. That is simply incorrect. State or local governmental works such as court decisions, statutes, regulations, ordinances, and attorney general opinions—in other words, the law—may *not* be copyrighted.[32]

Some words of caution: Although judicial decisions are not protected by copyright, two federal appeals courts had differing conclusions as to whether a publisher may claim copyright in a *compilation* of court decisions that are published as case reporters. In 1986, the U.S. Court of

---

[30] Although most states do not expressly claim copyright in all state publications, there are exceptions. Pennsylvania, for example, gives its Department of General Services the power and the duty "to copyright, in the name of the Commonwealth, all publications of the Commonwealth, or of any department, board, or commission or officer thereof, including the State Reports . . . ." PA. STAT. ANN. tit. 71, § 636(i) (West 2010).

[31] MYFLORIDA.COM COPYRIGHT STATEMENT: CONDITIONS OF USE, *available at* http://www.myflorida.com/myflorida/copyright.html.

[32] Banks v. Manchester, 128 U.S. 244, 253–54 (1888); Wheaton v. Peters, 33 U.S. 591, 668 (1834); Veeck v. S. Bldg. Code Cong. Int'l, 293 F.3d 791, 796 (5th Cir. 2002) (en banc).

Appeals for the Eighth Circuit held that West Publishing Company's arrangements of judicial decisions in its reporters were original works of authorship entitled to copyright protection.[33] But a decade later, the Second Circuit came to the opposite conclusion when it held that West Publishing could not claim copyright in the arrangement of its reporters because it lacked the creativity necessary for copyright protection.[34]

It seems clear that court records—the oral or written transcript of the trial proceedings—are in the public domain.[35] It appears that briefs submitted by attorneys to federal or state courts also may be freely copied; while no case has squarely decided the issue, at least two courts have indicated that court briefs enter the public domain when they become part of the judicial record.[36] In fact, briefs are commonly copied into microformat, and are digitized and made freely available on many websites.

Statutes and ordinances that emanate from state or local governments are not copyrightable. It is unclear, however, whether a privately published, subject-arranged compilation of state statutes or local ordinances—in other words, a "code"—is in the public domain.[37] Furthermore, it remains an open question whether statutes or administrative codes prepared by private entities (such as a building code) that are subsequently adopted by a state or local government enter the public domain when they are adopted into law.[38]

You may copy sections from a federal, state, or local code. It does not matter if you are a student, a teacher, or an attorney who charges $300 an hour. You also may copy sections from a privately prepared federal, state,

---

[33] West Publ'g Co. v. Mead Data Center, Inc., 799 F.2d 1219 (8th Cir. 1986), *cert. denied* 479 U.S. 1070 (1987).

[34] Matthew Bender & Co., Inc. v. West Publ'g Co., 158 F.3d 674 (2d Cir. 1998).

[35] Lipman v. Massachusetts, 475 F.2d 565 (1st Cir. 1973).

[36] In a case in which the court was deciding whether audiotapes played in court and introduced into evidence were in the public domain, the U.S. Court of Appeals for the District of Columbia wrote that "until destroyed or placed under seal, tapes played in open court and admitted into evidence—no less than the court reporter's transcript, the parties' brief, and the judge's orders and opinions—remain a part of the public domain." Cottone v. Reno, 193 F.3d 550, 554 (D.C. Cir. 1999). *See also* Krynicki v. Falk II, 983 F.2d 74, 77 (7th Cir. 1992).

[37] Texas v. West Publ'g Co., 882 F.2d 171 (5th Cir. 1989).

[38] In Building Officials & Code Adm'rs, Inc. v. Code Tech, Inc., 628 F.2d 730, 735 (1st Cir. 1980), a federal appeals court was doubtful that a privately prepared model building code would retain its copyright after enactment by a state. More recently, the Fifth Circuit held that after a model building code was adopted into law by two municipalities, the creator could not prevent a non-profit organization from posting the codes on its website. Veeck v. Southern Bldg. Code Cong. Int'l, Inc., 293 F.3d 791, 800 (5th Cir. 2002) (en banc).

or local code, for the law is not protected by copyright. But do not copy or scan an entire volume of a privately prepared code for any purpose—even an educational one—without permission. Remember that codes produced by private sector publishers (in the United States this generally is Lexis and West) include copyrightable information such as references, research aides, notes, and case summaries.

What about using photographs or scans that someone else has taken of works in the public domain? Do you need to get permission from the photographer or scanner to use their work? It depends. If a photographer takes a shot of the Venus de Milo, the photograph will almost certainly be protected by copyright, even though the sculpture itself is in the public domain. On the other hand, if a researcher scans a page from the *Congressional Record*, that scan almost certainly does not count as a copyrightable work. It's just a copy, which the public is free to use without permission.

What's the difference? A photograph of a sculpture involves some creativity in selecting the lighting, angle, exposure and so on. Conversely, scanning the *Congressional Record* is a mechanical process devoid of creativity, and so the scan doesn't qualify as an original work of authorship under Section 102. This doesn't mean that photographs of public domain works are always copyrightable and scans never are.[39] It means you have to consider the facts of each case. If in doubt, create your own photograph or scan of the public domain work instead of using someone else's.[40]

Compilations and Collective Works

1.5. Section 103 Compilations and Derivative Works

- Protection for original material contributed by the author
- Independent of and does not affect copyright status of pre-existing material

---

[39] *See* Bridgeman Art Library, Ltd. v. Corel Corp., 36 F. Supp. 2d 191, 197 (S.D.N.Y. 1999) (holding that photographs that are "slavish copies" of paintings are not copyrightable).
[40] We discuss this issue more when we cover digital repositories in Chapter Nine.

Copyright in compilations and collective works is a bit different from copyright in an individual work such as an article or a novel. Under the Copyright Act, a collective work is "a work, such as a periodical issue, anthology, or encyclopedia, in which a number of contributions, constituting separate and independent works in themselves, are assembled into a collective whole."[41] A compilation is "a work formed by the collection and assembling of pre-existing materials or of data that are selected, coordinated, or arranged in such a way that the resulting work as a whole constitutes an original work of authorship."[42]

There are two possible levels of protection for collective works. Take, for example, a compilation of twentieth-century poetry. Let's call it *The 100 Best Poems of the 20th Century*. The underlying materials—each individual poem—are protected by copyright. Furthermore, the entire work also may be protected as a copyrightable compilation if the editor exhibited sufficient skill and judgment selecting, organizing and arranging the poems. Here, copyright will extend only to the original material contributed by the editor: the selection and arrangement of the underlying content. Under the Act

> The copyright in a compilation or derivative work extends only to the material contributed by the author of such work, as distinguished from the preexisting material employed in the work, and does not imply any exclusive right in the preexisting material. The copyright in such work is independent of, and does not affect or enlarge the scope, duration, ownership, or subsistence of, any copyright protection in the preexisting material.[43]

This means that if you want to copy one of the poems from the anthology, then you will need permission from the person who holds copyright in the poem, *unless* the use is otherwise permitted under the Copyright Act as, say, a fair use. If *The 100 Best Poems of the 20th Century* is also protected as a compilation, someone who wants to copy a significant number of its poems may need to get permission from whomever has copyright in it as a compilation, generally the editor or the publisher.

---

[41] 17 U.S.C. § 101 (2006).
[42] *Id.*
[43] 17 U.S.C. § 103(b) (2006). The Copyright Act treats similarly protection for collective and derivative works. The copyright owner's right to prepare derivative works is addressed in the next chapter.

If the compilation consists of underlying material that is in the public domain, such as facts, the facts are not protected. Here copyright protection exists, if at all, in the particular selection or arrangement, not in the underlying content. For example, both *Guinness World Records* and *The World Almanac and Book of Facts* may record that Mt. Everest, at 29,035 feet, is the highest place on earth. The copyright owners of these two compilations cannot protect this information, nor any other facts in their almanacs. They may, however, copyright their works as compilations, where protection extends to the selection and arrangement of the facts in their respective publications.

Not all compilations may be copyrighted, however. Take, for example, the common white pages telephone directory. In *Feist Publications, Inc. v. Rural Telephone Service*,[44] the U.S. Supreme Court ruled that a garden-variety white pages telephone directory contained so little creativity in selecting, arranging or coordinating the unprotected underlying facts that it could not be copyrighted as a compilation. The *Feist* decision discredited what is called the "sweat of the brow" doctrine: effort alone will not make a work copyrightable. The Court made it clear that compilations require a certain level of creativity to be afforded copyright protection: the creator must exercise some skill and discretion in selecting and arranging the underlying information.[45]

Legislative efforts designed to effectively overturn the *Feist* decision have centered on database protection legislation. In the United States, such legislation was introduced in Congress, but never passed into law.[46] On the international front, although database protection legislation has not been enacted under the Berne Convention, a European Union directive creates *sui generis* protection of databases if there was a "substantial investment in either the obtaining, verification or presentation of the contents to prevent extraction and/or re-utilization of the whole or of a substantial part."[47]

---

[44] 499 U.S. 340 (1991).

[45] "Thus, even a directory that contains absolutely no protectable written expression, only facts, meets the constitutional minimum for copyright protection if it features an original selection or arrangement." 499 U.S. at 348.

[46] H.R. 3531, 104th Cong. (1996), H.R. 2652, 105th Cong. (1998), S. 2291, 105th Cong. (1998), H.R. 1858, 106th Cong. (1999), H.R. 354, 106th Cong. (1999), H.R. 3261, 108th Cong. (2003), H.R. 3872, 108th Cong. (2004).

[47] Legal Protection of Databases, Council Directive 96/9, 1996 O.J. (L 77) 20.

The Bottom Line: You may use the height of Mt. Everest and other facts from Guinness or any other source as much as you want. But if you scan *Guinness World Records*, rename it *My Big Book of Facts*, and publish it in print or on the web, you violate Guinness' compilation copyright.

Duration of Copyright Protection

Section 302 of the Act prescribes the term of copyright protection. Copyright protection lasts much longer today than it did under the original 1790 Copyright Act, which prescribed a term of fourteen years with a possible fourteen-year renewal.[48] In the period immediately prior to the 1976 Act, copyrights were issued for twenty-eight years, with an option to renew and extend the copyright for an additional twenty-eight-year term.[49] The 1976 Act changed the way we calculate copyright duration by factoring in the author's lifespan and eliminating the renewal requirement. In 1998, the Sonny Bono Copyright Term Extension Act further lengthened copyright duration.[50]

Here are the current terms for the most common types of work published or created after 1978, the effective date of the 1976 Act:

- For a work by a single author, protection lasts for the author's life plus another seventy years.
- When a work is authored by two or more individuals (called joint authorship), copyright lasts for seventy years after the death of last surviving author.
- Copyright in anonymous works, works by corporate authors, and works made for hire, last for ninety-five years from the year of first publication or 120 years from its creation, whichever expires first.

The length of copyright protection gets more complicated than this, particularly with regard to works created before January 1, 1978. Here are some other terms:

- A work published from 1923 to 1963 and that has a copyright notice is protected for twenty-eight years, with the possibility of an additional

---

[48] Act of May 31, 1790, ch. 15, § 1, 1 Stat. 124.
[49] 17 U.S.C. § 24 (1970).
[50] Pub. L. No. 105-298, 112 Stat. 2827 (1998).

sixty-seven years if the renewal option is exercised; if not, the work enters the public domain.

- A work published between 1964 and 1977 is protected, if it had a copyright notice, for ninety-five years from the date of publication.
- A work created before 1978 but not published by 1978 is protected for the author's life plus seventy years, unless the work was published between 1978 and 2002—in which case the work is protected for the author's life plus seventy years or through 2047, whichever is greater.

The crucial question for works published between 1923 and 1978 is whether all formalities—copyright notice, registration, and renewal—were fulfilled. Looking for a copyright notice is easy; just examine the work to see if there is a copyright notice anywhere.

Finding out if a work was registered or renewed is a bit trickier. For works published between 1923 and 1963, you need to check if the work was renewed, because if it was registered but not renewed, the copyright has expired. If the work was published in 1964 or later and has a copyright notice, it is going to be under copyright protection for quite some time.

Researching copyright renewals can be challenging, but some useful tools are available. The Copyright Office published the *Catalog of Copyright Entries*, a set of books containing copyright registrations and renewals. Many of these volumes have been digitized and are available on several web sites.[51] Search these databases by title and author to see if the copyright of the work you are interested in was renewed. The databases tend to each have parts of the entire set (for instance, all the book renewals for a certain period), so pay attention to their scope.

If you don't find evidence of the copyright being renewed, then the copyright most likely expired. We say most likely because digitized records are still incomplete and works by foreign authors had their copyrights restored by Congress to comply with the Berne Convention. Copyright Office Circular 22 has some advice and details how to request a search of the Copyright Office's records.[52] This is an expensive option, so it should be a last resort.

---

[51] The University of Pennsylvania has a helpful collection of links to and descriptions of the various collections at http://onlinebooks.library.upenn.edu/cce/.

[52] U.S. Copyright Office, Circular 22: How to Investigate the Copyright Status of a Work (rev'd Nov. 2010), *available at* http://www.copyright.gov/circs/circ22.pdf.

Unfortunately for users, a work that has fallen into the public domain will not necessarily stay there. In a recent case, the U.S. Supreme Court ruled that Congress can reinstate copyright protection for materials that were previously in the public domain.[53]

The Bottom Line: Copyright, like the Gary White tune (made famous by Linda Ronstadt), lasts a long, long time. To help you see things more clearly, we offer this simplified chart[54] and a more detailed chart in Appendix P.

1.6. Section 302
Term of Copyright

Works created in 1978 or later

Personal author	Life of the author plus 70 years
Joint authors	Life plus 70 years after last surviving author's death
Anonymous or corporate authors or works made for hire	95 years after date of first publication, or 120 years after date of creation, whichever expires first
Published 1964–1977	95 years after date of first publication with © notice
Published 1923–1963	28 years after date of first publication with © notice, plus 67 years if renewed
Published before 1923	In public domain
Created before 1978 and published 1978-2002	Life plus 70 (or 95/120 term) or thru 2047, whichever is greater
Created before 1978 and not published before 2003.	Life plus 70 (or 95/120 term)

---

[53] *Golan v. Holder*, 132 S. Ct. 873 (2012).
[54] Adapted from *When Works Pass Into the Public Domain*, by Professor Laura Gasaway, University of North Carolina School of Law, available at http://www.unc.edu/~unclng/public-d.htm. Adapted with permission from Prof. Gasaway.

International Issues

Intellectual property knows no geographic boundaries. Governing law may include national law (in our case, U.S. law), foreign law, and treaties. Notwithstanding international agreements, each nation creates its own copyright laws.

Many of the recent changes in United States law were enacted to align our laws more closely to the international arena, especially Europe. Examples include eliminating the requirement of a formal "notice of copyright" for a work to be copyrighted and extending the length of time a work is protected.

The United States is a party to two international copyright conventions. The United States ratified the Universal Copyright Convention (UCC),[55] which is administered by United Nations Educational, Scientific and Cultural Organization (UNESCO), in 1954. In 1988 the U.S. joined the Berne Convention,[56] which is administered by the World Intellectual Property Organization (WIPO), also a U.N. agency.

The core of these treaties is "national treatment." A country that belongs to a treaty agrees to protect works prepared in other countries that signed the treaty, as well as works created by authors from those countries, at the same level it protects works created by its own authors.[57] In a nutshell, this means that a work created by a foreign author who is a national of a country that signed the UCC or Berne convention is protected under U.S. law to the same extent as are works prepared in the United States.[58] The same is true for works published in those countries. Furthermore,

---

[55] Sept. 6, 1952, 6 U.S.T. 2731, 216 U.N.T.S. 132, revised July 24, 1971, 25 U.S.T. 1341, 943 U.N.T.S. 194.

[56] Sept. 9, 1886, S. Treaty Doc. No. 99-27, 1161 U.N.T.S. 3.

[57] Occasionally this produces somewhat strange results. For example, U.S. law provides that works of our federal government may not be copyrighted. However, Canadian law provides that works of the Canadian government *are* subject to copyright protection. Because a country must protect foreign works as it protects its own works, this means that works of the U.S. government are protected in Canada, though not in the United States.

[58] U.S. COPYRIGHT OFFICE, CIRCULAR 38A: INTERNATIONAL COPYRIGHT RELATIONS OF THE UNITED STATES (Nov. 2010). Many Copyright Office circulars can be found on the Copyright Office homepage at http://www.copyright.gov.

works published by the United Nations and by the Organization of American States also are protected.[59]

The Berne and UCC treaties do not provide an international forum to resolve disputes between litigants, and the treaties have no enforcement mechanism. Consequently, disputes must be resolved in a nation's courts. For example, a British author who claims that an American infringed her copyright will litigate her claim in a British or American court, under British or American law.

License Agreements

Finally, let's acknowledge the elephant in the room: license agreements. Over the past few decades, license agreements have been gradually displacing copyright law. Users and owners of copyrighted material have always been free to alter their copyright rights and responsibilities by mutual agreement. Publishers of print and microform sources rarely use license agreements. But digital publishers are compelled to rely on license agreements, partly because their products are more vulnerable to copying and other misuse, and partly because their users sometimes need rights that copyright law doesn't provide. As digital sources become more common, books like this one can no longer answer all of your questions about using copyrighted materials—increasingly, you'll have to look to your license agreements instead of copyright law.

In Chapter Seven, we'll take a closer look at license agreements and offer some advice on getting an agreement that's good for your library.

---

[59] The Berne Treaty also provides for so-called "moral rights." These include the right of attribution (the author has the right to claim authorship of his or her work) and integrity (the right of the author to object to any distortion, mutilation, other modification, or derogatory action in relation to the work that prejudices his reputation). Countries may waive out of, or modify, portions of the treaty, and sometimes they fail to fully honor the provisions they agree to. The U.S. does not protect moral rights at the same level as many other countries. We discuss moral rights in Chapter Two.

Chapter Two
RESTRICTIONS ON THE USE OF COPYRIGHTED MATERIALS

ℬℭ

2.1. Section 106
Copyright Owner's Rights

- Reproduction
- Derivative works
- Public distribution
- Public performance
- Public display
- Digital audio transmission of sound recordings
- Importation

For works of visual art (106a)

- Attribution
- Integrity

You may infringe someone's copyright when you reproduce a copyrighted work; prepare derivative works based on a work; or distribute, perform or display a work publicly.[1] But engaging in these activities without permission doesn't *necessarily* result in copyright infringement; sections 107 to 122 of the Copyright Act permit certain uses that would otherwise be infringing. We will address these exceptions later. For now, we will explain what types of use may result in copyright infringement.

---

[1] 17 U.S.C. § 106 (2006).

Reproduction (Section 106(1))

The most common type of copyright infringement is copying (or, as it's referred to in the Copyright Act, "reproducing"). Copies may be made in all sorts of different formats, such as paper, microform, or digital.

Before personal computers and the Internet became common, copying was a straightforward issue. You knew when you were making a copy, and most forms of communication didn't involve copying. If you wanted to share a document, you pinned it on a bulletin board, routed it through a distribution list, or sent it by mail, without making a copy. If you did copy, you had to use a photocopier, retype text, or engage in some similar physical activity.

Today, it's much easier to copy. We can create digital copies with the click of a button, and modern forms of communication encourage us to copy without thinking about it. If you post a document on the Web instead of a bulletin board, you've made a copy. If you send a document by e-mail instead of the postal service, you've made a copy. Unfortunately for users, e-mailing an infringing copy as an attachment is just as bad as making a photocopy.

Modern technology has changed what was once a straightforward issue into a somewhat difficult one, so today's users need to be especially alert when it comes to copying. Generally, any action that transfers a file from one electronic device to another involves making a copy, even if you intend to erase that copy at some point in the future.[2]

Remember that sharing material doesn't have to involve copying. Sharing a link to material on the Web is not a form of copying, nor is sharing an existing physical copy. Although some types of copying are

---

[2] The legal definition of "copy" in the electronic environment is complicated and, at times, surprising. Many users might think that an electronic copy is made only by saving a file, but a federal appellate court has held that copying can occur when information is merely loaded into a device's memory. MAI Systems Corp. v. Peak Computer, Inc., 991 F.2d 511, 518–19 (9th Cir. 1993). If the information exists in the device's memory for "more than a transitory duration," it's a copy. 17 U.S.C. § 101 (2006). This worrisome legal definition is mitigated by other rules. For example, under an implied license theory, you may browse Web pages, even though copies of the content are made in your computer's memory. We'll further discuss digital content in Chapter Six.

permitted without the owner's permission, the easiest way to avoid copyright infringement is not to copy when you don't have to.

Derivative Works (Section 106(2))

A derivative work is "a work based upon one or more preexisting works."[3] A derivative work may be created when someone recasts, reformats, or adapts an earlier work; obvious examples include translations and sequels. If the earlier work is protected by copyright, preparation of a derivative work without permission may infringe the copyright.[4]

For example, Elmore Leonard has the exclusive right to translate his novel *Get Shorty* to another language, and also to authorize a screenplay or film from the novel. If Mr. Leonard refuses to give permission to translate his novel, or to prepare a screenplay or film from it, someone who does so could be liable for infringement.

Be careful not to confuse derivative works with works that merely borrow ideas from earlier material. Remember that copyright only protects the *expression* of ideas.[5] A work that merely follows a formula or draws inspiration from earlier material is not a "derivative work" within the meaning of copyright law. Thus, the *Superman* movies are derivative works based on the *Superman* comic book character; the *Spider-Man* franchise, while it may follow the *Superman* genre, is not a derivative work based on *Superman* because it has its own names, storyline, and characters.

Like collective works, the copyright status of a derivative work is distinct from that of the original work from which it was derived.[6] This means that a screenplay based on a novel will be copyrighted independently of the novel, so long as it meets the requirements for protection: an original work of authorship fixed in a tangible medium of expression.

What about abridgments or abstracts? Whether a small portion or summary of a copyrighted work is a derivative work—and therefore requires permission from the original work's copyright owner—depends mostly on the extent to which the summary substitutes for the original. The more a

---

[3] 17 U.S.C. § 101 (2006).
[4] 17 U.S.C. § 106(2) (2006).
[5] SunTrust Bank v. Houghton Mifflin Co., 268 F.3d 1257, 1263–64 (11th Cir. 2001).
[6] 17 U.S.C. § 103(b) (2006).

person would be able to use the abstract *instead of* the original work, the more likely the abstract would be deemed a derivative work. The longer and more comprehensive the abstract is, the greater the chance it will be considered a derivative work. But even a short abstract that distills the essence of the original work—one which can substitute quite well for the original work—may also be considered a derivative work.

The Bottom Line: You *may* create a summary or abstract of a copyrighted work without permission if it is not a derivative work that can substitute for the original. A librarian may summarize individual journal articles, and also create annotated bibliographies from numerous articles on the same topic. But a one-page abstract that distills the essence of a five-page article and that can substitute for the original is probably a derivative work. Keep your abstracts brief. Whet the reader's appetite, but do not fill his or her stomach.

Distribution and the First Sale Doctrine (Sections 106(3) and 109)

> ### 2.2. Section 109
> ### First Sale Doctrine
> Owner may sell or otherwise dispose of a lawful copy:
> - but may not lease or lend sound recordings or computer programs for direct or indirect commercial advantage
> - library/school lending exemption of sound recordings and computer programs is permitted

Under section 106(3) of the Copyright Act, the right to distribute a copyrighted work is reserved to the copyright owner. But the distribution right is limited by the "first sale doctrine", found in section 109 of the Act.

The first sale doctrine permits the owner of a lawfully made copy of a copyrighted work to lease, lend, rent, sell, or otherwise dispose of the copy without permission.[7] The term "first sale" refers to the copyright owner's initial first sale of an authorized copy. Once the owner has made this first sale of a particular copy, the owner has no power under copyright law to control what happens to that particular copy, at least with respect to most types of material.[8]

For libraries, the first sale doctrine is probably the most important concept in all of copyright law, because libraries couldn't function without it. Any library open to the public "distributes" work under the meaning of the Copyright Act by lending it.[9] Thanks to the first sale doctrine, libraries generally don't incur any liability for these unauthorized distributions, but there's a catch. As we stated above, the first sale doctrine only applies to *authorized* copies. If a library distributes an *unauthorized* copy, the first sale doctrine is of no help and the library will incur liability absent some other defense such as fair use.

At this point, you might be thinking: "Yes, I already know that my library could be liable for *making* unauthorized copies, so why should I worry about *distributing* unauthorized copies?" It's important to understand that copying and distribution are two separate issues, because your library could incur liability for distribution even when it's not liable for copying. For example, if a donor offers your library a paper copy of a dissertation that he obtained from another library's microfiche collection, your library won't be liable for the copying, but it may be liable for distribution if it lends the copy.

Another way your library may be liable for distribution (and not copying) is when it distributes unauthorized copies that were made many years ago. For example, if your library's collection includes an unauthorized copy that a former staff member made thirty years ago, the statute of

---

[7] 17 U.S.C. § 109 (2006).

[8] For more background information on the first sale doctrine, see WILLIAM F. PATRY, PATRY ON COPYRIGHT § 13:15 (2006).

[9] One court has held that merely adding a work to the library's collection and cataloging it constitutes distribution. Hotaling v. Church of Jesus Christ of Latter-Day Saints, 118 F.3d 199, 203 (4th Cir. 1997) ("When a public library adds a work to its collection, lists the work in its index or catalog system, and makes the work available to the borrowing or browsing public, it has completed all the steps necessary for distribution to the public."). However, another court has criticized *Hotaling* for its conclusion that distribution occurs when a library merely makes a work available for lending, holding instead that distribution occurs when a work is actually distributed. Capitol Records, Inc. v. Thomas, 579 F. Supp. 2d 1210, 1224–25 (D. Minn. 2008).

limitations will probably shield you from liability for copying,[10] but the copyright owner could still obtain damages for distribution. When a work is in your collection, it's being distributed on an ongoing basis, and thus the statute of limitations won't protect you from a distribution claim.[11] For libraries, this is the most troublesome aspect of distribution, because you probably don't know how your library acquired certain items in the distant past. If you know that your collection includes unauthorized copies of protected works, you may want to consider discarding the copies, or at least remove them from the catalog and put them in storage.

So far, we've been talking about distribution and the first sale doctrine as they apply to most types of works. Under the original 1976 Copyright Act, all works were treated the same way with respect to distribution, but Congress later amended the Act to create special distribution rules for sound recordings and software.[12]

The Record Rental Amendment Act of 1984[13] and the Computer Software Rental Amendment Act of 1990[14] prohibit the unauthorized rental, leasing or lending of sound recordings or computer programs for a purpose of direct or indirect commercial advantage. The purpose of these acts was to stop stores like Blockbuster from renting sound recordings and software.[15] The Record Rental Amendment Act did not clearly define the term "sound recording", but a federal appellate court has ruled that the Act applies only to recordings of musical works, and not to recordings of literary works (i.e., audio books).[16]

---

[10] Generally, civil actions for copyright infringement must be filed within three years of the infringement. 17 U.S.C. § 507(b) (2006). We'll discuss the statute of limitations in more detail in Chapter Three.

[11] In *Hotaling*, a library incurred liability in exactly this way. Its collection included unauthorized copies of a work, and although the copyright owner's copying claim was time-barred, the distribution claim was not. 118 F.3d at 203–05.

[12] Congress considered, but did not include, a prohibition against lending computer game cartridges. This is why you can rent Nintendo and PlayStation games from video rental stores. *See* S. REP. NO. 101-265 (1990).

[13] Pub. L. No. 98-450, 98 Stat. 1727 (1984).

[14] Pub. L. No. 101-650, 104 Stat. 5134 (1990).

[15] H.R. Rep. No. 98-987, at 2 (1984) and S. Rep. No. 101-265, at 3 (1990).

[16] Brilliance Audio, Inc. v. Haights Cross Communications, Inc., 474 F.3d 365, 374 (6th Cir. 2007).

There are exceptions in both Acts that permit non-profit libraries and non-profit educational institutions to lend sound recordings and computer programs. Here is the language from the Act:

> Nothing in the preceding sentence [which prohibits the transfer of computer programs and sound recordings] . . . shall apply to the rental, lease, or lending of a phonorecord for nonprofit purposes by a nonprofit library or nonprofit educational institution. The transfer of possession of a lawfully made copy of a computer program by a nonprofit educational institution to another nonprofit educational institution or to faculty, staff, and students does not constitute rental, lease, or lending for direct or indirect commercial purposes under this subsection.[17]

This section indicates that non-profit libraries and non-profit educational institutions may lend phonorecords (CDs, tapes, etc.) to anyone. As for computer programs, it seems that the exemption applies only to non-profit educational institutions, which would include their libraries. They may lend software to other educational institutions, and to faculty, students and staff, because such lending is not "for direct or indirect commercial purposes." But read on, for later in section 109, we see this:

> Nothing in this subsection shall apply to the lending of a computer program for nonprofit purposes by a nonprofit library if each copy of a computer program which is lent by such library has affixed to the packaging containing the program a warning of copyright in accordance with requirements that the Register of Copyrights shall prescribe by regulation.[18]

Here, Congress writes that *any* type of non-profit library may lend a computer program so long as the library does so for non-profit purposes and if it includes on the package the following warning:

Computer Program Warning Label
Notice: Warning of Copyright Restrictions

The copyright law of the United States (Title 17, United States Code) governs the reproduction, distribution, adaptation, public performance, and public display of copyrighted material.

Under certain conditions specified in law, nonprofit libraries are authorized to lend, lease, or rent copies of computer programs to patrons on a nonprofit basis and for nonprofit purposes. Any person who makes

---

[17] 17 U.S.C. § 109(b)(1)(A) (2006).
[18] *Id.* § 109(b)(2)(A). The label prescribed by the Register of Copyrights can be found at 37 C.F.R. § 201.24 (2011).

an unauthorized copy or adaptation of the computer program, or redistributes the loan copy, or publicly performs or displays the computer program, except as permitted by Title 17 of the United States Code, may be liable for copyright infringement.

This institution reserves the right to refuse to fill a loan request if, in its judgment, fulfillment of the request would lead to violation of the copyright law.[19]

Note that you do not need to affix a warning label to sound recordings, as Congress did not include such a requirement in the Record Rental Amendment Act.

The exemption for lending software and sound recordings, then, applies both to non-profit libraries and non-profit educational institutions, if done for non-profit purposes. As for libraries in for-profit institutions, they may share software and sound recordings within their institutions, but should not lend them to outsiders.[20]

Another difference between software and other types of works is that software is often subject to a license agreement that may defeat the first sale doctrine. In itself, this is not surprising, but you may be surprised to learn that a license agreement could prevent you from relying on the first sale doctrine even when you didn't agree to any license agreement. In a recent case before the 9th Circuit U.S. Court of Appeals, an eBay merchant purchased copies of software from an end user and attempted to resell them, but was barred from doing so because the end user had acquired the copies through a license agreement that stated that the software developer retained ownership of the copies and merely licensed them to the end user. Although the eBay merchant had made no agreement with the software developer, he was nonetheless unable to assert the first sale doctrine in his defense because the software developer had never transferred ownership of the copies.[21]

Finally, we need to mention e-books, which are becoming increasingly important to libraries. Unfortunately, the first-sale doctrine is rarely applic-

---

[19] 37 C.F.R. § 201.24 (2011).

[20] As a Congressman noted with respect to the Computer Software Rental Amendment Act, "the transfer of copies within a single entity, whether nonprofit or for-profit, is exempt." 136 CONG. REC. H13315 (daily ed. Oct. 27, 1990) (statement of Rep. Kastenmeier). *See also* PAUL GOLDSTEIN, GOLDSTEIN ON COPYRIGHT § 7.6.1.2(c) (3d ed. 2005).

[21] Vernor v. Autodesk, Inc., 621 F.3d 1102 (9th Cir. 2010), *cert. denied*, 2011 U.S. LEXIS 6875, 80 U.S.L.W. 3182 (2011).

able to e-books, because the use of e-books is almost always controlled by license agreements. Just because your library purchases an authorized copy of an e-book doesn't mean you're free to share it with your patrons; you must look to your license agreement.[22]

Public Display and Public Performance (Sections 106(4) and 106(5))

Publicly displaying or performing copyrighted material without permission may infringe copyright. The owner's "public performance" right applies to literary, musical, dramatic, choreographic, pantomimes, motion pictures, and other audiovisual works.[23] The owner's "public display" right applies to those same works, and also to graphic and sculptural works.[24]

The performance right is a bit different from the display right, especially with regard to audiovisual works, such as films. The *performance* of an audiovisual work means showing the images in sequence.[25] The *display* of an audiovisual work involves showing individual images non-sequentially.[26] Showing the Marx Brothers' film *Duck Soup* would be a performance, while showing selected images of Groucho as Rufus T. Firefly, the President of Freedonia, would be a display.

Not all performances or displays are protected by copyright, but only those that are "public." Under the Copyright Act,

> To perform or display a work "publicly" means—
>
> (1) to perform or display it at a place open to the public or at any place where a substantial number of persons outside of a normal circle of family and its social acquaintances is gathered; or
> (2) to transmit or otherwise communicate a performance or display of the work to a place specified by clause (1) or to the public by means of any device or process, whether the members of the public are capable of

---

[22] For further reading on this topic, see Joseph Gratz, Digital Book Distribution: The End of the First-Sale Doctrine?, LANDSLIDE, May/June 2011, at 9.

[23] 17 U.S.C. § 106(4) (2006).

[24] *Id.* § 106(5).

[25] *Id.* § 101.

[26] *Id.*

receiving the performance or display receive it in the same place or in separate places and at the same time or at different times.[27]

The first sale doctrine, which we discussed in connection with the distribution right, permits the owner of a lawfully made copy to publicly display the copy.[28] This is why libraries are permitted to put books, photographs and other material in display cases, provided that they use authorized copies. But the first sale doctrine does *not* extend to public performances, and your library can't build a theater and show DVDs to the public without permission from the copyright owners. We'll discuss public performances in more detail in Chapter Eight.

What about images or text on a computer screen? This is a little tricky, because of the ability to display images simultaneously in multiple locations or to display them to remote viewers. The Act provides that the owner of a lawful copy may display the copy publicly "either directly or by the projection of no more than one image at a time, to viewers present at the place where the copy is located."[29] So although you may not send digital images from a computer to the world at large, you may display images on a projection device to a group, such as students in a classroom.

Digital Transmission of Sound Recordings (Section 106(6))

The Digital Performance Right in Sound Recordings Act of 1995 gives an owner of copyright in a sound recording the exclusive right to perform his or her work publicly by means of a digital audio transmission.[30] The right is qualified by numerous exceptions, which are spelled out in section 114 of the Act.

Unlike the other exclusive rights we've already described, this digital performance right is narrowly tailored to address specific types of situations, and is unlikely to affect your library. In passing this Act, Congress was attempting to protect the market for sound recordings by restricting subscription and "interactive" digital transmissions, the latter referring to

---

[27] *Id.*
[28] *Id.* § 109(c).
[29] *Id.*
[30] *Id.* § 106(6).

services that allow users to select the songs they want to hear. It has no application to libraries' traditional practice of lending sound recordings. The issue of sound recordings in electronic reserves will be addressed in Chapter Eight.

Moral Rights

Many countries recognize a category of authors' rights known as "moral rights", which the United States recognizes only in a very limited way. Moral rights, in their fullest sense, include the attribution right (i.e., the right to be known (or not known) as the author of a work), the integrity right (which restricts alterations to a work), and the right to begin or cease distribution of a work.[31] These rights are separate from the economic ownership of a work, and in some countries they cannot be waived or transferred by the author.[32] For example, in France, an author could sign away all rights to his novel, but still prevent anyone from issuing an abridged version.[33]

The Berne Convention, which we introduced in Chapter One, requires its members to recognize the attribution and integrity rights. But some signatories to the Convention, particularly the United States, have never fully complied with these requirements.[34] Long before joining Berne, the United States offered authors some protection similar to the attribution and integrity rights, but not under the traditional "moral rights" framework. Instead, the law of unfair competition, defamation, or invasion of privacy can sometimes be used in the United States to prevent distortions of authorship or damaging alterations to a work, even in situations where the author has already sold all economic rights.[35] Although this limited protection probably does not meet the requirements of the Berne Convention, the United States is unlikely to adopt full-fledged moral rights any time soon. So in contrast to France, in the United States, an author can sell *all* rights to a novel, including the right to approve alterations.

---

[31] 3 MELVILLE NIMMER, NIMMER ON COPYRIGHT § 8D.01 (2011).
[32] *Id.*
[33] *See* Robert Platt, *A Comparative Survey of Moral Rights*, 57 J. COPYRIGHT SOC'Y U.S.A. 951, 965 (2010).
[34] NIMMER, *supra* note 31, at § 8D.01.
[35] *Id.*

Visual fine art is the one type of material in the United States that receives certain "moral rights" protection beyond what is accorded to most types of work. The Visual Artists Rights Act of 1990 gives the creator of visual fine art the rights of attribution and integrity.[36] Under the Act, works of visual art include a single copy of a painting, drawing, print, photograph, or sculptural work, or if they are produced in multiple copies, to a limited edition of fewer than 200 numbered copies.[37] They do not include posters, maps, charts, technical drawings, motion pictures or other audiovisual works, electronic publications, or advertisements. And they do not include works made for hire.[38]

Generally, the Visual Artists Rights Act gives an author of a work of visual art the right (1) to claim authorship of the work; (2) to prevent the use of his or her name as the author of a work he or she did not create; (3) to prevent the use of the author's name on a work that was distorted, mutilated, or otherwise modified if those changes prejudiced the author's honor or reputation; (4) to prevent the intentional distortion, mutilation, or other modification of the work that prejudices the author's honor or reputation; and (5) to prevent the destruction of certain works.[39] The artist's rights are subject to certain exemptions.[40]

Although an artist's attribution and integrity rights may not appear to impact many libraries significantly, there is a bottom line: Whenever you "use" someone else's work—even if that use is permitted under fair use or another provision of the Copyright Act—you should credit the authors. If you modify the original work, you should provide credit, and also note the changes that were made from the original work. Not only is this smart legally, but it complies with scholarly and journalistic norms.

---

[36] Pub. L. No. 101-650, Title VI, 104 Stat. 5128 (1990).
[37] 17 U.S.C. § 101 (2006).
[38] *Id.*
[39] *Id.* § 106A.
[40] *Id.* § 113.

Chapter Three
LIABILITY FOR INFRINGEMENT
ℰℐℰℐ

Remedies and Damages (Section 504)

3.1. Section 504
Damages

- Actual damages and profits, or
- Statutory damages
  - $750 to $30,000 per infringement
  - $150,000 for willful infringement
  - $200 for innocent infringer
- Remission of damages
  - Employee or agent of a nonprofit educational institution, library, or archives
  - Acting within scope of employment
  - Reasonable belief the use was fair

Remedies and damages for infringement are governed by section 504 of the Copyright Act. In a nutshell, a copyright owner may seek actual or statutory damages, and also try to prohibit the infringing activity.

Actual damages are measured by what was lost as a result of the infringement. Statutory damages can range from $750 to $30,000 per infringing event, and usually will exceed actual damages. If the infringement was willful—if the defendant engaged in the infringing activity knowing that his or her conduct was infringing, or recklessly disregarded the copyright owner's rights—statutory damages can be as much as $150,000 per infringing act.

These amounts can quickly add up in cases that involve multiple infringing acts, which are becoming more common in the Internet era. In a recent case against a college student who willfully infringed the copyright of thirty songs he downloaded and shared online, the jury awarded statutory damages of $22,500 per song, for a total of $675,000.[1] The trial judge held that the damage award was so large that it violated the constitution's due process requirements and reduced the award to $67,500, but the 7th Circuit Court of Appeals disagreed and reinstated the jury's award.[2] The amount of the award is stunning considering that the student could have bought the songs for the cost of a few CDs, and it illustrates the power of statutory damages.

But before you start sweating, consider some other aspects of copyright law that work in favor of defendants. Even if a court finds that there was an infringement, statutory damages may be reduced significantly if the defendant was an "innocent infringer," someone who was not aware of and had no reason to believe that his or her acts were infringing. When this is the case, a court has discretion to reduce statutory damages to as little as $200.[3]

Furthermore, a court may not assess *any* statutory damages if the infringer is an employee of a non-profit educational institution, library, or archives who, acting under the scope of his or her employment, actually and reasonably believed that the use was fair under section 107.[4] Although section 504 does not expressly say so, one might reason that no statutory damages would be assessed against a library employee who believed that the use was permitted under the section 108 library exemption or any of the other statutory exemptions in the Act.

This does not, of course, give library employees a license to copy. The damage remission provision does *not* apply if the employee knew or should have known that his or her actions were infringing. For example, if a library employee knew she was violating the library's own policies when she copied material for a patron, it's unlikely that a court would view her as an innocent infringer.

---

[1] Sony BMG Music Entertainment v. Tennenbaum, 721 F. Supp. 2d 85 (D. Mass. 2010). Although the case focused on the thirty songs owned by the plaintiff, the defendant had downloaded and shared thousands of other songs as well. *Id.* at 87.
[2] Sony BMG Music Entertainment v. Tenenbaum, 660 F.3d 487 (7th Cir. 2011).
[3] 17 U.S.C. § 504(c)(2) (2006).
[4] *Id.*

Plaintiffs in an infringement lawsuit are not interested in getting damages from the person who runs the photocopier, of course. They want a judgment against the organization, which, if it has not already declared bankruptcy due to misconduct by its officers or accountants, has the "deep pockets." This brings us to the issue of the liability of an employer for the acts of its employees.

Institutional Responsibility: Vicarious Liability and Contributory Infringement

3.2. Institutional Liability
- Vicarious Liability
  - o Right to supervise
  - o Financial benefit
- Contributory Infringement
  - o Knowledge of infringing activity
  - o Induce, cause, or materially contribute

Whether a library or its parent institution may be responsible for an employee's infringement depends on the library's involvement in the infringing activity, or its relationship to the infringer. The institution may be liable under either of two legal theories: vicarious liability (sometimes called respondeat superior) or contributory infringement.

Vicarious liability generally means that an employer will be liable for harmful acts done by employees who acted within the scope of their employment. A library may be liable for the acts of its employees if it had the right and ability to supervise the employee, and also derived a financial benefit from exploiting the copyrighted work.[5] Knowledge of the infringing activity is not necessary. The financial benefit is found if the institution is getting something for free that it should have paid for, or even when there is an indirect benefit.[6]

---

[5] A&M Records, Inc. v. Napster, Inc., 239 F.3d 1004, 1022 (9th Cir. 2001).

[6] In the *Napster* case, the court found that Napster reaped a financial benefit when the availability of infringing materials acted as a draw for customers. 239 F.3d at 1023.

A library that provides guidance as to which activities are and are not permitted is less likely to be responsible for the acts of its employees. But it will not do the library any good if administrators and staff disregard the policy. The library, or any organization for that matter, cannot enforce its policy with a wink and a nod. This is what happened to the Kinko's Corporation when it was found liable for employees who photocopied copyrighted articles and book chapters to create coursepacks for students.[7] Kinko's had a policy, but failed to enforce it. The court found that Kinko's used the policy only to "cover" itself. It wrote:

> Kinko's instructions to its workers possessed little of the nuance of the copyright law. They provided no hypothetical situations nor any factual summary of the state of the law presently. . . . . This can hardly be considered a "good faith" effort on Kinko's part to educate their employees. To the contrary, it appears more to be a way to "cover" themselves while Kinko's remained willfully blind to the consequences of their activity.[8]

Contributory infringement is a little different. A library or its parent institution may be liable as a contributory infringer if it induces, causes, renders substantial assistance to, or materially contributes to the activity.[9] It doesn't matter whether the infringer is an employee or someone who walked in off the street. Actual knowledge is not necessary; it is enough if the library should have known that an infringement was taking place. But this doesn't mean that the library is on the hook if it merely provides patrons with an opportunity to infringe someone's copyright.

The U.S. Supreme Court has held that manufacturers of video cassette recorders aren't liable for contributory infringement simply for selling a device that could be used for both legitimate and illegitimate copying.[10] Likewise, no court would hold that a library is liable for contributory infringement simply because it provides patrons with computers that could be used for both infringing and non-infringing purposes. But if a library posted instructions on how to download pirated music files, it would be liable for contributory infringement because the instructions are clearly for an infringing purpose.

---

[7] Basic Books, Inc. v. Kinko's Graphics, 758 F. Supp. 1522 (S.D.N.Y. 1991).
[8] *Id.* at 1545.
[9] A&M Records, Inc. v. Napster, Inc., 239 F.3d at 1019; Cable/Home Communications Corp. v. Network Prods., Inc., 902 F.2d 829, 845 (11th Cir. 1990).
[10] Sony Corp. of America v. Universal City Studios, Inc., 464 U.S. 417, 442 (1984).

Equipment issues are discussed in greater detail in Chapter Five, but for now we'll just point out that a library isn't liable for infringing activities that take place on unsupervised photocopying equipment if the equipment has the following warning label.[11]

> **WARNING: THE MAKING OF A COPY MAY BE SUBJECT TO THE UNITED STATES COPYRIGHT LAW (TITLE 17 UNITED STATES CODE)**

It may be prudent to include a similar label on audio listening and video viewing equipment that the library makes available to patrons, such as

> **WARNING: THE MAKING OF A COPY AND PUBLIC DISTRIBUTION, PERFORMANCES OR DISPLAYS MAY BE SUBJECT TO THE UNITED STATES COPYRIGHT LAW (TITLE 17 UNITED STATES CODE)**

The Bottom Line: A library should give its staff guidance on what they may or may not do. Create a written policy, make sure that the staff is aware of it, and enforce it. Put a warning label on equipment. Do not provide assistance that facilitates copyright infringement.

Statute of Limitations (Section 507)

> ### 3.3 Statute of Limitations
> - Three years for civil actions
> - Five years for criminal actions

The Copyright Act includes a statute of limitations for both civil and criminal actions. In a civil action, a plaintiff must file suit within three years after the claim has accrued, while in criminal cases, the government must start a criminal proceeding within five years.[12]

That sounds pretty simple at first, but things get more complicated when you need to determine when the clock starts running. In some cases, the infringement is not a single act, but takes place over a period of time.

---

[11] 17 U.S.C. § 108(f)(1) (2006).
[12] 17 U.S.C. § 507 (2006).

For example, if your library infringed an author's copyright by keeping her article on the library's Web site for the past ten years, you can't use the statute of limitations to shield your library from liability. Because the article has remained on the library's Web site, the infringement is ongoing.[13] A more difficult question is whether your library is liable only for damages that resulted during the last three years, or if you're liable for damages during the entire ten-year period. On this question, courts are split, but most limit damages for continuing infringement to the three-year period.[14]

There is also some disagreement among courts on how to treat plaintiffs who are unaware of the infringement until after the statute of limitations has run. Some courts say that the clock starts running when the infringement occurs, while other courts say that the clock starts only when the plaintiff learns about, or has reason to learn about, the infringement. If the defendant has done something to conceal the infringement, courts will generally follow the latter approach—the clock doesn't start running until the plaintiff discovers or has reason to discover the infringement.[15]

As we noted in Chapter Two, the law regarding continuing infringements is particularly troublesome for libraries because any infringing work in a library's collection is being distributed on an ongoing basis. If your library has an infringing copy in its collection, it can be held liable no matter how long ago the copying took place, so long as the work itself continues to be protected by copyright.[16]

Government Immunity

What if the library is part of a federal, state, or local government, such as a city or county public library, a state-funded university library, or a federal agency library? Can the government be liable for acts of its employees? The answer is "maybe." In some circumstances a government has what is called sovereign immunity, meaning that a copyright owner cannot recover damages from it.

---

[13] Roley v. New World Pictures, Ltd., 19 F.3d 479, 481 (9th Cir. 1994).
[14] *See* 3 MELVILLE NIMMER, NIMMER ON COPYRIGHT § 12.05[B] (2011).
[15] *Id.*
[16] Hotaling v. Church of Jesus Christ of Latter-Day Saints, 118 F.3d 199, 203 (4th Cir. 1997).

Congress has passed legislation waiving the federal government's immunity for patent and copyright infringement.[17] A federal agency, therefore, may be sued for infringing acts committed by its employees. The situation differs for the states, because the Eleventh Amendment to the U.S. Constitution prohibits suits in federal court by an individual against a state without the state's consent. Congress has passed legislation abrogating Eleventh Amendment immunity, but court decisions have held that the legislation did not validly abrogate a state's immunity in copyright infringement suits.[18] Still, a state employee may be sued individually for infringement, may be subject to damages, and may have his or her activities enjoined by a court.[19]

The Bottom Line: If you work for the government and think your employer has immunity, *you* could be liable for infringement even though your employer may not.

---

[17] 28 U.S.C. § 1498 (2006).

[18] 17 U.S.C. § 511 (2006). *Chavez v. Arte Publico Press*, 157 F.3d 282 (5th Cir. 1998) and *Rodriguez v. Texas Comm'n on the Arts*, 199 F.3d 279 (5th Cir. 2000) held that the federal statute did not validly abrogate a state's sovereign immunity against infringement lawsuits.

[19] Redondo-Borges v. U.S. Dept. of Hous. and Urban Dev., 421 F.3d 1, 7 (1st Cir. 2005).

Chapter Four
FAIR USE (SECTION 107)

ଞ୍ଜେଓଃ

Copyright owners' rights are important, but Congress did not put copyrighted works in a lockbox. A copyright owner does not have an absolute monopoly over the use of his or her work; owners' rights are subject to other provisions of the Copyright Act that permit certain uses of copyrighted works. For those who work in libraries or schools, the most important of these rights are fair use (section 107 of the Act), the library exemption (section 108), the first sale doctrine (section 109), and the public performance exemptions (section 110).

Section 107 provides the broadest scope of protection for those who use copyrighted works. Unlike other sections of the Act that permit certain types of uses, or the use of certain types of materials, section 107 is an all-purpose exemption. Every use should be viewed under the section 107 microscope; when you try to determine whether a use is permitted under other exemptions, also consider whether it is a fair use.[1] And remember that when a use is allowed under section 107 or another exemption, you need not receive permission from the copyright owner nor pay royalties.

Most scholars trace the origin of fair use in the United States to an 1841 case, *Folsom v. Marsh*.[2] Jared Sparks, who had been assigned copyright in the letters of George Washington, edited them into a twelve-volume set. The Reverend Charles Upham used more than 300 pages from Sparks' set in his own 866-page biography of Washington. To determine whether Reverend Upham infringed, Justice Joseph Story decreed that the

---

[1] *See* 17 U.S.C. § 108(f)(4) (2006) (stating that nothing in section 108 affects libraries' fair use rights).
[2] 2 Story 100, 9 F. Cas. 342 (C.C. Mass. 1841) (No. 4,901).

court had to look at three things: (1) the nature and objects of the selection, (2) the quantity and value of the materials used, and (3) the degree in which the use may prejudice the work, diminish the author's profits, or supersede the objects of the original work. After examining these factors, Justice Story concluded that Upham's use was not fair.

Fair use remained exclusively within the judiciary until Congress codified it in the 1976 Copyright Act. Congress understood the complexity of legislating fair use; the legislative history notes that Congress intended to restate the fair use doctrine as it had developed in the courts, not to change, narrow, or enlarge it.[3] Recognizing the difficulty in defining fair use, the House Judiciary Committee wrote

> Although the courts have considered and ruled upon the fair use doctrine over and over again, no real definition of the concept has ever emerged. Indeed, since the doctrine is an equitable rule of reason, no generally applicable definition is possible, and each case raising the question must be decided on its own facts.[4]

Fair use, then, is an equitable concept that attempts to balance the rights of copyright owners with the needs of those who use copyrighted works. The courts ultimately determine which uses are "fair uses." American jurisprudence is guided by precedent, and a court deciding a case today will look at earlier decisions involving similar facts and issues for guidance. But because fair use determinations are fact-specific, it is difficult to generalize what is, and what is not, fair. A federal appellate court wrote in 1939 that "the issue of fair use . . . is the most troublesome in the whole law of copyright."[5] That is no less true today. The Judiciary Committee noted the freedom courts have in deciding whether a particular use is fair. It wrote

> The statement of the fair use doctrine in section 107 offers some guidance to users in determining when the principles of the doctrine apply. However, the endless variety of situations and combinations of circumstances that can arise in particular cases precludes the formulation of exact rules in the statute.... Beyond a very broad statutory explanation of what fair use is and some of the criteria applicable to it, the courts

---

[3] H.R. Rep. No. 94-1476, at 66 (1976).
[4] *Id.* at 65.
[5] Dellar v. Samuel Goldwyn, Inc., 104 F.2d 661, 662 (2d Cir. 1939).

must be free to adapt the doctrine to particular situations on a case-by-case basis.[6]

4.1. Section 107
Fair Use Purposes

- Criticism
- Comment
- News reporting
- Teaching (including multiple classroom copies)
- Scholarship
- Research
- Other possible uses

Let's move to the Act. Section 107 begins with the statement that the fair use of a copyrighted work, including reproduction for purposes such as criticism, comment, news reporting, teaching (including multiple copies for classroom use), scholarship, or research is not an infringement. The Supreme Court has written that this list is not intended to be exhaustive, nor intended to single out any particular use as presumptively "fair."[7] And although the uses noted in the preamble are favored, you will see that not all copying done for such purposes is necessarily fair.

The Four Factors

Under the statute, a court deciding whether a use of a copyrighted work is a "fair use" must consider no less than four factors. Section 107 provides that:

> In determining whether the use made of a work in any particular case is a fair use the factors to be considered shall include—
>
> (1) the purpose and character of the use, including whether such use is of a commercial nature or is for nonprofit educational purposes;
>
> (2) the nature of the copyrighted work;
>
> (3) the amount and substantially of the portion used in relation to the copyrighted work as a whole; and

---

[6] H.R. REP. NO. 94-1476, at 66.
[7] Harper & Row v. Nation Enters., 471 U.S. 539, 561 (1985).

(4) the effect of the use upon the potential market for or value of the copyrighted work.[8]

4.2. Section 107
Fair Use Factors

- Purpose and character of the use
- Nature of the copyrighted work
- Amount and substantiality
- Effect on potential market or value

Non-publication does not bar fair use

The first factor examines two different things—the purpose of the use, and the character of the use. With regard to *purpose*, a court will consider whether the use is of a commercial nature or, instead, for non-profit educational purposes. Although non-profit educational uses are favored over commercial uses, this means neither that all non-profit educational uses are fair, nor that all commercial uses are infringing. For example, a court has held that extensive copying of PBS programs by a public school system for distribution to schools within the system—an obvious educational use—was infringing.[9] Another court ruled that it was not a fair use when a teacher copied eleven pages from a thirty-five-page copyrighted booklet on cake decorating, and incorporated those eleven pages into a twenty-four-page booklet she prepared for her class.[10]

The second part of the first factor requires an examination of the *character* of the use, including whether the use is transformative. The character/transformative issue was discussed at great length in *Campbell v. Acuff-Rose Music,* where the U.S. Supreme Court found that the band 2 Live Crew's parody of Roy Orbison's "Oh Pretty Woman" was a fair use.[11] The Court wrote that the central purpose of the first factor is whether

---

[8] 17 U.S.C. § 107 (2006).
[9] Encyclopedia Britannica Educ. Corp. v. Crooks, 542 F. Supp. 1156 (W.D.N.Y. 1982).
[10] Marcus v. Rowley, 695 F.2d 1171 (9th Cir. 1983).
[11] 510 U.S. 569 (1994).

the new work merely supplants the original—a non-transformative use—or instead

> adds something new, with a further purpose or different character, altering the first with new expression, meaning, or message; it asks, in other words, whether and to what extent the new work is "transformative." . . . [T]he more transformative the new work, the less the significance of the other factors, like commercialism, that may weigh against a finding of fair use."[12]

The concept of transforming a work was explored in great detail by a federal appeals court in *American Geophysical Union v. Texaco*,[13] which is discussed below.

The second fair use factor is the nature of the work copied. Because the purpose of copyright is to "promote the progress of science and the useful arts," there is more freedom to copy or otherwise use informational, scientific, or factual works than there is for creative or expressive works.[14] For example, articles on the First Amendment, Google, and the Middle East may be more freely copied than a short story from the *New Yorker* or a Charles Schultz comic strip. This does not mean that a person may copy a "favored" work anytime he or she wants, nor that someone may *never* copy a *Peanuts* comic strip. A fair use analysis requires examination of all four factors, and sometimes others.

For example, courts often consider whether the work is published, unpublished, or out of print. In 1987, a federal appeals court ruled that a biographer of J.D. Salinger could not include Salinger's private letters because, even though they were deposited in the archives of several university libraries, they were unpublished.[15] Following the *Salinger* decision, after several other courts also restricted copying from unpublished works, it became apparent that some tinkering with the fair use provision was necessary. Consequently, in 1992 Congress amended section 107 with the following, simple clause: "The fact that a work is unpublished shall not itself bar a finding of fair use if such finding is made upon consideration of all the above factors."

---

[12] 510 U.S. at 579.
[13] 60 F.3d 913 (2d Cir. 1994).
[14] Harper & Row v. Nation Enters., 471 U.S. at 563.
[15] Salinger v. Random House, 811 F.2d 90 (2d Cir. 1987), *opinion supplemented and reh'g denied*, 818 F.2d 252 (1987).

Today, the fact that a work is out-of-print may work for, or against, fair use. That a work is out-of-print may work in favor of the copyright owner because royalties from copying are the only source of income from the work.[16] In other situations, however, the fact that a work is out-of-print may actually work in favor of the user, particularly if the copyright owner has not set up a handy mechanism to collect royalties.[17] Of course, if a work is available through print-on-demand, it is not out-of-print.

The third fair use factor considers the amount of the copyrighted work that was copied, performed, or otherwise used. As a general matter, the more that is copied, the less likely this factor will favor the user. But you must look beyond quantity. Courts may conclude that this factor favors the copyright owner even when a very small portion of a copyrighted work is used—less than 1%, in some cases—if what is used constitutes the heart of the work.

In *Harper & Row v. Nation Enterprises*,[18] *The Nation* magazine scooped an article on the memoirs of President Gerald Ford that was to appear in *Time* magazine. Harper & Row, which was to publish a book on the Ford memoirs, negotiated a prepublication agreement with *Time* in which the magazine would excerpt 7,500 words from the book dealing with Ford's account of his pardon of former President Nixon. Before the *Time* article appeared in print, someone provided *The Nation* with a copy of the

---

[16] Basic Books, Inc. v. Kinko's Graphics Corp., 758 F. Supp. 1522 (S.D.N.Y. 1991).

[17] In *Maxtone-Graham v. Burtchaell*, 803 F.2d 1253, 1264 n. 8 (2d Cir. 1986), the appeals court wrote:

> We also note that *Pregnant by Mistake* was out of print when *Rachel Weeping* was published. While this factor is not essential to our affirmance of the district court's finding of fair use, it certainly supports our determination. The legislative reports have provided some guidance on this issue: "A key, though not necessarily determinative, factor in fair use is whether or not the work is available to the potential user. If the work is 'out of print' and unavailable for purchase through normal channels, the user may have more justification for reproducing it than in the ordinary case, . . . S. Rep. No. 94-473, 94th Cong., 1st Sess. 64 (1965); H.R. Rep. No. 94-1476, 94th Cong., 2d Sess. 67 (1976) . . . ."

In *Sony Computer Entm't Am., Inc. v. Bleem, LLC*, 214 F.3d 1022, 1028 (9th Cir. 2000), the Ninth Circuit wrote the following:

> For instance, if the copyrighted work is out of print and cannot be purchased, a user may be more likely to prevail on a fair use defense. . . . On the other hand, if the copyrighted material is unpublished and creative while the copy is a commercial publication, courts would be less receptive to the defense of fair use.

[18] 471 U.S. 539 (1985).

Ford manuscript. A few weeks before the publication of the *Time* article, *The Nation* published a 2,250-word article that included about 300 copyrighted words (verbatim quotes, actually) from the as yet unpublished manuscript. With its article scooped, *Time* cancelled its agreement with Harper & Row, and Harper & Row sued *The Nation*. Although *The Nation* used less than 1% from the Harper & Row manuscript, Harper & Row won.

A court may consider not only the amount taken from the first work, but also how much of the new work includes material that was copied from the first one. In other words, if the author of a twenty-page article copies twelve pages from another person's work, 60% of the new work (twelve of the twenty pages) really is someone else's. Needless to say, "the more the merrier" does not bode well for defendants in such cases.

Because much library copying involves copying articles, it is important to understand that there are usually two levels of copyright protection for periodicals. First, the publisher holds a copyright in the entire periodical issue as a "collective work", provided that the selection and arrangement of the contents meet the originality requirements for copyright protection.[19]

Second, there is copyright in each individual article. Copyright in an article is held by its author, unless the author transfers the copyright to another person or entity. If you want to use an article, and that use is *not* permitted by section 107 or another provision of the Copyright Act, you will need permission from whoever holds copyright in the article. In most cases it probably is the author, but many journals require authors to transfer copyright in their articles to the publisher. If you are copying an entire issue of a periodical, you may need to secure permission from whoever holds copyright in the articles, as well as from whoever owns copyright in the issue as a whole.

Copying from newsletters is even more problematic, and copying entire issues of newsletters is particularly frowned upon. A library should *not*

---

[19] "[T]o the extent that the compilation of a journal issue involves an original work of authorship, the publishers possess a distinct copyright in each journal issue as a collective work." American Geophysical Union v. Texaco, 60 F.3d 913, 918 (2d Cir. 1994). Issues of illustrated magazines such as *Rolling Stone* or *Time* clearly warrant copyright protection as collective works because of the creativity involved in selecting and arranging the articles, photographs and graphics. Other periodicals (such as law reviews) may arguably lack such creativity, but the safest approach is to treat all periodical issues as collective works.

subscribe to only one copy of a newsletter and use it to make additional copies for others in the organization. Neither should an individual subscribe to a newsletter and make copies for his or her friends or professional colleagues. Several court decisions indicate the risk of making cover-to-cover copies of newsletters in both the for-profit and non-profit sectors.

In 1991, a Washington, D.C.–area law firm was sued for making multiple copies of a newsletter for several attorneys in the firm, even though there were discounts available for multiple subscriptions.[20] The law firm reportedly paid a huge amount of money to settle the suit.[21] A year later, another newsletter publisher succeeded in getting an injunction against a for-profit corporation that was making cover-to-cover copies for employees in its branch offices.[22] And one year after that, a non-profit association was held to have infringed for doing the same thing.[23] In 2004, in a more up-to-date twist to this scenario, a brokerage firm was held liable for nearly $20 million in damages for repeatedly forwarding an e-mail newsletter to its employees and posting it on its intranet.[24]

For newsletters, do not make cover-to-cover copies (either paper or electronic), even if you work in a non-profit educational institution, unless you have an agreement with the publisher that allows you to do so. This does not mean that you cannot copy *anything* from a newsletter. Occasional, isolated copying of small portions—not a significant portion, and not regularly—might be considered fair use. Even an entire newsletter issue may occasionally be copied, within limited circumstances, under the section 108 library exemption. (See Chapter Five.) Finally, your license

---

[20] Washington Bus. Info., Inc. v. Collier, Shannon & Scott, No. 91-CV-305 (E.D. Va., filed Feb. 26, 1991). *See* James Gibbs, *Copyright and Copy Rights*, LEGAL TIMES, May 3, 1993, at S33.

[21] The *New York Times* wrote that the settlement, including legal fees, "may have cost Collier, Shannon $1 million." David Margolick, *When a Firm Tries to Cut Corners, It Is Caught in Copyright Embarrassment*, N.Y. TIMES, Dec. 6, 1991, at B-7.

[22] Pasha Publ'ns, Inc. v. Enmark Gas Corp., 22 U.S.P.Q.2d (BNA) 1076, 1992 Copyright L. Dec. (CCH) ¶ 26,881, 19 Media L. Rep. (BNA) 2062, 1992 U.S. Dist. LEXIS 2834 (N.D. Tex. 1992).

[23] Television Digest v. United States Tel. Ass'n, 1994 Copyright L. Dec. (CCH) ¶ 27,191, 28 U.S.P.Q.2d 1697, 21 Media L. Rep. (BNA) 2211, 1993 U.S. Dist. LEXIS 19143 (D.D.C. 1993).

[24] Lowry's Reports, Inc. v. Legg Mason, Inc., 302 F. Supp. 2d 455 (D. Md. 2004); Lowry's Reports, Inc. v. Legg Mason, Inc., 271 F. Supp. 2d 737 (D. Md. 2003).

agreement may permit you to distribute electronic copies within your institution.

Fair Use in the For-Profit Sector: The *Texaco* Case and Beyond

Here we need to talk about *Texaco*, a case coordinated by the Association of American Publishers in the name of five publishers. In 1992, a federal district court in New York held that Texaco's routing of journals to researchers within the corporation, who subsequently photocopied articles and filed them away for later use, was not a fair use.[25] Two years later the U.S. Court of Appeals for the Second Circuit upheld the lower court decision.[26]

Although Texaco employed hundreds of scientists, before trial the parties agreed that the trial would focus on the activities of one, Dr. Donald H. Chickering, who photocopied eight articles from the *Journal of Catalysis* and placed them in his personal filing cabinet. Let's see how the trial and appellate courts addressed the main issue in *Texaco*: Was the routing of journals to corporate scientists, who copied articles and filed them away for possible later use, a fair use under section 107 of the Act?

The trial court judge spent considerable time examining the first factor —the purpose and character of the use. As for the *purpose* of the use, the judge wrote that because the defendant was a for-profit company, its copying was "commercial." As for the *character* of the use, the judge was struck by the fact that Dr. Chickering did not transform the copyrighted articles in any way. Chickering copied the articles and filed them away for possible later use, but there was no evidence that he ever used the articles in his research.

The appeals court had to decide if Dr. Chickering's copying was, as the district court concluded, commercial copying. Noting that Texaco did not directly profit from the copying, the court concluded that the purpose was neither "for-profit" nor "non-profit educational," calling it instead an "intermediate" use.[27] The appeals court also pointedly called into question

---

[25] American Geophysical Union v. Texaco, Inc., 802 F. Supp. 1 (S.D.N.Y. 1992).

[26] American Geophysical Union v. Texaco, Inc., 60 F.3d 913 (2d Cir. 1994).

[27] The court pointedly distinguished copying at corporations such as Texaco from those whose business is to make copies, such as copyshops, when it wrote

the library's systematically routing journals to Texaco scientists so that each person could build a mini-library of photocopied articles. It called this

> "archival"—*i.e.*, done for the primary purpose of providing numerous Texaco scientists each with his or her own copy of each article without Texaco having to purchase another additional journal subscriptions. The photocopying "merely supersede[s] the objects of the original creation" [quoting *Campbell and Folsom v. Marsh*] and tilts the first fair use factor against Texaco.[28]

Weighing its words carefully, the court continued

> We do not mean to suggest that no instance of archival copying would be fair use, but the first factor tilts against Texaco in this case because the making of copies to be placed on the shelf in Chickering's office is part of a systematic process of encouraging employee researchers to copy articles so as to multiply available copies while avoiding payment.[29]

As for the *character* of the use, the appeals court agreed with the district court that the copying was not transformative. Chickering had merely made copies. As the court explained, the transformative use concept is important when considering the character of the use, because a transformative use creates something new, thereby contributing to copyright's goal of promoting the arts and sciences.[30]

The second fair use factor, you will recall, examines the nature of the work copied. Both the district and appeals courts characterized the articles in the *Journal of Catalysis* as factual in nature, and concluded that the second factor favored Texaco. As for the third factor—the amount used—

> Our concern here is that the [trial] court let the for-profit nature of Texaco's activity weigh against Texaco without differentiating between a direct commercial use and the more indirect relation to commercial activity that occurred here. Texaco was not gaining direct or immediate commercial advantage from the photocopying at issue in this case, i.e. Texaco's profits, revenues, and overall commercial performance were not tied to making copies of eight *Catalysis* articles for Chickering. . . . Rather, Texaco's photocopying served, at most, to facilitate Chickering's research, which in turn might have led to the development of new products and technology that could have improved Texaco's commercial performance.

Texaco, 60 F.3d at 921.
[28] *Id.* at 919–20.
[29] *Id.* at 920.
[30] *Id.* at 922–24.

both courts concluded that it favored the plaintiffs because entire articles were being copied.

On to the fourth factor, the effect of the use upon the potential market for or value of the copyrighted work. Courts are more likely to find an infringement when the copyright owner incurs financial harm due to unauthorized or uncompensated copying. In 1985, the Supreme Court called the fourth factor the most important element of fair use.[31] But since the 1994 *Campbell* decision, as the appeals court noted, the fourth factor no longer is more important than the others.[32]

In assessing how copying affects the potential market or value of a work, courts will consider markets beyond journal subscriptions and book sales, such as the secondary market for article and book chapter reprints, and royalty or licensing fees.[33] Furthermore, not only will a court examine the market impact of the individual defendant's copying, but also "whether unrestricted and widespread conduct of the sort engaged in by the defendant . . . would result in a substantially adverse impact on the potential market for the original."[34] In other words, what would be the impact if a lot of other people do what this particular defendant did?

Both the district and appellate courts in *Texaco* noted that the publishers lost sales of additional journal subscriptions, back issues and back volumes, and also licensing revenue and fees. Like the district court, the appeals court also thought it significant that the publishers of the journals from which articles were copied were registered with the Copyright Clearance Center, thereby making it easy to pay royalties.[35] Both the trial court and the appeals court found that the fourth factor favored the publishers.

---

[31] *Harper & Row*, 471 U.S. at 566.

[32] "Prior to *Campbell*, the Supreme Court had characterized the fourth factor as 'the single most important element of fair use,' Harper & Row, 471 U.S. at 566. . . . However, *Campbell's* discussion of the fourth factor conspicuously omits this phrasing. Apparently abandoning the idea that any factor enjoys primacy, *Campbell* instructs that '[a]ll [four factors] are to be explored, and the results weighed together, in light of the purposes of copyright.'" *Texaco*, 60 F.3d at 926.

[33] *Id.* at 927–29.

[34] *Campbell*, 510 U.S. at 590.

[35] "Though the publishers still have not established a conventional market for the direct sale and distribution of individual articles, they have created, primarily through the CCC, a workable market for institutional users to obtain licenses for the right to produce their own copies of individual articles via photocopying. The District Court found that many major

As Texaco lost the first, third, and fourth factors, the appeals court upheld the lower court decision and found that Texaco had infringed. But you should not conclude from the *Texaco* decision that a corporate library or any library in a for-profit organization can *never* copy journal articles for researchers; the court did *not* say that all copying in for-profit companies is infringing. Indeed, the court limited its ruling "to the institutional, systematic, archival multiplication of copies revealed by the record—the precise copying that the parties stipulated should be the basis for the District Court's decision now on appeal and for which licenses are in fact available."[36]

Remember that fair use is an equitable concept; whether a use is or is not fair depends on the particular facts of each case. A company that fails to purchase as many subscriptions or licenses as it needs and uses large-scale copying or distribution—either by the library or by employees—as a substitute for subscriptions risks liability as an infringer. This is true not only in for-profit corporations such as Texaco, but even for non-profit educational institutions. The lesson from *Texaco* is not that fair use doesn't exist in the corporate sector, but instead that there are limits as to what libraries and employees of an organization may do.

Let's take a closer look at fair use in the for-profit sector. We need to recognize first that there are different types of for-profit entities, and that they are not all created equal under copyright law. Two of the earliest infringement lawsuits against corporations for internal copying were orchestrated by the Association of American Publishers in the early 1980s. Both resulted in out-of-court settlements. American Cyanamid, the defendant in the first suit, relinquished all fair use rights and agreed to make payments to the Copyright Clearance Center for internal copying. The other corporation, Squibb, also joined the CCC, but under its settlement did not have to pay royalties for a small amount (6%) of their copying that was considered fair use.[37]

---

corporations now subscribe to the CCC systems for photocopying licenses." *Texaco*, 60 F.3d at 930.

[36] *Id.* at 931.

[37] Michael C. Elmer & John F. Harnick, *In-House Photocopying Subject to New Challenges*, LEGAL TIMES, Apr. 25, 1983, at 11.

As noted earlier, publishers sued several organizations in the 1990s for copying newsletters and won substantial settlements.[38] And in 1999, LeBoeuf, Lamb, Greene & MacRae, a large New York–based law firm, purchased a multi-year photocopying license with the CCC and paid an undisclosed settlement to avoid an infringement suit brought by four publishers.[39] Also noted earlier, in 2004 a brokerage firm was held liable for nearly $20 million in damages for copying an electronic newsletter.[40]

Then we have litigation against the for-profit information brokers. In the early 1990s, the West Publishing Company, the largest U.S. legal publisher, sued several for-profit information brokers for infringement as a response to their copying and distributing the proprietary features in West's court reporters.[41] These cases resulted in victories for West, either through injunction or settlement.

We ought not to forget litigation against copyshops for producing coursepacks for college students. The first was a successful suit against the Gnomon Corporation, which operated several stores in the Northeast. In 1980 Gnomon entered into a consent decree enjoining the company from making multiple copies of journal articles and book chapters to produce coursepacks unless they had written permission from the copyright owners, or written certification from the faculty member that the copying complied with the *Classroom Guidelines*, which are part of the legislative history of the 1976 Copyright Act.[42] A year later, Harper & Row brought a successful suit against Tyco Copy Service. Tyco settled the case on terms similar to the Gnomon settlement.[43]

A case that received more publicity than either *Gnomon* or *Tyco* involved a lawsuit by Addison-Wesley Publishing against New York University, several members of its faculty, and a private copyshop for creating coursepacks. The parties settled, with NYU agreeing to inform its faculty

---

[38] *See infra* p. 48.

[39] Anna Snider, *Firm Settles Photocopy Charges*, NAT'L L.J., Mar. 22, 1999.

[40] *See infra* p. 48.

[41] West Publ'g Co. v. California Law Retrieval Serv., No. 93-7137 (C.D. Cal., filed Nov. 24, 1993); West Publ'g Co. v. Aaron/Smith, No. 89-CV-2693 (N.D. Ga., filed Dec. 1, 1989); West Publ'g Co. v. Faxlaw, No. 91-CV-293 (S.D. Fla., filed Feb. 12, 1991).

[42] Basic Books, Inc. v. Gnomon Corp., Copyright L. Dec. (CCH) ¶ 25,145, at 15,847, 1980 U.S. Dist. LEXIS 10981 (D. Conn. 1980).

[43] Harper & Row, Publishers, Inc. v. Tyco Copy Serv., Inc., Copyright L. Dec. (CCH) ¶ 25,230, at 16,361, 1981 U.S. Dist. LEXIS 13113 (D. Conn. 1981).

members of NYU's photocopying policies and to encourage them to comply with the *Classroom Guidelines*.[44]

A few years later came the case with real staying power: Kinko's, once found in every college town, was sued for copying articles and portions of books and compiling them into coursepacks.[45] Kinko's argued that the copying was educational because it was done for students at the request of their instructors. Unfortunately for Kinko's, the court did not agree. Not only did the court describe the copying as non-educational and commercial, but it also criticized Kinko's internal policies and procedures and its failure to educate and adequately supervise its employees, and held that Kinko's was a willful infringer.

Michigan Document Services (MDS), an Ann Arbor copyshop, apparently failed to learn any lessons from the *Kinko's* decision. In the MDS case, a three-judge panel of the U.S. Court of Appeals for the Sixth Circuit considered MDS's copying "educational" and held that it was a fair use. But MDS's happiness was short-lived. In an en banc decision (in which all the judges of a circuit sit together),the Sixth Circuit reversed the panel's decision, holding that the copyshop's systematic and premeditated copying for commercial motivation was infringing, noting also that MDS's copying went beyond the *Classroom Guidelines*.[46]

Litigation against copyshops did not end with the MDS case. The Copyright Clearance Center coordinated separate lawsuits in 2002 and 2003 against copyshops located near universities, with the earlier suit filed against Gainesville, Florida's Custom Copies & Textbooks,[47] and the latter against Los Angeles–based Westwood Copies.[48] Both defendants settled.[49] In 2005, ten major publishers sued copy shops in the Boston Area that

---

[44] Addison-Wesley Publ'g v. New York Univ., 1983 Copyright L. Dec. (CCH) ¶ 25,544, at 18,203 (S.D.N.Y. 1983).

[45] Basic Books, Inc. v. Kinko's Graphics Corp., 758 F. Supp. 1522 (S.D.N.Y. 1991).

[46] Princeton Univ. Press v. Michigan Document Servs., 99 F.3d 1381 (6th Cir. 1996).

[47] Steven Zeitchik & Judith Rosen, *CCC Charges Copy Shop with Infringement*, PUBLISHERS WKLY., Oct. 21, 2002, at 9.

[48] Steven Zeitchik, *Four Publishers Sue L.A. Copy Shop*, PUBLISHERS WKLY., Jan. 27, 2003, at 113.

[49] Judith Rosen, *CCC Settles with Copy Shop*, PUBLISHERS WKLY., Mar. 10, 2003, at 18; Judith Rosen, *CCC Settles One Suit, Files Another*, PUBLISHERS WKLY., July 14, 2003, at 12.

were making coursepacks for college students;[50] one of the lawsuits reportedly settled for $40,000.[51]

On first blush, looking at all of these cases may give those who work in the private sector more shivers than actors performing *Hair* in Central Park in February. But remember that every fact counts in a fair use analysis, and no two cases are the same.

Take, for example, the status of the defendants. In the lawsuits against the pharmaceutical companies, the defendants were corporations that were *not* in the business of directly profiting from making copies. These lawsuits resulted in settlements, not in court decisions. By contrast, the other lawsuits targeted for-profit document delivery companies and for-profit copyshops which directly profit from making copies of copyrighted works. The latter group—companies whose business is making money from making copies—are on much thinner ice than pharmaceutical or oil companies or other businesses that do *not* directly profit from copying copyrighted works.

So what should we make of *Texaco*? The court of appeals did *not* say that all copying in for-profit companies is infringing. The Association of American Publishers and the Copyright Clearance Center might believe—and they also may want librarians to believe—that *all* corporate copying requires permission or payment of royalties. But that is not what the court wrote, and it is not how fair use is applied. The appeals court noted that its decision was limited to the facts before it:

> Our ruling does not consider photocopying for personal use by an individual. Our ruling is confined to the institutional, systematic, archival multiplication of copies revealed by the record—the precise copying that the parties stipulated should be the basis for the District Court's decision now on appeal and for which licenses are in fact available.[52]

The Bottom Line: If you have a situation identical to that in *Texaco*— (1) systematic and extensive routing of journals to corporate researchers; (2) who make copies of entire articles; (3) without even reading them or otherwise using them for any purpose; and (4) merely file them away for

---

[50] Jesse Noyes, *Suit Targets Shops Copying for Classrooms*, BOSTON HERALD, Nov. 16, 2005, at 34.
[51] Christian B. Flow, *What's in a Gnomon?*, HARVARD CRIMSON, Oct. 13, 2006.
[52] *Texaco*, 60 F.3d at 931.

possible later use (archiving) such that the effect is to multiply the number of subscriptions without actually subscribing to the needed number of copies; and (5) if there is an easy way to pay royalties, such as through the CCC—then the copying is not a fair use. If you do not have this same factual situation, you should examine *your* facts under the fair use test. *Texaco* did not eliminate fair use in the commercial sector. Now let's see how *Texaco* might play out in the non-profit educational sector.

Fair Use in the Educational Sector

In its decision in *Texaco*, the court of appeals wrote:

> We do not deal with the question of copying by an individual, for personal use in research or otherwise (not for resale), recognizing that under the fair use doctrine or the *de minimis* doctrine, such a practice by an individual might well not constitute an infringement. In other words, our opinion does not decide the case that would arise if Chickering were a professor or an independent scientist engaged in copying and creating files for independent research, as opposed to being employed by an institution in the pursuit of his research on the institution's behalf.[53]

Does a professor act independently of her university when she writes a book or an article? Our answer is yes. Unless the professor was hired by the university to create a particular work under circumstances that would make it a "work made for hire," or unless the university otherwise owns or shares copyright with the professor in the work (which, under university policies, is more likely when a professor or researcher uses significant university funding and other resources), we think that a professor does act independently of the university when she writes a book or an article.[54] And as the court in *Texaco* wrote, its opinion did not address that issue.

---

[53] *Id.* at 916.

[54] "Works made for hire" are owned by the employer. If the creator is an independent contractor, the work is considered a "work made for hire" if it comes within one of nine categories listed in section 101 of the Act and if there is also a written agreement specifying that the work is a "work made for hire." If the work was prepared by an employee, whether it is a work made for hire depends on (1) control by the employer over the work, such as whether the work was prepared at the employer's location, whether the employer determined *how* the work was done, and whether the employer provided equipment or other means that supported the creation of the work; (2) control by the employer over the employee; and (3) the status and conduct of the employer, such as the employer being in the business of producing these kinds of works. *See* U.S. COPYRIGHT OFFICE, CIRCULAR 9: WORKS MADE FOR HIRE UNDER

Would the court have reached a different conclusion if Dr. Chickering was a college professor rather than a researcher in a for-profit corporation? As noted above, the court took great pains to limit the *Texaco* decision to its facts. Libraries may continue to route journals to their faculty, and their faculty may copy individual articles. But there are limits. A court might very well decide against a university if the copying is systematic, extensive, and archival—if, for example, a university library routes issues to the dozen members of the economics department, and the faculty extensively copy articles from the issues for later use. The same would hold true if the university's license to an e-journal permitted access to a small group of faculty researchers, but copies were made available to many others by electronic messaging. Here there could be both infringement and violation of the license agreement.

The Classroom Guidelines and the ALA Model Policy

4.3. Agreement on Guidelines for Classroom Copying in Not-for-Profit Educational Institutions

For teachers
- Single copy for research or teaching

For students
- One copy
- Brevity and spontaneity limitations
- Cumulative effect not harmful,

But
- No anthologies, compilations, or collective works

House Report No. 94-1476

Section 107 of the Copyright Act provides that "the fair use of a copyrighted work . . . for purposes such as criticism, comment, news reporting,

---

THE 1976 COPYRIGHT ACT (rev'd April 2010), *available at* http://www.copyright.gov/circs/circ09.pdf.

Most university policies assume that a professor owns his or her scholarly work unless there is significant investment by the university. *See, e.g.*, University of California, Office of Technology Transfer, Copyrighted Works Created at the University of California, *available at* http://www.ucop.edu/ott/faculty/crworks.html.

teaching (including multiple copies for classroom use), scholarship, or research, is not an infringement." The Act itself sheds no more light on what is fair use in an educational setting. We do have some guidelines, however, courtesy of a 1976 agreement by the Ad Hoc Committee of Educational Institutions and Organizations on Copyright Law Revision, the Authors League of America, and the Association of American Publishers. The *Agreement on Guidelines for Classroom Copying in Not-for-Profit Educational Institutions* was part of the 1976 Act's legislative history.[55] Here are its highlights:

(1) A single copy of a journal or newspaper article, a book chapter, or a drawing may be made by or for a teacher for research or to help teach or prepare to teach a class.

(2) A teacher may provide one copy of a copyrighted work to each pupil in his or her class (i.e., multiple copies) under the following conditions:

A. Brevity: (1) a 2,500 word article, or, if article is greater than 2,500 words, a 1,000 word excerpt or 10%, whichever is less (but at least 500 words).

B. Spontaneity: (1) The copying is made at the teacher's insistence and inspiration (rather than being directed from above by a principal, department chair, or dean); and (2) There was no time to get permission from the copyright owner.

C. Cumulative effect: (1) The copying is done for a single course (but multiple sections of the same course are okay); (2) No more than one article from a single author or three articles from a journal volume are copied during a class term; and (3) There are no more than nine instances of copying during a term, and the same materials are not copied from term to term.

D. You cannot copy to create anthologies, compilations, or collective works (i.e., "coursepacks").

We believe the *Guidelines* are overly restrictive. For example, a teacher may not copy for her students an entire article if it is longer than 2,500 words. Although the typical *Newsweek* or *Time* article will fit comfortably within the 2,500-word limit, that is not true for articles in scholarly journals.

---

[55] H.R. REP. NO. 94-1476, at 68–70. The Guidelines are reproduced in Appendix C to this book.

The American Association of University Professors and the Association of American Law Schools criticized the *Guidelines* "particularly with respect to multiple copying, as being too restrictive with respect to classroom situations at the university and graduate level" and would not endorse them.[56] Acknowledging this criticism, the House Judiciary Committee noted that the "purpose of the . . . guidelines is to state the minimum and not the maximum standards of educational fair use," and that "there may be instances in which copying which does not fall within the guidelines . . . may nonetheless be permitted under the criteria of fair use."[57]

You will note that the *Guidelines* do not permit the creation of coursepacks. As you read earlier, many courts agree, and so do we. When you create a coursepack that serves as the primary text for students in a class, get permission for each item that is protected by copyright, regardless of who does the copying—a for-profit copyshop, a non-profit university copy center, or a teacher. Coursepacks require permission. Period. If a teacher cannot get permission to include an article or book chapter in a coursepack, then leave it out.

4.4. ALA Model Policy (March 1982)

Single copy of a chapter or article for research or for reserve

Multiple copies
- Reasonable: amount of reading, number of students, timing . . .
- Notice of copyright
- No detrimental effect

Generally
- Less than six copies
- Not repetitive
- Not for profit
- Not for consumable works
- Not anthologized

---

[56] *Id.* at 72.
[57] *Id.*

The *Classroom Guidelines* did not address copying for library "reserve." In response to librarians' wish for some guidance, and also the belief that the *Classroom Guidelines* were unrealistic in the university setting, in 1982 the American Library Association prepared a *Model Policy Concerning College and University Photocopying for Classroom Research and Library Reserve Use.*[58]

Like the *Classroom Guidelines*, the ALA *Model Policy* provides that an instructor may, for scholarly research or use in teaching or preparing to teach a class, make a single copy of a chapter of a book; a journal or newspaper article; a short story, short essay, or short poem; or a chart, diagram, graph drawing, cartoon or picture.

With respect to copies for students, the *Model Policy* follows the *Classroom Guidelines*, permitting the distribution of a single copy to students in a class without permission so long as (a) the same material is not distributed every semester, (b) the material includes a copyright notice on the first page of the item, and (c) students are not assessed a fee beyond the actual cost of the copying.

After repeating the *Classroom Guidelines'* brevity standards, the *Model Policy* notes that they are not realistic in a university setting and that faculty "should not feel hampered by these guidelines, although they should attempt a 'selective and sparing' use of photocopied, copyrighted material." The Policy notes that copying should not have a significant detrimental impact on the market for copyrighted works, and, therefore, that instructors usually should restrict using an item to one course and not repeatedly copy excerpts from one journal or author without permission.

Copies for Librarians and Administrators

Some copying in the educational sector has no direct connection with teaching or scholarship. For example, if an academic librarian copies an excerpt about librarians using Twitter from *Library Journal* to share with her colleagues at a staff meeting, would she be protected by the fair use exception? Neither the *Classroom Guidelines* nor the ALA *Model Policy*

---

[58] The Model Policy is reproduced in Appendix D to this book and is available at http://library.ucmo.edu/circulation/Model_Policy.pdf.

addresses this situation, so we will use the four-factor test set forth in section 107.

Under the first factor, which considers the purpose and character of the use, the example described above appears to be neutral. Although the use is not directly connected to traditional fair use purposes such as teaching, criticism or scholarship, it is nonetheless a non-profit use that indirectly supports education. However, the character of the use is non-transformative, and thus not favored. The second factor, which involves the nature of the copyrighted work, also appears to be neutral. *Library Journal* isn't as creative as the *New Yorker*, but it's more than a mere factual report. Under the third factor, which depends on the amount copied in relation to the work as a whole, copying only a short excerpt from an issue of *Library Journal* would weigh in favor of fair use. Finally, the fourth factor, which considers the effect of the copying on the market for the work, seems to weigh in favor of fair use, assuming that the library already has a paid subscription and the copying doesn't substitute for a need to purchase multiple subscriptions.

The Bottom Line: Copying of this sort is going to be a closer call than copying that has a more direct connection with educational or scholarly purposes, but it should still qualify as a fair use provided that the original copy is purchased by the institution and the amount of copying is modest.

Copies for Library Reserve and Course Web Sites

4.5. E-Reserves

- Legal copy
- Copyright (©) notice and credits
- Reasonable amount
- For teacher and enrolled students
- Non-repetitive
- Course/faculty name retrieval

Many instructors make copies of course materials available to students outside the classroom. When the ALA's *Model Policy* was developed, this copying was done in paper format and placed on reserve in the library. Now it's more likely to be done electronically and posted online, sometimes on a site controlled by the library (i.e., library e-reserves), but more often on a site controlled by the instructor or an IT staff member using course management software such as Blackboard. This change has shifted some of the responsibility for reserve away from libraries, but libraries will still face copyright questions when instructors ask for guidance or ask for electronic copies to post online.

We think that course Web sites and library e-reserves are not very different from paper reserves, and that the *Model Policy* can provide a framework for electronic copies. The *Model Policy* views library reserve as an extension of the classroom, and provides that at the request of a faculty member, a library may copy and place on reserve an entire article, a book chapter, or a poem. Some of the *Model Policy*'s guidelines apply equally in a print or online environment:

- The amount of material copied should be reasonable in relation to the total amount of reading assigned for the course;
- The material should include a notice of copyright;
- The effect of copying should not be detrimental to the market. To this end, the library should own an authorized copy of the work;
- Avoid repetitive copying: do not copy the same materials semester after semester;
- Do not copy consumable works (such as workbooks); and
- Do not create anthologies (including coursepacks).

We can also borrow some ideas from the Conference on Fair Use's (CONFU) *Fair-Use Guidelines for Electronic Reserve Systems*, even though the conferees never reached consensus on them,[59] and *The Code of*

---

[59] THE CONFERENCE ON FAIR USE, FINAL REPORT TO THE COMMISSIONER ON THE CONCLUSION OF THE CONFERENCE ON FAIR USE (Nov. 1998). The *Final Report* notes (at pp. 15–16) that the working group reached an impasse over the scope and language of possible electronic reserve guidelines. However, some members of the working group continued to meet, and drafted for comment proposed guidelines. At the CONFU plenary session on September 6, 1996, several organizations, including the American Association of Law Libraries, the American Council on Learned Societies, the Music Library Association, and the Special Libraries Association, supported the draft. Others, including ASCAP, the Association of American Publishers, the Authors Guild/Authors Registry, and the Association of Research Libraries, did not. It was ultimately decided that the proposed electronic reserve guidelines would not be disseminated as a formal work product of CONFU.

The *Final Report*, which does not include the draft electronic reserve guidelines, can be found at the Patent and Trademark Office website http://www.uspto.gov. The preferred

Best Practices in Fair Use for Academic and Research Libraries, developed by the Association of Research Libraries and American University.[60] Although we mostly agree with the CONFU guidelines, we disagree with an introductory statement: "The complexities of the electronic environment, and the growing potential for implicating copyright infringements, raise the need for a fresh understanding of fair use." Horse Feathers! Electronic reserve issues are not terribly complex, and do not require a fresh understanding of fair use. Although it is easy to send a digital copy to lots of people, that does not mean that an entire university community wants to receive—let alone read—the article Professor Quincy Wagstaff assigns to his Huxley College students. With appropriate controls you can minimize the risk of abuse. As an equitable concept, fair use is flexible enough to apply to nearly any type of situation and any type of format; that is its elegance.

A different perspective is offered by the Copyright Clearance Center's *Using Electronic Reserves: Guidelines and Best Practices for Copyright Compliance*.[61] The CCC advocates for copyright owners, so we can expect their guidelines to be more conservative. Although we agree with many of the CCC's recommendations, we think there are a few that go too far in asserting the rights of copyright owners. Here are a few of the CCC guidelines with our comments:

E-reserves require the same permissions as coursepacks. While there are obvious savings—financial and environmental—from eliminating paper copies of reserves or coursepacks, traditional copyright rules still apply when using digital technology such as e-reserves: the institution must obtain permission from the rightsholder or its agent, who may charge a fee for such permission based on the amount of material and number of people viewing the material (i.e. students).

> *Comment:* Yes, traditional copyright rules still apply when using digital technology, but the rest of this guideline is misleading. The lawsuits that publishers brought against off-campus copy centers selling coursepacks, which we discussed earlier in this chapter, involved facts patterns that are

---

draft electronic reserve guidelines may be found on the University of Texas's Web site at http://copyright.lib.utexas.edu/rsrvguid.html and are reproduced in Appendix F.

[60] Available at http://www.arl.org/bm~doc/code-of-best-practices-fair-use.pdf and reproduced in Appendix M.

[61] Available at http://www.copyright.com/content/dam/cc3/marketing/documents/pdfs/Using-Electronic-Reserves.pdf.

different from e-reserves: (i) the coursepacks were sold by the copy centers for a profit, whereas e-reserves are typically produced by non-profit institutions at no cost to the user; and (ii) coursepacks generally contain a large part of the reading for a course, while e-reserves are more likely to feature short pieces that make up only a small part of the assigned reading. While coursepacks almost always require permission from copyright owners, e-reserves can often use copyrighted material without permission as a fair use.

"First semester free." The "first use is free" standard invoked by many libraries is not part of the Copyright Act or any subsequent rulings or agreed-upon guidelines. Any content posted in an e-reserve channel always requires copyright permission, unless it is covered by fair use, public domain, or other exception.

> *Comment:* The "first semester free" standard does come from agreed-upon guidelines, although it may be open to misinterpretation. The Agreement on Guidelines for Classroom Copying in Not-for-Profit Educational Institutions, which was approved by a Congressional committee and is one of the most authoritative (and conservative) set of guidelines available, describes several factors to be considered in a fair use analysis, one of which is whether material is used only once (which supports a finding of fair use) or is used repeatedly. So you can sometimes use material for free the first time and pay for use thereafter. Of course, this doesn't mean that you can always use material for free the first time. Frequency of use is just one factor in the analysis.

Get permission before posting. Unlike inter-library loans, you need to secure copyright permissions prior to posting content. Reposting of the same material for use in a subsequent semester requires a new permission.

> *Comment:* Again, the CCC sweeps with a wide broom, and sweeps fair use under the rug. The truth is that sometimes you need to obtain permission to post copyrighted content, and sometimes you don't, depending on the facts of your situation. However, the CCC is correct in pointing out that reposting in a subsequent semester will require a new permission if you needed to get permission the first time.

Incorporating the "best of" the CONFU Guidelines, the CCC guidelines, the ALA Model Policy, and ARL's Code of Best Practices, here are our suggested guidelines for posting online copies on course Web sites or library e-reserves without permission. At the outset, it's important to understand that these guidelines only apply to copies of copyrighted material that you want to post online. If the material is already accessible online, whether on a free site or in a database your institution subscribes to, you should post a link to the material instead of posting a copy. By posting only a link, you avoid making a copy. You may post as many links as you like, and for any purpose. Also, there are no restrictions on posting copies of works in the public domain.

The Librarian's Copyright Companion E-Reserve Guidelines

1. At the request of an instructor, e-reserves may include entire articles, book chapters, or poems, but they should not include entire issues of a journal or an entire book.
2. The amount of material on reserve for a course should be reasonable in relation to the total amount of reading assigned for the course.
3. Preferably, materials should be posted on only one occasion, for a single course. But materials may be posted repeatedly if other factors weigh in favor of fair use.
4. Access to e-reserve documents is limited to the instructors and to students registered in the particular course for which the materials are placed on reserve.
5. Documents on reserve for a specific course should remain in the e-reserve system only during the semester in which the course is taught, but short-term access to e-reserve documents may be provided to students who have not completed the course.
6. Simultaneous access to a particular document is limited to a maximum of five individuals.
7. The introductory screen to the e-reserve system shall include the following notice:

   > WARNING: THE E-RESERVE DATABASE INCLUDES COPYRIGHTED WORKS. THE MAKING OF A COPY MAY BE SUBJECT TO THE UNITED STATES COPYRIGHT LAW (TITLE 17 UNITED STATES CODE). DO NOT FURTHER DISTRIBUTE COPYRIGHTED WORKS INCLUDED IN THIS DATABASE.

8. If a copyright notice appears on the copy of the work, that notice should be included on the digital copy.
9. Documents in the e-reserve system should include accurate copyright management information, including (but not necessarily limited to) the author, source, and date of publication.
10. The instructor or the library should possess a lawfully made copy of any document placed on e-reserve.
11. Students should not be charged a fee to access or use the e-reserve system.

12. If possible, disable any download features and allow students only to view material without downloading.

We can see how a court interprets fair use in the context of e-reserves in a recent decision from a U.S. District Court in Georgia.[62] A group of publishers sued Georgia State University officials over copyrighted material posted on Georgia State's e-reserves. Instructors at Georgia State had posted the material for students to read, sometimes relying on fair use instead of obtaining permission. The publishers alleged that Georgia State's policies on the use of copyrighted material were too lax and not properly enforced, and that the publishers' copyrighted materials were infringed as a result.[63] Because of sovereign immunity, the publishers did not seek damages, but sought an injunction ordering Georgia State to change its practices.

A few months before this book went to press, the trial court issued a 350-page ruling that mostly favored Georgia State. Out of ninety-nine alleged instances of infringement, the court sided with the publishers only five times.[64] Before we take a closer look at the federal district court's analysis, it's important to note that the publishers have already appealed this decision to the United States Court of Appeals for the 11th Circuit. At the time you read this, there may already be a decision from the appellate court, which you definitely will want to look at.

In the Georgia State case, all the alleged infringements the court considered involved chapters and other excerpts from nonfiction books used as supplemental reading in courses (in addition to assigned textbooks), with access limited to students enrolled in the applicable course.[65] The court found that the first factor in the fair use test (character and purpose of the use) favored Georgia State in all instances because the copying was done for nonprofit educational purposes. The court also found that the second factor (nature of the work) always favored Georgia State because all the works copied were nonfiction.[66]

On the third factor (amount and substantiality of the portion used), the court held that the limits suggested by the *Classroom Guidelines* were too

---

[62] Cambridge University Press v. Becker, No. 08-01425, slip op. (N.D. Ga. May 11, 2012).
[63] *Id.* at 1–3.
[64] *Id.* at 338–39.
[65] *Id.* at 36, 40–41.
[66] *Id.* at 48–54.

restrictive.[67] Like the American Association of University Professors, the American Association of Law Schools, the American Library Association, and the authors of this book,[68] the court believed that classroom copying could be considered a fair use even if it goes beyond the *Classroom Guidelines*. In place of the *Guidelines'* much more restrictive standards, the court held that copying not more than 10% of a book or, in books with ten or more chapters, not more than one chapter, would indicate fair use under factor three.[69] In this case, Georgia State's copying was mostly within the limits set by the court.[70]

Does that mean you can always copy up to 10% of a book and call it a fair use? No. The court made it clear that its 10%-or-one-chapter rule was specific to the facts of this case.[71] Does that mean you can never copy more than 10%? Again, the answer is no. Remember that the third factor is just one part of the fair use test.

As for the fourth factor (effect on potential market or value), the court found that the plaintiffs had not lost any book sales as a result of the copying and only a very small amount of permissions revenue.[72] Nonetheless, the court held that if a digital license for an excerpted work was readily available and reasonably priced, the fourth factor would favor the publishers.[73] In this case, digital licenses typically were not readily available, and so the fourth factor usually favored Georgia State.[74]

Because the first and second factors always favored Georgia State, and the third and fourth factors usually did too, nearly all the instances of copying in this case were fair uses. The court's fairly liberal limits on the amount of copying and its skepticism about the publisher's lost sales were the key to Georgia State's win. Now we must wait to see what the U.S. Court of Appeals says.

Finally, we'll address one last question that sometimes comes up: by asking the owner for permission, are you giving away any fair use rights

---

[67] *Id.* at 58–59.
[68] *See infra* pp. 58–59.
[69] *Cambridge University Press* at 87–88.
[70] *Id.* at 6.
[71] *Id.*
[72] *Id.* at 33, 74.
[73] *Id.* at 79–80.
[74] *Id.* at 78.

you might have? In *Campbell v. Acuff Rose*, the Supreme Court said no.[75] You may still use a copyrighted work under the fair use doctrine, even if you've asked for and been denied permission. Just be sure that your use *is* a fair use. Remember that nothing a copyright owner says can diminish your fair use rights without your consent.

---

[75] "Being denied permission to use a work does not weigh against a finding of fair use." *Campbell*, 510 U.S. at 585.

Chapter Five
THE LIBRARY EXEMPTION
(SECTION 108)
❧❧

In addition to fair use, libraries and archives have certain rights to use copyrighted works without permission under section 108 of the Copyright Act. As we discussed in Chapter One, copyright law balances the rights of creators and users of information, with the ultimate goal of disseminating and promoting knowledge. Because libraries and archives play a special role in this goal, section 108 gives them certain privileges not afforded to other users.

Section 108 is in some ways a flawed and outdated piece of legislation. Some of its provisions are unclear, and changes in technology have added to the confusion. In 2004, the Copyright Office and the Library of Congress convened a study group to suggest ways of improving section 108. The study group released its report in March 2008,[1] in which it recommended substantial changes to the section, but Congress has taken no action to implement the recommendations.

Section 108 has several subsections which address various library activities. We'll discuss each in turn, starting with subsection (a), which sets forth some general requirements that apply to exempted copying by libraries and archives. Other subsections set forth further rights and restrictions that vary depending on the purpose of the copying and the material being copied.

---

[1] SECTION 108 STUDY GROUP REPORT, *available at* http://www.section108.gov/docs/Sec108StudyGroupReport.pdf.

> ### *5.1. Section 108(a)*
> ### *The Library Exemption*
>
> A library or employee acting within the scope of employment:
> - One copy
> - No direct or indirect commercial advantage
> - Open or available collection
> - Personal access or interlibrary loan
> - Copyright notice
>   - from the copy reproduced, or
>   - legend

Qualifying for the Exemption (Section 108(a))

Nowhere in the Copyright Act are the key terms *library* or *archives* defined. Some institutions are unquestionably libraries or archives under the everyday meaning of those terms. But for other entities, such as archives that exist only online, the application of section 108 is unclear.

Section 108(a) does make it clear that not every instance of copying by libraries qualifies for the 108 exemption. To qualify for the library exemption:

- the library or archives' collection must be open to the public or to researchers;
- copying or distribution must be made without any purpose of direct or indirect commercial advantage; and
- the copy must include a notice of copyright.

Each of these requirements merits discussion.

Open or Available Collection

Here's the language from 108(a):

> ... the collections of the library or archives are (i) open to the public, or (ii) available not only to researchers affiliated with the library or archives

or with the institution of which it is a part, but also to other persons doing research in a specialized field.[2]

The exemption is not limited to "public" libraries. Permitting visitors to use the collection, or participating in interlibrary loan arrangements under which a library makes its collection available to others, will meet the "open or available" requirement. This means that libraries whose doors are not wide open, such as corporations and law firms, many governmental and trade association libraries, and private college and university libraries, may qualify for the section 108 exemptions.

No Direct or Indirect Commercial Advantage— As Applied to Libraries in the For-Profit Sector

Again, here's the language from 108(a):

> ... the reproduction or distribution must be made without any purpose of direct or indirect commercial advantage.[3]

The Senate and House committees considering the proposed legislation had different interpretations of this requirement. The Senate Judiciary Committee wrote that this clause prohibited libraries in the for-profit sector from providing copies to their employees unless the copying qualified as a fair use or the organization received permission.[4] The House Judiciary Committee had a different opinion. It wrote that "the 'advantage' referred to in this clause must attach to the immediate commercial motivation behind the reproduction or distribution itself, rather than to the ultimate profit-making motivation of the enterprise in which the library is located."[5] Unlike the Senate, the House believed that libraries in the for-profit sector *could* qualify for the library exemption when making copies for company employees. It wrote

> Isolated, spontaneous making of single photocopies by a library in a for-profit organization, without any systematic effort to substitute photo-copying for subscriptions or purchases, would be covered by section 108, even though copies are furnished to the employees of the organization for

---

[2] 17 U.S.C. § 108(a)(2) (2006).
[3] *Id.* § 108(a)(1).
[4] S. Rep. No. 94-473, at 67.
[5] H.R. Rep. No. 94-1476, at 75.

use in their work. Similarly, for-profit libraries could participate in interlibrary arrangements for exchange of photocopies, as long as the production or distribution was not "systematic." These activities, by themselves, would ordinarily not be considered "for direct or indirect commercial advantages," since the "advantage" referred to in this clause must attach to the immediate, commercial motivation behind the reproduction or distribution itself, rather than to the ultimate profit-making motivation behind the enterprise in which the library is located. On the other hand, section 108 would not excuse reproduction or distribution if there were a commercial motive behind the actual making or distributing of the copies, if multiple copies were made or distributed, or if the photocopying activities were "systematic" in the sense that their aim was to substitute for subscriptions or purchases.[6]

The House Judiciary Committee's interpretation was supported by the Conference Committee, which was composed of members of both the House and the Senate. The Conference Committee concluded

> Another point of interpretation involves the meaning of "indirect commercial advantage," as used in section 108(a)(1), in the case of libraries or archival collection within industrial, profit-making, or proprietary institutions. As long as the library or archives meets the criteria in section 108(a) and the other requirements of the section, including the prohibitions against multiple and systematic copying in subsection (g), the conferees consider that isolated, spontaneous making of single photocopies by a library or archives in a for-profit organization without any commercial motivation, or participation by such a library or archives in interlibrary arrangements, would come within the scope of section 108.[7]

The Bottom Line: Libraries affiliated with for-profit organizations may qualify for the library exemption. But all libraries—those in for- and non-profit institutions—must avoid the section 108(g) prohibitions against multiple and systematic copying, discussed below.

---

[6] *Id.* at 75.

[7] H.R. Rep. No. 94-1733 (Conf.), at 73–74 (1976), *reprinted in* 1976 U.S.C.C.A.N. at 5810. If you're tempted to use the *Texaco* case for further guidance on section 108, remember that *Texaco* was decided under fair use and *not* under section 108.

No Direct or Indirect Commercial Advantage—
As Applied to Fee-Based Document Delivery

The direct or indirect commercial advantage prohibition means that a library loses section 108 protection if it profits from its document delivery service. The first step, then, is comparing how much it costs your library to make a copy with how much you charge. You may go beyond the obvious costs of paper and toner, and include all direct and indirect costs, such as equipment, supplies, and personnel.

An Association of Research Libraries (ARL) study from the late 1990s may help you determine if you are within this mandate.[8] In its report, the ARL noted that it cost research libraries, on average, $18.35 to borrow an item, and $9.48 to lend an item (the average cost for *all* libraries was $12.02 to borrow and $7.25 to lend). Costs obviously vary from one library to the next, and presumably are higher today.

We can hear some librarians saying, "We're not making money on document delivery; the revenue we receive just enables us to enhance our collection." Stop! If your document delivery activities enable you to "enhance your collection," you are either making money from document delivery (which you cannot do), or you are not counting all of your expenses (which indeed may be the case).

There is no definitive answer as to how much you may charge, but for some guidance, we offer these university library document delivery hypotheticals.

Example 1
Freedonia State College has a base document delivery transaction charge of $5.00, plus $.25 per page.

> *Comment:* Freedonia State, then, charges $7.50 for a 10-page article, and $10.00 for a 20-page article. We doubt that the college is making any money from its document delivery services.

---

[8] ASSOCIATION OF RESEARCH LIBRARIES, INTERLIBRARY LOAN AND DOCUMENT DELIVERY (ILL/DD) PERFORMANCE MEASURES STUDY, EXECUTIVE SUMMARY LL/DD PERFORMANCE MEASURES STUDY (May 1998), *available at* http://www.arl.org/bm~doc/illdds.pdf.

Example 2

The University of Freedonia charges $5.00 plus $.50 per page.

Comment: If UF has determined that it costs $10 to supply a 10-page article and $15 to supply a 20-page article, it does not violate the "direct or indirect advantage" prohibition.

Example 3

The library at the Freedonia School of Medicine charges non-profit institutions $10 per article, and for-profit institutions $20.

Comment: Again, if this merely recovers actual costs, the pricing structure is fine. The library may choose to subsidize document delivery to the non-profit sector, but it cannot profit from its services to the for-profit sector.

Example 4

The University of Freedonia Law Library has a minimum copying charge of $15 for individuals and non-profit institutions, and $20 for businesses. To that it adds a $.50 per-page photocopying charge. For business requests it also adds a $1 per-minute labor fee, with a minimum labor charge of $15.00. In other words, a ten-page article costs a business at least $40.00.

Comment: The law library's charges certainly appear to be beyond what is permitted under section 108. This does not mean that the library cannot provide document delivery services. It may, but it must pay royalties. The library would be wise to register with the Copyright Clearance Center and pay royalty fees to the CCC.

Example 5

The Freedonia Institute of Technology (FIT) Library sets up a fee-based document delivery unit (FIT-DOC). It has its own budget and hires its own staff. It advertises its document delivery services throughout the state and the region, especially to the corporate and scientific communities. It charges non-profits a flat $25 per article charge, and for-profit organizations $35 per article, plus whatever royalties it pays for copying. It also does online research at a charge of $50 per half hour. FIT-DOC is a member of the CCC and pays royalties to the CCC.

Comment: This certainly looks and smells like a business, even though it operates out of a state-supported university. It is appropriate for FIT-DOC to pay royalties and belong to the CCC.

Notice of Copyright

> ### 5.2. Section 401(b)
> ### Notice of Copyright
>
> Notice Requirements
> - © or Copyright or COPR.
> - Date of first publication
> - Name of copyright owner
> - Stamp:
>
> "THIS MATERIAL IS SUBJECT TO THE UNITED STATES COPYRIGHT LAW; FURTHER REPRODUCTION IN VIOLATION OF THAT LAW IS PROHIBITED."

The third and final requirement imposed by subsection (a) is the copyright notice requirement:

> ...the reproduction or distribution of the work includes a notice of copyright that appears on the copy or phonorecord that is reproduced under the provisions of this section, or includes a legend stating that the work may be protected by copyright if no such notice can be found on the copy or phonorecord that is reproduced under the provisions of this section.[9]

First, understand that you may not always be able to find a formal copyright notice. The United States joined the Berne Convention in 1989, and works first published on or after March 1 of that year do not need the notice to be copyrighted. If a work qualifies for protection, it is copyrighted when it is created, whether or not it has the formal notice.[10]

When you copy journal articles and the article itself includes a copyright notice, include it. If you are lucky, the copyright notice will appear on the first page of the article, either right after the author's name or perhaps as a footnote. Unfortunately, many journal publishers do not include a

---

[9] 17 U.S.C. § 108(a)(3) (2006).
[10] 17 U.S.C. §§ 401–405 (2006).

copyright notice with each specific article, but instead only a general notice at the beginning of the issue, or elsewhere.

Finding the notice may not be easy. The U.S. Copyright Office lists ten places where a copyright notice may appear in a book, and an additional three places for periodical issues.[11] Looking for the copyright notice is like being At the Circus. Make a diligent search for the formal notice, but do not make yourself crazy trying to find it.

If you cannot readily locate the formal copyright notice, stamp the article: "THIS MATERIAL IS SUBJECT TO THE U.S. COPYRIGHT LAW; FURTHER REPRODUCTION IN VIOLATION OF THAT LAW IS PROHIBITED." In fact, you should use the stamp *every time* your library makes a copy under the section 108 exemption. Here is what you should do:

- Prepare this notice in large (13-point) type;
- Put a box around it so it looks like this:

> THIS MATERIAL IS SUBJECT TO THE
> U.S. COPYRIGHT LAW;
> FURTHER REPRODUCTION IN
> VIOLATION OF THAT LAW IS
> PROHIBITED

- Send this to a stamp company and ask them to make you a stamp (in fact, make an extra stamp);
- Purchase a red ink pad and extra red ink;
- Whenever you make a copy—even when you *do* include the formal copyright notice—stamp the copy in the upper right hand corner.

What about chapters from books? Whenever you copy a book chapter, look for the formal notice. It usually appears on the verso of the title page (although as you read above, Copyright Office regulations permit an Easter egg-like hunt). You should include the copyright notice with the copy you are making. Also include the title page from the book, as it indicates where the chapter came from.

If a book consists of a variety of chapters written by different authors, it is a collective work, and each author may have copyright in his or her own chapter. The Copyright Office notes that a single notice applicable to the entire collective work indicates copyright protection for all of the con-

---

[11] 37 C.F.R. § 201.20 (2011).

tributions, regardless of who owns copyright in each separate contribution.[12] Therefore, treat all books the same: When you copy a chapter, also copy the title page and the general copyright notice. And use the red stamp, too.

As for journals, although the publisher typically has copyright in each issue as a collective work, the authors have copyright in their articles unless they signed those rights away. Although many publishers do in fact require authors to transfer copyright to them, do not assume that the publisher of a journal holds copyright in the articles.

What about digital information? If you want to make a paper copy of a document that you find on a computer, look for the copyright notice on the screen, just as you would if the article was in print. If you find the notice, copy it, too. And use the red stamp.

If you electronically forward the digital article to someone, in your introductory e-mail message include the "THIS MATERIAL IS SUBJECT TO THE U.S. COPYRIGHT LAW; FURTHER REPRODUCTION IN VIOLATION OF THAT LAW IS PROHIBITED" notice. It will be easy to include this notice on a generic "Here is the article you requested" e-mail message that you send to everyone who requests copies.

The Bottom Lines on section 108(a):

- The copying or distribution must be done with no purpose of direct or indirect commercial advantage. You may not profit, but you may recoup your costs. These may include costs of staff time, equipment, supplies, and delivery.
- The library collection must be open to the public or available to researchers in a specialized field. Your library qualifies if it offers in-person access to the collection, or if you make your collection available through interlibrary lending. A library need not be open to the general public to fulfill this requirement.
- Include a notice of copyright on all copies provided, or a legend that the work may be protected. You will not always be able to find the statutory notice on the work copied. Whether you find the formal notice or not, use the "This Material Is Subject to the U.S. Copyright Law; Further Reproduction in Violation of That Law Is Prohibited" stamp (red, 13-point typeface, upper-right- hand corner of the first page of each document copied). Stamp . . . Stamp . . . Stamp . . .

---

[12] U.S. COPYRIGHT OFFICE, CIRCULAR 3: COPYRIGHT NOTICE (rev'd Aug. 2011).

Copying Unpublished Works
(Section 108(b))

> ### *5.3. Section 108(b) Copying Entire Unpublished Works*
>
> - Three copies
> - For preservation and security, or for deposit for research use in another § 108(a) library
>
> If
>
> - The work is owned by the library asked to make the copy, and
> - The digital version is used internally

Section 108(b) permits a library to reproduce an unpublished work for the purpose of preservation and security, or for deposit for research use in another library, if the library making the reproduction owns a copy of the work. The three copies may be in any format, including digital. But a Congressional committee expressed concern that "uncontrolled public access to the copies or phonorecords in digital formats could substantially harm the interests of the copyright owner by facilitating immediate, flawless and widespread reproduction and distribution of additional copies or phonorecords of the work."[13] To address this concern, Congress included some restrictions regarding further distribution of digital copies and where digital copies may be accessed.

Under section 108(b)(2), copies reproduced in digital format may not be "otherwise distributed in that format," nor "made available to the public in that format outside the premises of the library or archives." The provision prohibiting further distribution in digital format might seem to preclude a library that owns an unpublished work from sending a digital copy to another library for research purposes. The legislative history, however, indicates otherwise. The Senate Judiciary Committee wrote that

> subsection (b) permits a library or archive to make (for itself or another library or archive of the type described by clause (2) of subsection (a)) up

---

[13] S. Rep. No. 105-190, at 61 (1998).

to 3 copies or phonorecords for these purposes, rather than just one, and permits such copies or phonorecords to be made in digital as well as analog formats.[14]

It seems pretty clear that a library that owns a copy of an unpublished work may make an analog *or* a digital copy "for deposit for research use in another library."

The language mandating that digital copies may be used only within the library premises seems less ambiguous. A library that has made or received a digital copy of an unpublished work under 108(b) apparently may not make it available in that format to the public outside the premises. A library patron may use a digital copy onsite, but the library should not send a digital copy to an individual, nor permit access to a digital version outside the walls of the library.[15]

If a library receives a copy of an unpublished work under 108(b), may a researcher copy the work? The answer depends on the results of a section 107 analysis. Whether a use is a "fair use" depends on the facts, so the answer is a definite "maybe." There probably is less room to copy an entire unpublished work than there is to copy a published work,[16] but section 107 itself says that "the fact that a work is unpublished shall not itself bar a finding of fair use if such a finding is made upon consideration of all the

---

[14] *Id.*

[15] The Section 108 Study Group recommended that libraries should be permitted to make digital copies available outside the library if the original unpublished work was also digital. SECTION 108 STUDY GROUP REPORT 61, *available at* http://www.section108.gov/docs/Sec108StudyGroupReport.pdf.

[16] In 1983, David Ladd, Register of Copyrights, citing the Senate Judiciary Committee's report (S. REP. NO. 94-473, at 106), wrote that "there is *no* fair use copying [of unpublished works] permitted beyond that authorized by 108(b)." U.S. COPYRIGHT OFFICE, REPORT OF THE REGISTER OF COPYRIGHTS: LIBRARY REPRODUCTION OF COPYRIGHTED WORKS (17 U.S.C. § 108) 106 (1983) [hereinafter REGISTER'S REPORT]. However, one of the premier treatises on copyright law includes this passage: "The scope of the fair use doctrine is considerably narrower with respect to unpublished works that are held confidential by their copyright owners. Note that 'confidential' differs subtly from 'unpublished.' If the author does not seek confidentiality, fair use is not necessarily precluded even as to an unpublished work." MELVILLE B. NIMMER & DAVID NIMMER, NIMMER ON COPYRIGHT § 13.05[A][2][b] (2011). Nimmer continues "The amendment thus reaffirms the holding in the *Nation* case— in particular, that the unpublished nature of a work . . . is a 'key, though not necessarily determining factor tending to negate a determination of fair use' . . ." *Id.*

above factors."[17] And in some cases, a library may copy an entire unpublished work for a patron under section 108(e), which is discussed later in this chapter.

The Bottom Line: A library may copy an unpublished work it already owns for preservation and security. The library may make up to three digital copies of the work, but the digital copies may only be used on-site. A library that owns an unpublished work may send a digital copy to another section 108 library. A library that receives a digital copy under 108(b) for research use similarly must limit access to the digital copy to within the library's walls.

Replacing Lost, Stolen, Damaged, or Deteriorating Copies of Published Works (Section 108(c))

> ### 5.4. Section 108(c) Copying
> ### Entire Published Works
> - Three copies
> - To replace a damaged, deteriorating, lost or stolen copy, or
> - Obsolete format
>
> If
>
> - Unused replacement unobtainable at a fair price
> - Digital version is used internally

Section 108(c) permits a library, under some circumstances, to replace a lost, stolen, damaged, or deteriorating copy of a published work by copying, if after reasonable efforts it determines that an unused replacement cannot be obtained at a fair price. As with section 108(b), the copy can be

---

[17] Section 107 was amended in 1992 to address the problem users had copying from unpublished works after the *Salinger* decision, discussed earlier. Pub. L. No. 102-492, 106 Stat. 3145 (Oct. 24, 1992).

in any format, including digital, but digital copies may be used only within the library premises.

Before a library may make a copy under section 108(c) it must have made a reasonable effort to acquire an *unused* replacement copy, and must not have been able to find such a copy at a fair price. The legislative history notes that a reasonable effort varies according to the circumstances, but that a library should contact commonly-known trade sources such as dealers and jobbers, and generally the publisher or other copyright owner.[18] You do not need to contact *used* book dealers; you must only determine that you cannot get an unused copy at a fair price.

What is a fair price? In 1983, the Register of Copyrights wrote that a fair price for a book or periodical is that which is charged by a publisher, a dealer specializing in remainders, or a jobber or dealer in bulk issues of periodicals, but not if the only unused copies are available at high prices from rare or antique dealers.[19] The Register's statement makes more sense for books than for journals when you consider the following scenarios.

Example 1. The Case of the Missing Issue
You are ready to bind the six issues from a scholarly journal, and discover that the July/August issue is missing. The subscription price was $40 for six issues, or about $7.00 per issue.

> *Comment*: If the publisher or jobber charges $10 to $15 to replace the July/August issue, the price seems fair. If it costs $20 or more to replace one issue, you might conclude that it is not. (Of course if you consider what it costs two libraries to request, reproduce, receive, and do the bookkeeping for an ILL request, it makes sense to just buy the issue.)

Example 2. The Case of the Missing Article
Someone cut out one article from the same journal. Each of the six issues has eight to ten articles. In other words, you "lost" about 2% of the volume.

> *Comment*: If it will cost $15 to $20 to replace the issue in which the article appeared, or $10 just for a reprint of the article, you may conclude that the price is not fair and ask another library to copy the article for you under section 108(c).

---

[18] H.R. REP. No. 94-1476, at 75–76; S. REP. No. 94-473, at 68.
[19] REGISTER'S REPORT, *supra* note 16, at 107–08.

Libraries may also copy a published work "if the existing format in which the work is stored has become obsolete." A format is obsolete "if the machine or device necessary to render perceptive a work stored in that format is no longer manufactured or is no longer reasonably available in the commercial marketplace." If you cannot see or hear the work because you are unable to acquire the equipment that enables you to see or hear it—if the equipment is no longer manufactured or not reasonably available —then you can make a copy of it.

Example 3. Sound Recordings

Your library has a collection of 78 r.p.m. blues records from artists like John Lee Hooker and Elmore James, but only one ancient record player.

> *Comment*: Under section 108(c), if you cannot acquire at a reasonable price a record player that plays 78s, you can copy the records onto a different format. This does not end the inquiry, however. If you can buy the recordings in a different format—if they are available on CD, for example —then you should do so and not make a copy.

Example 4. Videos

Your library has some old videos in Betamax format and you no longer have Betamax equipment.

> *Comment*: If you cannot purchase Betamax equipment at a reasonable price, you can copy the videos onto a different format unless, as in Example 2, you can purchase a video in a "current" format such as DVD.

The Bottom Line: If at a reasonable price a library can buy the equipment that enables it to play its old format "stuff," or if it can buy the old "stuff" in a current format, it should. If the library cannot do either, then it may make a copy under 108(c).

Articles or Excerpts for Users (Section 108(d))

> ## 5.5. Section 108(d) Articles and Excerpts
> - Single copy
> - Becomes user's property
> - No notice of impermissible purpose
> - Warning of copyright
>   - where orders are accepted
>   - on order form

Most section 108 copying by libraries takes place under subsection (d). Section 108(d) permits a library to make a single copy of an article, or of another contribution to a collection or periodical issue such as a book chapter, for a patron. It also permits library-to-library copying to fill a patron's request—what we call interlibrary loan, or perhaps more appropriately, document delivery. Section 108(d) has four conditions.

First, you can only make one copy. What if the requestor asks for two copies, one to read and mark up, and one for her files? Follow Nancy Reagan's advice, and just say no.[20]

Second, the copy must become the property of the user. You may not add it to the library's collection. Say, for example, that African explorer Jeffrey T. Spaulding[21] is hired to teach courses at your university. Professor Spaulding asks a reference librarian for an article from the *Ghana Journal of Science*, and also one from *JASSA: Journal of Applied Science in Southern Africa*, neither of which the library owns. The reference librarian asks the ILL librarian to get copies of the two articles from another library. The professor really likes one of the articles. He gives it back to the reference librarian and asks her to add it to the library's collection. Just say no.

---

[20] *See* http://www.reaganfoundation.org/her-causes.aspx.
[21] "At last we are to meet him, the famous Captain Spaulding. From climates hot and scalding, the Captain has arrived . . . ." "Hooray for Captain Spaulding", from the film *Animal Crackers* (music and lyrics by Bert Kalmar & Harry Ruby (1936)).

Third, the library must have no notice that the use will be for a purpose other than private study, scholarship, or research. Congress did not explain what this means, but it is reasonable to conclude that a library may do for a library patron what that person could do for him or herself as a fair use. You may decide—wisely, we think—that your library will not make copies for fee-based information brokers. Information brokers do not request copies for "private study, scholarship, or research." To the contrary, they are in the business of supplying copies to others. Even if the information broker says "We will pay royalties," it is *your* library that is making the copy. If you feel more comfortable not offering document delivery services to fee-based information brokers—and that is how we feel—just say no.

The final condition under 108(d) requires the library to display prominently at the place orders are accepted, and include on its order forms, a warning of copyright as prescribed by the Register of Copyrights. Here is what you have to do: (1) Copy the warning below and tape it near the door of the office where people request copies; (2) include the warning on the form people fill out when they ask for copies; and (3) for electronic ILL requests, include the warning on your electronic ILL form.

Section 108(d) Warning
Copyright Restrictions

The copyright law of the United States (Title 17, United States Code) governs the making of photocopies or other reproduction of copyrighted material.

Under certain conditions specified in the law, libraries and archives are authorized to furnish a photocopy or other reproduction. One of these specified conditions is that the photocopy or reproduction is not to be "used for any purpose other than private study, scholarship, or research." If a user makes a request for, or later uses, a photocopy or reproduction for purposes in excess of "fair use," that user may be liable for copyright infringement.

This institution reserves the right to refuse to accept a copying order if, in its judgment, fulfillment of the order would involve violation of copyright law.

Source: 37 C.F.R. § 201.14

In addition to the four requirements imposed by section 108(d), remember the rule in 108(a)(1) against copying or distributing for a direct or indirect commercial purpose. As we explained earlier in this chapter, profit-making document delivery services are not compatible with section 108. Another taboo is "systematic" copying, which is prohibited by section 108(g), and which we'll discuss later in this chapter.

Because there are many copyright pitfalls when it comes to ILL and document delivery, we've prepared some guidelines to help you navigate this difficult terrain. But first, let's discuss what publishers and the courts have to say.

The publishing industry has weighed in on document delivery and ILL. As one would expect, they take a restrictive view of these practices. The Association of American Publishers has written that the activities of "fee-based and technology-enhanced copying and distribution services of libraries . . . are indistinguishable in purpose and effect from those of commercial document delivery suppliers."[22] We don't agree. Nothing in section 108 bars a library from charging fees to recover the cost of document delivery and interlibrary loan. Section 108 merely excludes commercial activity.[23] A commercial document delivery supplier is indeed distinguishable from a library engaged in nonprofit, fee-based interlibrary loan and document delivery services.

The AAP's statement seems modest compared to the document delivery guidelines released in 2011 by the International Association of Scientific, Technical & Medical Publishers (STM). STM advises limiting ILL and document delivery to print documents, and only to on-site patrons.[24] STM characterizes this proposal as a "good compromise" between libraries and publishers; we would characterize it as overreaching on the part of STM. Section 108 clearly allows ILL and document delivery, and STM's acknowledgement of this fact does not amount to a compromise. Although section 108 was originally drafted in the pre-digital era, it doesn't bar the electronic delivery of documents.

---

[22] ASSOCIATION OF AMERICAN PUBLISHERS, STATEMENT OF THE ASSOCIATION OF AMERICAN PUBLISHERS ON DOCUMENT DELIVERY (Apr. 1994).

[23] 17 U.S.C. § 108(a)(1).

[24] INTERNATIONAL ASSOCIATION OF SCIENTIFIC, TECHNICAL & MEDICAL PUBLISHERS, STATEMENT ON DOCUMENT DELIVERY 2 (May 31, 2011), *available at* http://www.stm-assoc.org/industry-news/stm-statement-on-document-delivery/.

Electronic delivery makes publishers nervous because it can facilitate additional copying by the patron (which could be infringing), but if publishers want to eliminate electronic document delivery and ILL under section 108, they'll have to convince Congress to amend the law. In the meantime, if your library has obtained an article through ILL and you want to e-mail it to a patron, we say go ahead. Just remember the other restrictions we've mentioned.

While publishers wage a propaganda war against ILL, their friend the Copyright Clearance Center has introduced a fee-based service, called Get It Now, to compete with traditional ILL. Libraries that need articles from journals they don't subscribe to can pay a fee to the CCC, in return for which the CCC will supply the library with PDFs of the requested articles.[25] The CCC's service is licensed by publishers, who in return receive a portion of the fees.

Although we have no quarrel with libraries that wish to use this service, we are concerned that a licensing model such as this may come to replace traditional ILL, the result being a dilution of users' rights and more expense for libraries and patrons. The danger can be seen in an article from *Information Today* lauding the Get It Now service; in fine print at the end of the issue, *Information Today* advises libraries to contact the CCC for permission if they need to make copies of the article for ILL.[26] This is nonsense. Libraries might choose to use Get It Now because of its convenience, but they don't need the CCC's permission to fill an ILL request.

Of course, what the courts say is more important than publishers' guidelines. Unfortunately, we have only one appellate court decision—an old one at that—that involves library document delivery. In *Williams & Wilkins Co. v. United States*,[27] the U.S. Supreme Court upheld, by a four-to-four vote, a U.S. Court of Claims decision holding that large scale copying by the National Library of Medicine and the National Institute of Health was a fair use. Although the NIH copied only for their own staff, about 12% of NLM's requests came from private or commercial organizations, drug companies in particular.

---

[25] *See* http://www.copyright.com/content/cc3/en/toolbar/productsAndSolutions/getitnow. html.

[26] Barbara Brynko, *Armstrong: The Voice of Copyright*, INFORMATION TODAY, Oct. 2011, at 1.

[27] 487 F.2d 1345 (Ct. Cl. 1973) (*aff'd* by an equally divided Court, 420 U.S. 376 (1975)).

How *William & Wilkins* would be decided today is anyone's guess. At the time *Williams & Wilkins* was decided in 1975, section 108 had not yet been enacted and libraries could rely only on the fair use defense to avoid liability for unauthorized copying. To some extent, section 108 reflects preexisting case law on fair use, including *William & Wilkins*, but it was intended to go beyond fair use in some respects.[28] On the other hand, you should also consider what the appellate court in *Texaco* wrote about the advent of licensing since the *Williams & Wilkins* decision:

> Whatever the situation may have been previously, before the development of a market for institutional users to obtain licenses to photocopy articles [citing *Williams & Wilkins*] . . . it is now appropriate to consider the loss of licensing revenues in evaluating "the effect of the use upon the potential market for or value of" journal articles. It is especially appropriate to do so with respect to copying of articles from *Catalysis*, a publication as to which a photocopying license is now available. We do not decide how the fair use balance would be resolved if a photocopying license for *Catalysis* articles were not currently available.[29]

The dissenting judge in *Texaco* had a different opinion. Referring (as did the majority) to *Williams & Wilkins*, he wrote that he disagreed with the majority that "a reasonable and customary use becomes unfair when the copyright holder develops a way to exact an additional price for the same product," and that what Dr. Chickering (the Texaco scientist) did was a customary fact of copyright life that should be considered a fair use.[30] We happen to agree with Judge Jacobs. That a publisher or the CCC makes it easy for you to pay royalties does not abrogate fair use, section 108, or other user rights.

Nearly forty years after it was decided, what remains instructive about *Williams & Wilkins* are the NIH's and NLM's policies and practices. NIH made only single copies of articles, and generally would copy only forty or fifty pages, although longer articles would be copied with permission of a high level supervisor. As a general rule they copied only a single article from a journal issue. Exceptions were routinely made, but NIH would not copy more than half of an issue.[31]

---

[28] S. REP. 94-973, at 67 (1975).
[29] *Texaco*, 60 F.3d 913, 931.
[30] *Id.* at 934 (Jacobs, J., dissenting).
[31] *Williams & Wilkins*, 487 F.2d at 1348.

NLM would make only single copies of articles, and would not copy an entire issue. Nor would they copy articles from 104 journals that were included on a "widely available" list. NLM would not honor what it considered an excessive number of requests from an individual or an institution: not more than twenty requests from an individual or thirty from an institution, within a month. NLM would copy no more than one article from a single issue, or three from a volume. Generally, they would not copy more than fifty pages.[32]

With NIH's and NLM's policies in hand, as well guidelines from other librarians[33] and publishers,[34] here are our guidelines for when you can provide document delivery without paying royalties or obtaining permission. If they seem too liberal or conservative to you, adjust them to suit your taste. And remember that if the library is paying royalties, none of these guidelines are necessary.

Document Delivery Guidelines[35]

1. The library will not make more than one copy of an item at a time.
2. The library will not make multiple copies of an item for the same user (including the institution with which the user is affiliated) whether made simultaneously or over a period of time.
3. The library will not copy more than one article from a periodical issue for the same user.
4. The library will include with the copy it makes, if readily available, the "notice of copyright" from the work copied. The library will include on every copy it makes the following notice: "This Material Is Subject to the United States Copyright Law; Further Reproduction in Violation of That Law Is Prohibited."
5. The library will not fill a request if it knows that the requestor plans to sell the copy.

---

[32] *Id.* at 1348–49.

[33] The American Association of Law Libraries' (AALL) GUIDELINES ON THE FAIR USE OF COPYRIGHTED WORKS BY LAW LIBRARIES (rev'd 2001) is reproduced in Appendix J. The AALL's MODEL LAW FIRM COPYRIGHT POLICY (rev'd 2001) is reproduced in Appendix K.

[34] In addition to the AAP's statement and STM's guidelines, we also considered COPYRIGHT CLEARANCE CENTER, INTERLIBRARY LOAN: COPYRIGHT GUIDELINES AND BEST PRACTICES (March 2011).

[35] Guidelines adapted from James S. Heller, *The Impact of Recent Litigation on Interlibrary Loan and Document Delivery*, 88 L. LIBR. J. 158, 176–77 (1996).

6. If the library first photocopies materials for subsequent faxing or scanning, it will destroy the photocopy after the transmission is complete.
7. If the library downloads or scans a document to transmit it to a requestor, it will delete its electronic copy after the transmission is complete.
8. The library will not honor an excessive number of requests from an individual or an institution for articles from the same journal title. The CONTU Guidelines, which we discuss later in this chapter, may provide some guidance as to when requests are excessive.
9. Requests from other libraries include an attestation that the request complies with the Copyright Act or the CONTU Guidelines. The library will not provide copies if it knows that the request exceeds fair use or the section 108 exemption.

Out-of-Print and Unavailable Works (Section 108(e))

> ### 5.6. Section 108(e)
> ### Copying Entire Works for Patrons
> From the collection of a library where the user makes the request or from another library if:
> - New or used copy is unobtainable at a fair price
> - Becomes the user's property
> - No notice of impermissible purpose
> - Warning of copyright

Section 108(e) permits in some situations the copying of an entire work—a complete book, a substantial part of a book, or a journal issue—for a library patron if the library cannot obtain either a new or used copy at a fair price, and if the library meets the other requirements of subsection (d) discussed above (the copy becomes the property of the user; the library has no notice that the copy will be used for a purpose other than private study, scholarship, or research; and the library displays the copyright warning).

Like section 108(c), subsection (e) requires that the library make a reasonable effort to find a copy at a fair price. But the "unavailable copy" requirement for 108(e) is stricter than it is under 108(c). Under 108(c), Library A may ask Library B to make a copy of a damaged, deteriorating, lost, or stolen work if Library A cannot find a new copy at a fair price.

Under 108(e), however, Library A must be unable to find either a new *or used* copy. The library, therefore, must contact both new and used dealers.

Example 1

Ronald Kornblow,[36] a professor of hotel management, finds out that the International Journal of Hospitality Management recently published a symposium issue devoted to managing hotels in Islamic countries. He asks the library to photocopy every article from that issue for him.

> *Comment*: You cannot do this under 108(e). You could, of course, tell the professor that he may keep the library's issue, and then order another issue for the library. The professor will love you, he will love the library, and he will support you when the library wants something really important, like $100,000 to replace its fraying carpeting. If you cannot afford to purchase another issue, check out the issue to the professor and give him plenty of time to read it.

Example 2

Professor Spaulding wants to read a book published in 1983 on architectural ruins in North Africa. You borrow the book from another library, and when it needs to be returned the professor tells you it is the best book he ever read on that topic and he wants to purchase a copy. Unfortunately, the book is out of print. You contact numerous new and used book dealers, but none have the book, nor can they locate one.

> *Comment*: Under these circumstances, you may copy the entire book for the professor under 108(e).

Example 3

Same fact pattern as Example 2, except that an electronic version of the book *is* available for purchase from Google Books.

> *Comment*: It doesn't matter whether the copy available for purchase is print or electronic. If it's available, the library can't copy it. Professor Spaulding will have to buy a copy from Google Books.

---

[36] From A NIGHT IN CASABLANCA (Loma Vista Productions 1946).

Library Reproducing Equipment (a.k.a. Photocopiers and Scanners) (Section 108(f)(1) and (2))

A library is not liable for infringing activities done on library-owned reproducing equipment that is not "supervised."[37] Joe Student checks out a book from the Reserve Desk. He begins reading it, and decides to copy the entire book. We will assume that Joe's actions are infringing. The library is not liable as a contributory infringer if (1) Joe's copying is unsupervised, and (2) there is a notice on the machine that says:

> **WARNING: THE MAKING OF A COPY MAY BE SUBJECT TO THE UNITED STATES COPYRIGHT LAW (TITLE 17 UNITED STATES CODE)**

Your equipment does not come with this warning, so you must create a label yourself. Make it prominent—use large, bolded typeface—and tape it to the machine, close to the "copy" button. Put a label on every copier in the building, even machines in staff-only areas.

Should you affix warning notices to library computers as well? Section 108(f)(1) doesn't refer explicitly to computers, only to "reproducing equipment", a term that is not defined in the Copyright Act. An argument could be made that computers are "reproducing equipment" because they can be used to make digital copies, but in the absence of a statutory definition, words are assumed to have their common meanings.[38] We don't think that "reproducing equipment" refers to computers in everyday English, so we don't think that Section 108(f)(1) applies to computers. There's no harm in affixing copyright warnings to your library computers, but it's probably not worth the effort. Moreover, as we explained in Chapter Three, we don't think a library would incur any liability simply for letting patrons use library-owned computers.

Under section 108, a library is absolved from liability only for "unsupervised use of reproducing equipment located on its premises." If the equipment is available for walk-up use and the library merely adds toner or

---

[37] 17 U.S.C. § 108(f)(1) (2006).
[38] *See* Johnson v. U.S., 130 S. Ct. 1265, 1270 (2010); NORMAN J. SINGER & J.D. SHANDIE SINGER, 2A STATUTES AND STATUTORY CONSTRUCTION § 47:7 (7th ed. 2007).

paper, replaces cartridges, and fixes paper jams, the copying is not supervised. Copying *is* supervised when library staff (or the library's agents if the library outsources copying services) make the copies, or when the equipment is under such close supervision that the library can control what patrons actually copy. The most obvious examples are copy centers in university or corporate libraries that make copies for students and employees. If the copying is infringing, then the library can be liable.

Do the same rules apply in both for- and non-profit organizations? The legislative history to the Copyright Act says that "a library in a profit-making organization could not evade these obligations by installing reproducing equipment on its premises for unsupervised use by the organization's staff."[39] In other words, if an employee in a for-profit organization infringes copyright, both the employee and the institution can be held liable because businesses and corporations are assumed to have control over the actions of their employees.

The person who makes unauthorized copies on an unsupervised walk-up machine could be liable for infringement, of course. Section 108(f)(2) provides that a person who uses unsupervised equipment to make copies that exceed fair use is not excused from liability for infringement. Furthermore, a person who *requests* that the library make a copy for him or her under 108(d) is not excused from liability for infringement if the copying exceeds fair use.[40]

Contracts, Licenses, and Fair Use (Section 108(f)(4))

Tiny subsection (f)(4) of section 108 has a lot of oomph, just like Maria Callas or Leontyne Price performing a Night at the Opera. Here is what it says:

> Nothing in this section [108] in any way affects the right of fair use as provided by section 107, or any contractual obligations assumed at any time by the library or archives when it obtained a copy or phonorecord of a work in its collections.

---

[39] H.R. REP. NO. 94-1476, at 75.
[40] 17 U.S.C. § 108(f)(2) (2006).

First, this means that libraries, in addition to having rights under the section 108 exemption, also have fair use rights. This interpretation is supported by the legislative history of the Copyright Act.

> Nothing in section 108 impairs the applicability of the fair use doctrine to a wide variety of situations involving photocopying or other reproduction by a library of copyrighted material in its collections, where the user requests the reproduction for legitimate scholarly or research purposes.[41]

You should be wary of contrary messages from the publishing industry. Soon after passage of the Copyright Act, the Association of American Publishers and the Authors League of America asserted that libraries could copy materials *only* under section 108.[42] The then Register of Copyrights also had a restrictive, although somewhat different, interpretation of the relationship between sections 107 and 108. The Register wrote that library photocopying beyond section 108 may be permitted as a fair use, but only if the copying would be a fair use absent section 108, and then, only if the library first accounted for any section 108 copying that already took place.[43]

The AAP/Authors' League and the Register were wrong. Section 108(f)(4) cannot be clearer: "Nothing in this section in any way affects the right of fair use as provided by section 107." The legislative history is equally clear. Library copying and distribution may be permitted under section 107 even if it does not come within the section 108 exemption.

But there is another side of subsection (f)(4): Section 108 rights do not affect any contractual obligations assumed by a library when it obtained a copy of a work. In plain English, this means that by signing a license a library may agree to give up specific rights provided for in the Act, such as fair use and the section 108 exemption. Licenses and contracts are addressed in greater detail in Chapter Seven. For now, just remember this: you *may* contract away your rights. Review carefully all license agreements, and do not sign what you do not understand.

---

[41] H.R. REP. NO. 94-1476, at 78–79.
[42] ASSOCIATION OF AMERICAN PUBLISHERS & THE AUTHORS LEAGUE OF AMERICA, PHOTO-COPYING BY ACADEMIC, PUBLIC AND NONPROFIT RESEARCH LIBRARIES 4, 16 (1978).
[43] REGISTER'S REPORT, *supra* note 16, at 98–99.

The Section 108(g) Provisos

> ### 5.7. Section 108(g)
> Section 108 rights do not apply to:
> - Related or concerted reproduction
>   - o   Multiple copies
>   - o   Same material
> - Systematic reproduction
>   - o   Single or multiple copies
>   - o   Same or different material

Related or Concerted Copying or Distribution (Section 108(g)(1))

Fasten your seatbelts, secure your tray tables, and place your seats in an upright position. If you think that libraries can do most anything under section 108, you are wrong. Section 108(g)(1) and (2) govern section 108. No Monkey Business is allowed. There are two parts to subsection (g), and we begin with the first part.

Section 108(g)(1) prohibits related or concerted copying or distribution of multiple copies of the same material, whether at one time or over a period of time, either for aggregate use by one or more individuals or for separate use by individual members of a group. Congress did not define what "related or concerted" means, so we will use some examples.

Example 1
Mary N. Librarian reads an article on insurance bad faith—when an insurance company places its own interests above those of its insured clients and unreasonably denies a claim. Mary thinks the article might interest several people: professors if she works in a law school, attorneys if she is in a law firm, or agents if she works for an insurance company.

Comment: The "related or concerted" limitation in 108(g)(1) may be implicated if, on her own initiative, Mary copies the articles for numerous individuals. The easy (and also effective) alternative would be to notify them of the article. If any ask to see the article, Mary could route them the issue, or she may be able to make a copy under section 108(d). If the article is available online, she can send a link. Here copyright isn't implicated because Mary didn't make a copy. But if the library accesses the digital copy under a license, forwarding it must not be prohibited under the contract.

Example 2

Mary is on a listserv and receives an e-mail message about the insurance bad faith article. The message has a link to the article, which the author posted on the Web.

Comment: Mary should not download the article and send digital copies to professors, attorneys, or insurance agents. She should instead send an e-mail message that includes the link to the article.

Example 3

Mary presents continuing education workshops for several different library and education associations each year. She wants to give every attendee a packet of materials that includes several copyrighted articles.

Comment: This looks and smells like related copying and distribution of multiple copies of the same material at one time (for a specific workshop) and over a period of time (the different workshops). It is precisely what subsection (g)(1) proscribes, and Mary needs to get permission from the copyright owners.

Systematic Copying or Distribution (Section 108(g)(2))

Section 108(g)(2) is a bit different from (g)(1). Subsection (g)(1) addresses related and concerted copying of the *same* copyrighted work. Subsection (g)(2) paints with a broader brush. It prohibits the systematic making of multiple copies, and in some cases even single copies, of articles or short excerpts from the same publication. Here is the precise language.

The rights of reproduction and distribution under this section . . . do not extend to cases where the library or archives, or its employee—

(2) engages in the systematic reproduction or distribution of single or multiple copies or phonorecords of material described in subsection (d): Provided, That nothing in this clause prevents a library or archives from participating in interlibrary arrangements that do not have, as their

purpose or effect, that the library or archives receiving such copies or phonorecords for distribution does so in such aggregate copies as to substitute for a subscription to or purchase of such work.44

Subsection (g)(2) addresses copying for library users, and also copying *between* libraries. It expressly permits library-to-library copying, but there are limits. The big question: When is library copying systematic? A long, long time ago, the Register of Copyrights wrote that

> [t]he fundamental concern with respect to (g)(2) has been and continues to be the lack of statutory precision or common consensus about what copying is (and is not) 'systematic.' The meaning of that term has been vigorously debated since before the enactment of the statute, but not even the rudiments of agreement have emerged.[45]

The Register did offer this helpful advice: "the extent to which library photocopying services are large-scale operations, with full time photocopying staff, advertisements soliciting patronage, and consistently substantial output, bear directly on the extent to which such services are 'systematic.'"[46] The typical library (if one exists) photocopies or scans documents—mostly journal articles—for other libraries, and occasionally for the commercial sector. Other libraries offer extensive document delivery services that may operate as a separate division within their institution (typically a university library), with their own budget and staff. The latter arrangement is closer to what the Register of Copyrights warned about and may not fall under the section 108 exemption or qualify as a fair use. Libraries that do engage in "systematic" copying or distribution need to get permission or pay royalties.

The Senate Judiciary Committee offered specific examples of what it considered systematic copying.[47] Do not take these as gospel; the Senate Committee was more conservative than the House Committee with regard to library copying. That said, here are the Senate Committee's examples, and our comments.

---

[44] 17 U.S.C. § 108(g)(2) (2006).
[45] REGISTER'S REPORT, *supra* note 16, at 130.
[46] *Id.* at 140.
[47] S. REP. NO. 94-473, at 70.

Senate Example 1

A library with a collection of journals in biology informs other libraries with similar collections that it will maintain and build its own collection and will make copies of articles from these journals available to them and their patrons on request. Accordingly, the other libraries discontinue or refrain from purchasing subscriptions to these journals and fulfill their patrons' requests for articles by obtaining photocopies from the source library.

> *Comment*: The real test is one of degree: How many copies are being requested by the libraries that cancel their subscriptions? Each library certainly may request copies within the CONTU Guidelines, which we will get to shortly. Also remember that the first sale doctrine allows a library to freely lend its material to other libraries, regardless of section 108 limitations, as it isn't making any copies. Nowadays, it's more likely that the library will get the journal electronically via a license agreement. In this case, the license will control. You will want to review carefully its terms, especially those dealing with lending and document delivery.

Senate Example 2

A research center employing a number of scientists and technicians sub-scribes to one or two copies of needed periodicals. By reproducing photo-copies of articles the center is able to make the materials in these perio-dicals available to its staff in the same manner which otherwise would require multiple subscriptions.

> *Comment*: This sounds like Texaco, except here the library makes the copies rather than the scientist. If the library makes so many copies that copying does, indeed, substitute for additional subscriptions—if but for the copying the library would need additional subscriptions—then the copying is systematic and violates 108(g)(2).
>
> Reactive is better than proactive. A library that actively promotes its copying services is engaging in risky business. If your library sends out weekly or monthly tables of contents from recently published journals to professors or lawyers, you would be wise not to advertise that the library will photocopy articles upon request. A library that becomes a copying factory will run afoul of the related or concerted copying prohibitions of 108(g)(1), and perhaps the systematic copying proscribed by 108(g)(2). Remember that section 108(g) begins with these words: "The rights of reproduction and distribution under this section extend to the isolated and unrelated reproduction or distribution of a single copy or phonorecord of

the same material on separate occasions." For digital content, check your license. If all staff are "authorized users," everyone can access the content without intervention by the library.

Senate Example 3

Several branches of a library system agree that one branch will subscribe to particular journals in lieu of each branch purchasing its own subscriptions. The one subscribing branch will copy articles for users in any branch.

> ***Comment***: This differs from the first example in that it involves a single library system that decides to reduce its number of subscriptions to the same title. Should transactions between libraries within a single library system be considered "interlibrary" transactions? We think the answer is yes. If the central library sends lots of copies to its branches—so many that the single subscription substitutes for subscriptions the branches really should have—the copying is systematic. As in Senate Example 1, consider lending the issue rather than making copies.
>
> Subscriptions to most periodicals subscribed to by city and county public libraries are not expensive. Do not be penny-wise and pound-foolish. Money saved by cancelling a subscription to a $50 magazine will be quickly eaten up by photocopying or shuttle costs. If a title is used frequently in each branch of a library system, you should have multiple subscriptions. You will make your users happy, and probably will save money in the long run.
>
> As for digital journals, the licensing agreement may make the content available to one library, to several libraries, or to all libraries in the system. Similarly, the content may be available to some, or all, of the library system's users. Don't plan on using section 108 or any other aspect of copyright law to get around the license agreement, because the license agreement overrides regular copyright rules. Whatever agreement you sign is what you will live by, so negotiate for broad access rights.

The CONTU Guidelines

5.8. Section 108(g)(2)
The CONTU Guidelines

- Journal published within last five years
- Maximum of five articles from same title in one year
- Exceptions
  - issue is missing
  - journal is on order
- Attestation by requesting library
- Maintain three years of "borrowing" records

After writing that section 108 struck the appropriate balance between the rights of creators and the needs of users, the Senate Judiciary Committee continued:

> However, neither a statute nor legislative history can specify precisely which library photocopying practices constitute the making of "single copies" as distinguished from "systematic reproduction." Isolated single spontaneous requests must be distinguished from "systematic reproduction." The photocopying needs of such operations as multi-county regional systems must be met. The committee therefore recommends that representatives of authors, book and periodical publishers and other owners of copyrighted material meet with the library community to formulate photocopying guidelines to assist library patrons and employees.[48]

The House Judiciary Committee's Report, submitted nine months after the Senate Report, noted the "storm of controversy" provoked by the addition of subsection (g)(2) proscribing the "systematic reproduction or distribution of single or multiple copies or phonorecords," and that 108(g)(2) was then amended to include the proviso "that nothing in this clause prevents a library or archives from participating in interlibrary arrangements that do not have, as their purpose or effect, that the library or archives receiving such copies or phonorecords for distribution does so in such aggregate quantities as to substitute for a subscription to or purchase

---

[48] *Id.* at 70–71.

of such work."[49] The Committee wrote that the National Commission on New Technological Uses of Copyrighted Works (CONTU) offered to help develop "more or less specific guidelines establishing criteria to govern various situations."[50] The CONTU Guidelines, which were included in the House Committee Report,[51] follow.

Guidelines for the Proviso of Subsection 108(g)(2)

1. As used in the proviso of subsection 108(g)(2), the words ". . . such aggregate quantities as to substitute for a subscription to or purchase of such work" shall mean:

(a) with respect to any given periodical (as opposed to any given issue of a periodical), filled requests of a library or archives (a "requesting entity") within any calendar year for a total of six or more copies of an article or articles published in such periodical within five years prior to the date of the request. These guidelines specifically shall not apply, directly or indirectly, to any request of a requesting entity for a copy or copies of an article or articles published in any issue of a periodical, the publication date of which is more than five years prior to the date when the request is made. These guidelines do not define the meaning, with respect to such a request, of ". . . such aggregate quantities as to substitute for a subscription to [such periodical]."

(b) With respect to any other material described in subsection 108(d), (including fiction and poetry), filled requests of a requesting entity within any calendar year for a total of six or more copies or phonorecords of or from any given work (including a collective work) during the entire period when such material shall be protected by copyright.

2. In the event that a requesting entity—

(a) shall have in force or shall have entered an order for a subscription to a periodical, or

(b) has within its collection, or shall have entered an order for, a copy of phonorecord of any other copyrighted work, materials from either category of which it desires to obtain by copy from another library or archives (the "supplying entity"), because the material to be copied is not reasonably available for use by the requesting entity itself, then the fulfillment of such request shall be treated as though the requesting entity made such copy from its own collection. A library or archives may request a copy or phonorecord from a supplying entity only under those

---

[49] H.R. REP. NO. 94-1476, at 77–78.
[50] *Id.* at 78.
[51] *Id.* at 68–70.

circumstances where the requesting entity would have been able, under the other provisos of section 108, to supply such copy from materials in its own collection.

3. No request for a copy or phonorecord of any materials to which these guidelines apply may be fulfilled by the supplying entity unless such request is accompanied by a representation by the requesting entity that the request was made in conformity with these guidelines.

4. The requesting entity shall maintain records of all requests made by it for copies or phonorecords of any materials to which these guidelines apply and shall maintain records of the fulfillment of such requests, which records shall be retained until the end of the third complete calendar year after the end of the calendar year in which the respective request shall have been made.

5. As part of the review provided for in subsection 108(i), these guidelines shall be reviewed not later than five years from the effective date of this bill.

The CONTU drafters apparently had grand illusions of being in Congress. Let's use plain English, and some examples and comments, to explain what the Guidelines really say.

- The Guidelines apply only to journal articles published within the last five years.
- In any one year, the Guidelines expressly permit a library to request from another library copies of five articles from the same journal title. Some call this the "Rule of 5" or "Suggestion of 5."

Example 1

You work in a college library. Professor Spaulding, a visiting professor for one semester, needs articles from several journals your library does not own. Are you absolutely limited to requesting from other libraries no more than five copies from each title?

Comment: No. Here is what the Conference Committee wrote about the Guidelines:

> The conference committee understands that the guidelines are not intended as, and cannot be considered, explicit rules or directions governing any and all cases, now or in the future. It is recognized that their purpose is to provide guidance in the most commonly encountered interlibrary photocopying situations, that they are not intended to be limiting or determinate in themselves or with respect to other situations, and that they deal with an evolving situation that

will undoubtedly require their continuous reevaluation and adjustment. With these qualifications, the conference committee agrees that the guidelines are a reasonable interpretation of the proviso of section 108(g)(2) in the most common situations to which they apply today.[52]

As for Professor Spaulding's request, remember that these are guidelines. You may exercise some judgment. We think that a short-term project is a good example of when you may go beyond the "five article" guideline. Requesting six articles from the same journal title from other libraries does not bother us and, frankly, neither does a few more. We do not feel the least bit queasy until it moves into double figures.

Example 2

The requestor is an attorney who is working on a quick turnaround, one-time project.

> *Comment:* Same answer as above.
>
> - You do not need to count requests if your library subscribes to the journal and the issue you need happens to be unavailable.
> - You do not need to count requests if your library has entered an order for a subscription to the journal.
> - The requesting library must attest that the request conforms to the guidelines.

Example 3

The requesting library confirms that the request complies with another provision of the Act, such as section 108(c)—to replace a damaged or lost copy.

> *Comment:* This is fine. The American Library Association's Interlibrary Loan Request Form, and both the WorldCat and ILLiad electronic ILL protocols, require that the requesting library indicate that the request complies with either the 108(g)(2) Guidelines (CCG) or other provisions of the copyright law (CCL).[53]

---

[52] H.R. Rep. No. 94-1733 (Conf.), at 71–72 (1976).

[53] The ALA reminds requesting libraries that they are responsible for complying with section 108(g)(2) and the CONTU Guidelines. American Library Association, Interlibrary Loan Code for the United States, Explanatory Supplement § 4.8 (May 2008) [hereinafter ALA Interlibrary Loan Code]. The ALA's interlibrary loan request form is available at http://www.ala.org.

Example 4

The requesting library does not include any attestation.

Comment: Just say no.

- The requesting library should keep records of its document delivery requests for three full calendar years, plus the current year.

Example 5

Your interlibrary loan clerk read the USA Patriot Act[54] and is concerned about privacy. She wants to discard all borrowing records more than three months old.

Comment: The ALA notes that ILL transactions are confidential library records, but that including a user's name on an ILL request does not violate their Interlibrary Loan Code.[55] To monitor requests, we suggest that libraries record (1) the date of the request; (2) the title and author of the article; and (3) the title of the journal, its volume number, and the publication date. Three full calendar years plus the current year means just that: Keep records for the entire time period.

The Patriot Act treats library records, including borrowing transactions, as business records that must be disclosed to law enforcement officials who present a subpoena or search warrant from a duly authorized court as part of a criminal investigation. After an ILL transaction has been completed, libraries may want to delete from their records the name of the person who requested the item.

In the end, there is no exact answer as to how much copying is permitted under section 108. Even non-profit academic libraries that arguably have "gold club" status cannot make copies for faculty or students, or use document delivery, in quantities such that the copying substitutes for needed subscriptions or purchases. Because section 108 really is a fair use–like provision that permits a library to, in effect, act as an agent for the person who needs a copy, the answer to the question "How much may I copy?" depends on the facts.

So here you are, in the gray zone. What is the bottom line when your library receives a request from a library patron—a teacher, a judge, a corporate CEO, whomever—and are unsure whether the use is permitted under section 108 or as a fair use? If you thought about this a lot and *still* think it is a close call, you may recall that the primary purpose of copyright is not to reward copyright owners but instead to enhance knowledge and promote the creation of other works. Just say yes.

---

[54] Pub. L. No. 107-56, 115 Stat. 272 (2001).
[55] ALA INTERLIBRARY LOAN CODE, *supra* note 53, § 4.2.

Preservation and Term Extension (The Return of Sonny Bono) (Section 108(h))

> ### 5.9. Section 108(h) Preservation and Term Extension
>
> May copy, distribute, display, or perform the work during last twenty years of term for preservation, scholarship, or research
> - The work is not exploited commercially
> - A copy is unobtainable at a fair price
> - No owner notification

The Sonny Bono Copyright Term Extension Act added twenty years to the copyright term. Congress tried to appease the library and academic communities with a tiny bone: During the last twenty years of copyright of a published work, a library or archives, or a non-profit educational institution that functions as a library or archives, may copy, distribute, display, or perform a work—in either facsimile or digital form—for preservation, scholarship, or research if (a) the work is not subject to normal commercial exploitation, and (b) a copy cannot be obtained at a reasonable price. The library may not take advantage of the exemption if the copyright owner notifies the Copyright Office that either (a) or (b) apply.[56]

The "normal commercial exploitation" language appears to mean that the copyright owner has decided there is no commercial value in the work. If the copyright owner makes the work available on the Web for a fee—either as part of a database or as a stand-alone product—or if the library can purchase reprints, the work *is* being commercially exploited and the exemption does not apply. And even if the work is not being commercially exploited, the exemption only applies if the library cannot acquire a copy at a reasonable price.

The Bottom Line: This exemption is not worth the paper it was printed on, nor the bits and bytes it takes up in the digital world. Works that have

---

[56] 17 U.S.C. § 108(h)(1)–(3) (2006).

value will be commercially exploited. And in any event, by the time a work is in the last twenty years of its term, it is pretty darn old.

Non-Print Works (Music, Pictures, Graphs, and Sculptural Works) (Section 108(i))

5.10. Section 108(i) Non-Print Works

Except for subsections (b) and (c), Section 108 does not apply to:

- Musical works
- Pictorial, graphic or sculptural works, or
- Motion pictures or other AV works other than news

But

- May include illustrations and diagrams within articles or chapters

---

Section 108 is designed primarily for print works and sound recordings. Most of the library exemption does not apply to the following: (1) musical works, (2) pictorial works, (3) graphical works, (4) sculptural works, (5) motion pictures, and (6) audiovisual works that do not deal with the news.[57]

Section 108(i), however, provides that each of these six types of works may be reproduced or distributed under certain circumstances. First, section 108(b), which permits the copying of an unpublished work for purposes of preservation, security, or for deposit for research use in another library, applies to works in these non-print formats. Second, section 108(c) also applies to these types of works, thereby permitting the copying of a published work in these formats to replace a damaged, deteriorating, lost, or stolen copy if the library cannot obtain an unused replacement copy at a fair price. Third, section 108(c) also permits the making of a copy if the

---

[57] *Id.* § 108(i). A "musical work" is different from a "sound recording." The musical work is the composition; the sound recording is what we hear by playing a disk, tape, phonorecord, etc.

format in which the work is stored is obsolete and you cannot acquire an unused replacement of the work at a fair price.

Articles and book chapters often are accompanied by illustrations, diagrams, graphs and charts. You *may* include illustrations, diagrams, etc., when you copy an article or book excerpt under section 108(d) or (e).

Section 108 and Fair Use (Reprise) (Section 108(f)(4))

Section 108, as you have seen, has its limitations. But remember that fair use may still apply. Section 108(f) reads "[n]othing in this section . . . in any way affects the right of fair use as provided by section 107. . . ." This is reinforced by the House Judiciary Committee:

> Nothing in section 108 impairs the applicability of the fair use doctrine to a wide variety of situations involving photocopying or other reproduction by a library of copyrighted material in its collections, where the user requests the reproduction for legitimate scholarly or research purposes.[58]

---

[58] H.R. REP. NO. 94-1476, at 78–79.

Chapter Six
DIGITAL INFORMATION
AND SOFTWARE

ഇൗരു

This chapter will discuss how licenses and copyright law interact to control libraries' use of digital information. Today, software and digital products generally are transferred under license. That is, unlike books you purchase, you generally will not own the digital products that publishers license to you.

Licensing information is more like renting an apartment than buying a house. Just as landlords may ban dogs or loud music in their rentals, publishers and information vendors may add a number of conditions to your use of their digital resources. These conditions may be more restrictive than copyright law requires. The most important thing to remember about licenses is to read them carefully. Contracts can override default copyright rules; if you are not vigilant, you may sign away the privileges that libraries are allowed under copyright law.

Some publishers have begun offering "digital ownership" or "perpetual access" to digital resources. These options usually involve a large payment with smaller annual fees to maintain access to publisher services and updates. An advantage of these arrangements is that you own the digital copies and don't lose access to them if you cancel the database subscription. But these purchases will be governed by a contract, too; examine it closely so you know exactly what you are buying. Do you get continued access to the database search functions? If you just get thousands of digital articles, it might be difficult to access them without a search mechanism. Buying digital copies can make sense, but you want to be sure you can use what you own in case you cancel your subscription or the publisher stops supporting the resource.

A recent article describes a case where a law library purchased digital ownership to a database and then had to cancel the subscription due to budget cuts.[1] The library received the files in the database on two 500GB hard drives. Because owning the files did not include access to the vendor's search mechanisms, the library had to hire a computer engineering doctoral student to create a basic search interface. The library ultimately had a functional database, but cancelling the database still affected the patrons' experience accessing the resource.

Now let's cover some basic questions.

Question: Is information on the World Wide Web subject to copyright protection?

Answer: Yes.

Question: Do the same rules apply to digital content and information in book or magazine format?

Answer: Generally, yes, but there are exceptions, such as sections 108(b) (unpublished works duplicated for purposes of preservation and security or for deposit for research use in another library or archives) and 108(c) (a replacement copy of a damaged, deteriorating, lost, or stolen published work) which restrict the places where digital copies may be read.

Question: May I send information from the Web to anyone I want, such as members of a listserv?

Answer: Think about the print world. You may not, under either fair use or the library exemption, photocopy a copyrighted journal article and send paper copies to an untold number of people without permission. That you can easily distribute digital articles to lots of people via e-mail does not mean that you can do so without infringing. This is true even when an author posts his or her article on the Web. Rather than download the text, send an e-mail message that includes a link. You achieve the same result,

---

[1] Sallie Smith, Susanna Leers, & Patricia Roncevich, *Database Ownership: Myth or Reality?*, 103 Law Lib. J. 233 (2011).

but you have not made any copies. Even e-mail messages are copyrightable. There may be an unwritten assumption that someone who sends an e-mail message to a huge list impliedly gives his or her permission to send it to the rest of the world, but this may not always be the case.

Question: John Bit and I are fellow members of list A. John sends a draft article to the list, and invites everyone to share their comments with other members. May I send a reply to the list, along with John's article?

Answer: Yes. John sent out his article and invited comments. Consent to make copies can be inferred when one knows of a use and encourages it.[2] John's conduct gives an implied license to list members to make copies of his article for purposes of accessing it and providing comments.

Question: I am a member of list B. My colleague Mary Byte subscribes to both list A and list B. Mary received a copy of John's article from list A and forwarded it to me. May I share John's article with other members of list B?

Answer: John's sharing his article with list A impliedly gave permission to the members of list A to make copies for the purpose of reviewing the paper and offering comments. John's actions don't indicate he intended to share copies with list B members, so you cannot rely on implied consent to justify making copies. You'd have to rely on some other exception to make copies. The best way of handling this is to ask John if he wants his article circulated to list B. If he doesn't, don't.

---

[2] Field v. Google, Inc., 412 F.Supp.2d 1106, 1116 (D. Nev. 2006). *See also* John S. Sieman, Comment, *Using the Implied License to Inject Common Sense into Digital Copyright*, 85 N.C. L. Rev. 885 (2007).

Click and Shrinkwrap Licenses (Section 117)

6.1. Click and Shrinkwrap Licenses

Click and shrinkwrap licenses may
- Prevent libraries and patrons from using materials in ways copyright law would otherwise permit, and
- Specify the forum for any disputes.

Shrinkwrap and click licenses refer to unsigned agreements between a purchaser of digital products or software and the creator or vendor that define the respective rights of the parties. Shrinkwrap refers to the plastic wrap that encases software; upon opening the program the first thing the user sees is the license agreement that sets out the terms of use. A purchaser who opens the shrinkwrap or other packaging, or begins using the software, is presumed to have read the license and assented to its terms.

Click licenses are found on Web-based products. The user cannot access the information or use the program until he or she agrees to the terms by clicking a box. Licenses frequently include terms that prohibit uses otherwise permitted under copyright law or state consumer protection law, such as the right to make fair use of the work. Courts are split on whether shrinkwrap or click licenses are enforceable.

Compare *Vault v. Quaid*,[3] a 1988 decision of the United States Court of Appeals for the Fifth Circuit, with *Pro-CD v. Zeidenberg*,[4] a 1996 decision from the United States Court of Appeals for the Seventh Circuit. In *Vault*, the court held unenforceable a license provision that was not disclosed to the purchaser at the time of purchase. By contrast, the *Pro-CD* court held that shrinkwrap licenses *are* enforceable unless their terms are objectionable on grounds applicable to contracts in general. The fact that copyright law permits uses that might be precluded under a license did not convince the court to reach a different conclusion. Likewise, in *Bowers v.*

---

[3] 847 F.2d 255 (5th Cir. 1988).
[4] 86 F.3d 1447 (7th Cir. 1996).

Baystate Technologies, Inc.,[5] the United States Court of Appeals for the Federal Circuit held that copyright law did not override a shrinkwrap provision that prevented reverse engineering of a template used with a computer program. Even if copyright law allowed reverse engineering, the license prevented it. Other cases have had mixed results. Relevant factors included the form of notice, methods by which assent was indicated, and each state's contract laws.

Despite the differing cases, it is clear that a library *can* contract away its rights, so read licensing agreements carefully. Also pay attention to how the contract affects those who use the digital products. A license agreement between a library and a vendor may limit a library patron's right to copy or otherwise use an article in the licensed database, even though the use would be a permissible fair use.

Computer Programs (Section 117)

6.2. Section 117
Computer Programs

Owner may make a copy or adapt the program
- To utilize it
- For archival purposes, or
- To repair or maintain equipment

Section 117 of the Copyright Act permits the owner of a computer program—"a set of statements or instructions to be used directly or indirectly in a computer in order to bring about a certain result"[6]—to make a copy under three circumstances. First, the owner may make a new copy of the program, or an adaptation of the program, if it is an essential step in order to use the program in conjunction with a machine. For example, if the software you purchased cannot run on your equipment or operating system, you may make a copy in order to adapt it to make it work. This sec-

---

[5] 320 F.3d 1317 (Fed. Cir. 2003).
[6] 17 U.S.C. § 101 (2000).

tion also permits the automatic loading of a copy onto a computer's random access memory (RAM).

A software owner may also make a copy for archival purposes, so long as the archival copy is destroyed if possession ceases to be legitimate. Remember that the archival copy is just that. You may not make an archival copy under section 117 for use on another computer. Furthermore, when possession is no longer legitimate—for example, if you give the original software to someone else—you must destroy the archival copy.

Finally, the Digital Millennium Copyright Act amended section 117 to permit someone who owns or leases a computer to make a temporary copy of a program that was loaded on the machine for the purpose of repairing or maintaining the equipment. The new copy must be destroyed after the maintenance has been completed.

Section 117 was drafted in the days of floppy disks. It is much less important now that software is held on CD's or sent through the web. So let's move on to what really engages libraries and information vendors, the matter of licenses. We are going where the wild things are, so let the wild rumpus begin.[7]

Single-User and Site Licenses

The typical single-user license agreement prohibits use of software on more than one piece of equipment at one time. Unless the license so provides, you should not load the software on a network accessible to several different users, even if only one person can access the software at a time. However, installing software on a single computer that is used by several different people is permissible.

Site licenses permit group access to software, to databases, or to other digital products. Because cost is directly related to the number of users, you should determine how many people really need access. Although a public library may serve a population of 50,000 and a law firm library may serve 500 attorneys, this does not mean that the product needs to be accessible to everyone at one time. A public library may do quite well with a site license to a genealogy database that allows a few patrons simul-

---

[7] MAURICE SENDAK, WHERE THE WILD THINGS ARE (1963).

taneous access to the database. Similarly, a firm's license to a labor law database may only need to be accessed by a handful of lawyers at any one time.

Downloading

When you download a piece of information, a copy is being made. Copying the results of a database search onto a hard drive or saving a PDF copy of an article are good examples. Copyright principles, including fair use, apply, so you will want to answer the following questions: Is the work being used for private study, scholarship, or research? Is the use for a commercial or a non-profit educational purpose? Is the use transformative? Is the information factual or creative? How much is being downloaded? Will the copying significantly affect the market for the original work? And, of course, what does the license say?

We sense you are not satisfied, so here are some guidelines. The more transformative your use, the more likely it is to be fair. Downloading a work and then copying and distributing it without any changes would be frowned upon. Even worse would be selling the copies for profit. On the other hand, if you download some works and then recompile them, deleting material that is not relevant to the end user, reorganizing the material for easier use, and adding your own original comments, then that use would be more favored.

Downloading works that are freely available online or available through licensed databases and keeping copies until your need for them has ended is better than keeping copies permanently. If the work comes with a license that prohibits even temporary retention of copies, you may be stuck, so don't agree to such terms.

Database Protection (Redux)

We know that some information—facts and works of the U.S. government, for example—are not protected by copyright. However, *databases* of federal governmental works and other works in the public domain, such as facts, might receive protection as compilations.

As noted in Chapter One, in *Feist v. Rural Telephone Service*[8] the U.S. Supreme Court rejected the "sweat of the brow" doctrine and held that a white pages telephone directory could not be copyrighted because it lacked originality. But a database may be eligible for protection if the compiler exercised sufficient skill and judgment in selecting, organizing, and arranging the data.

Although many database providers thought that *Feist* would bring the apocalypse to their businesses, subsequent to that decision many lower courts have held that databases consisting of factual information (a Yellow Pages directory,[9] a database of used vehicles values,[10] or a price guide for yachts,[11] for example) may be copyrightable compilations. Remember that compilation copyright extends only to the material contributed by the author, not to the underlying materials that are compiled. For instance, data collected by tax assessors about real estate is not eligible for copyright protection, but its creative arrangement in a database is. The data may be extracted from the database and used freely.[12] However, using the copyrighted arrangement and compilation of the information may be infringing. Fair use, of course, is a possible defense.

The Bottom Line: You may use unprotected factual information from a printed work (like an almanac) or an online database that is copyrighted as a compilation. But if you copy or download a significant amount of that information in its compiled form—more than that which is allowed under fair use—you may violate the copyright that protects how the information is selected, arranged, and presented. For online products, remember to check your license.

---

[8] 499 U.S. 340 (1991).

[9] *See, e.g.*, BellSouth Adver. & Publ'g Corp. v. Donnelly Info. Publ'g, Inc., 999 F.2d 1436 (11th Cir. 1993); Key Publ'ns, Inc. v. Chinatown Today, Publ'g, 945 F.2d 509 (2d Cir. 1991).

[10] CCC Info. Servs., Inc. v. Maclean Hunter Mkt. Reports, Inc., 44 F.3d 61 (2d Cir. 1994).

[11] BUC Int'l Corp. v. Int'l Yacht Council Ltd., 489 F.3d 1129 (11th Cir. 2007).

[12] Assessment Technologies of WI, LLC v. WIREdata, Inc., 350 F.3d 640 (7th Cir. 2003).

The First Sale Doctrine (Reprise) (Section 109)

Section 109 of the Copyright Act—the First Sale Doctrine—permits libraries to lend their materials. We discussed this earlier in chapter two, but let's visit section 109 again in the context of digital information.

Lending Software

> ### 6.3. Lending Software and Sound Recordings
> - May not lend for direct or indirect commercial advantage
>
> But
> - Nonprofit library or educational institution may lend
>   - o   To another educational institution
>   - o   To faculty, staff, or students
> - For-profit entity may lend internally
> - Include copyright notice for software

Remember that the copyright owner has the right to copy, to publicly distribute, and to publicly display the copyrighted work. The Computer Software Rental Amendments Act of 1990[13] amended section 109 to prohibit the owner of a copy of computer software from lending that copy for a purpose of direct or indirect commercial advantage. The prohibition does not, however, bar a non-profit library or a non-profit educational institution from lending software to another educational institution, or to faculty, staff or students, so long as the software has the requisite notice prescribed by the Register of Copyrights.[14] Affix the notice on the computer disk or its container, whether it is a stand-alone product or if the software comes with a book.

---

[13] Pub. L. No. 101-650, Title VIII, §§ 802, 803, 104 Stat. 5134 (1990).

[14] 37 C.F.R. § 201.24 (2011) ("The copyright law of the United States (Title 17, United States Code) governs the reproduction, distribution, adaptation, public performance, and public display of copyrighted material.").

Public Display (Section 109(c))

Notwithstanding the copyright owner's right to display the work publicly, if you own a lawfully-make copy you may publicly display it, either directly or by projection. If you display by projection, you can only show one image at a time, and it must only be visible to viewers present at the place where the copy is located.[15]

Question: The library purchased a sculpture from a local artist. Do we need written permission to display the sculpture in our lobby?

Answer: You can certainly display the sculpture without further permission. Section 109(c) says you do not need permission to display copies that you own and are legitimately made.

Question: What about showing a picture of the sculpture on a screen on another floor?

Answer: Taking a photograph of the sculpture and displaying that image is a different question. The simplest solution is to ask the artist to grant the library permission to make and display images of the sculpture for promotional purposes. Without such permission, though, making and displaying an image that does not substantively replace the sculpture would probably be fair use. The more the image could replace the sculpture, the less likely using it would be fair use. Posting a small thumbnail image, or even a somewhat larger image, on a monitor is very likely to be fair use, while hanging a high-resolution, life-size poster is less likely to be fair use. Displaying the picture on a public billboard or in a different building is less likely a fair use. But fair use is still possible for some public uses, such as posting a small, low-resolution image.

Question: The library subscribes to a Web-based product. Absent a license agreement that specifically permits or prohibits any of the following uses, which of these is permitted under section 109(c)?

---

[15] 17 U.S.C. § 109(c) (2006).

A. A group of people may view an image from the product at the same computer terminal or from a projection device.
B. The image may be transmitted simultaneously to computers throughout the library so lots of people may see it at the same time.
C. You may transmit the image throughout the library to multiple pieces of equipment, but no more than one computer can show the image at any one time.

Answer: "A" and "C." A group of people may view the image on one screen because section 109(c) permits displaying one image of a lawfully obtained work. As long as one image is made, any number of people can view it. For instance, you could display the image on a large projection screen for a group. "C" is an option because only one image is being made at a time, even though the image is being displayed in different places within the library. Crucial for "C" is that only one image can be displayed at any time and that all display equipment is within the library.

"B" isn't permissible under section 109(c) because projecting the image on more than one screen, even if all the screens are in the same building or room, counts as displaying more than one image at a time.[16] If you want multiple, simultaneous access, get those terms in a license. Remember that fair use could apply to some uses beyond what is covered by section 109(c). For example, displaying the image in a way that does not substitute for the work (say, as a thumbnail image) could be a fair use.

The Digital Millennium Copyright Act

6.4. Digital Millennium Copyright Act
- Digital copies for preservation
- Online service provider protections
- Anti-circumvention provisions

The 1998 Digital Millennium Copyright Act (DMCA)[17] addresses several matters that affect librarians and educators. In addition to the amendments to sections 108(b) and (c) that permit some digital copying, the DMCA

---

[16] WILLIAM F. PATRY, 5 PATRY ON COPYRIGHT § 15:10 (2011).
[17] Pub. L. No. 105-304, 112 Stat. 2860 (1998).

provides some protection for service providers who have infringing materials on their Web sites, or temporarily store or link to such materials. The DMCA also includes two important prohibitions. One proscribes the circumvention of devices that limit access to digital works, and the other bans interference with copyright management information.

Under the DMCA, a service provider is "an entity offering the transmission, routing, or providing connections for digital online communications, between or among points specified by a user, of material of the user's choosing, without modification to the content of the materials sent or received."[18] Most libraries have parent institutions that supply Internet connectivity. Whether you work for an independent library or one with a parent institution, it is important to understand the DMCA and help your institution stay within the DMCA's safe harbor. The DMCA uses "service provider", and that is what we use here, but "internet service provider" and "online service provider" are synonyms.

In a nutshell, there are four situations where the DMCA protects service providers: (1) transitory digital communications, (2) caching, (3) materials stored on a network at the direction of a user (including hosting Web sites), and (4) information location tools (linking). Very generally, under certain circumstances a service provider that infringes because its Web site routes, stores, or links to infringing material will be liable neither for monetary damages nor subject to injunctive relief.[19]

Transitory Digital Network Communications (Section 512(a))

Section 512(a) of the DMCA addresses a service provider that "merely acts as a data conduit, transmitting digital information from one point on a network to another at someone else's request" when the information transmitted happens to be infringing.[20] This protects the service provider for simply routing or providing connections that enable the information to be

---

[18] 17 U.S.C. § 512(k) (2006).

[19] 17 U.S.C. § 512(j) (2006) (spells out the limited injunctive relief available to a plaintiff).

[20] U.S. COPYRIGHT OFFICE, THE DIGITAL MILLENNIUM COPYRIGHT ACT OF 1998, at 10 (Dec. 1998), *available at* http://www.copyright.gov/legislation/ dmca.pdf [hereinafter DMCA SUMMARY].

transmitted, and also for any intermediate and transient copies that are made automatically during regular network operations.

The key is passivity, and several things must (or must not) take place: (1) the service provider does not initiate the transmission; (2) the transmission, routing, connecting, or copying is automatic (that is, the service provider did not select the materials transmitted); (3) the service provider does not determine who receives the materials transmitted; (4) intermediate copies are accessible only to anticipated recipients of the transmission; (5) the service provider does not retain the materials transmitted; and (6) the service provider does not modify the materials that are transmitted.

System Caching (Section 512(b))

System caching is an automatic process that stores data from other networks temporarily on the service provider's system so that data need not be retrieved over and over again from the original source. Caching, which technically involves making a copy, saves bandwidth. Section 512(b) provides some protections for a service provider if (1) the caching process is automatic; (2) the content of the data was not modified; (3) the data is refreshed with more current materials according to industry standards; (4) the service provider does not interfere with "hit" information (which is used for advertising revenue); and (5) the service provider limits or blocks access to the data when the original poster uses access control devices, such as passwords.[21]

Information Residing on Systems or Networks at the Direction of Users (Section 512(c))

6.5. DMCA Service Provider Protections

Generally limits liability for infringing content or links to infringing content if:
- No actual knowledge
- No financial benefit
- Designated Institutional Agent
- Take down

---

[21] 17 U.S.C. § 512(b) (2006).

The DMCA also provides some protection for a service provider that has infringing material stored on its system or network—including hosting a Web site—at the direction of a user. The service provider is protected when it does not have the right and ability to control the infringing activity, and it did not have actual knowledge that the material or the activity using the material on the network was infringing. If the service provider *can* control the infringing activity, the protections apply if it does not receive a financial benefit due to the infringing activity. Should the service provider receive notice that infringing materials are on its system or network, it must remove or block access to that material.[22]

Designated Agent, and Notice and Takedown

The service provider is protected under section 512(c) only if it has filed with the Copyright Office the name and contact information for its designated agent, someone who can receive complaints from copyright owners.[23] Neither Congress nor the Copyright Office specifies what role the designated agent must have in your organization. A university, for example, may appoint its director of information technology, a law firm its managing partner, a public library its chief librarian, and a corporation its general counsel. It's totally up to you.

Protection under the DMCA is conditional on having a designated agent, so if your library is independent, you must choose one and file their contact information with the Copyright Office. If your parent institution handles DMCA complaints for the library, be sure you know who your institution's agent is.

The designated agent will receive complaints from copyright owners, such as a poet who discovers her poem on your Web site, or that your Web site links to an infringing copy of her poem. Section 512(c) also spells out the required elements of notification of a claimed infringement, including that the notification must (1) be in writing with a physical or electronic signature; (2) identify the infringing work or materials; (3) include information on how to contact the complainant; and (4) include statements that the complainant has authority to act on behalf of the copyright owner, has

---

[22] 17 U.S.C. § 512(c)(1) (2006).
[23] 17 U.S.C. § 512(c)(2) (2006).

a good faith belief that the use complained of is not authorized, and that the information in the complaint is accurate.

This begins the "notice and takedown"—takedown, not shakedown—process. Assuming that the copyright owner follows the statutory notification requirements, the service provider must remove or block access to the material, and also notify the subscriber who posted the allegedly infringing materials of the complaint. The subscriber may then file a counter notification. If that happens, the service provider must restore the materials unless the complainant notifies the provider that it has sought a court order to enjoin the alleged infringement.[24]

Information Location Tools (Linking) (Section 512(d))

Finally, the DMCA protects a service provider that provides information location tools. A service provider will not be liable for referring or linking users to a Web site that contains infringing content if the service provider did not have knowledge of the infringing link and, if it had the right and ability to control the activity, it does not receive a financial benefit from doing so. As in 512(c), the service provider must remove the link if it receives notice that it is linking to a site that has infringing content.[25]

Non-Profit Educational Institutions (Section 512(e))

Non-profit educational institutions are included in the DMCA's definition of "service provider." But some faculty or graduate students engaged in teaching and research activities are not considered activities of the institution itself, so DMCA protection can apply as it does for the activities of students and patrons. The protection will apply when

---

[24] 17 U.S.C. § 512(c) and (g) (2006). *See* DMCA SUMMARY, *supra* note 20, at 12; Casey Lide, *What Colleges and Universities Need to Know about the Digital Millennium Copyright Act*, 22 CAUSE/EFFECT 1 (1999), *available at* http://net.educause.edu/ir/library/html/cem/cem99/cem9913.html.

[25] 17 U.S.C. § 512(d) (2006).

- the faculty or graduate student's activity does not involve access to instructional materials for a course taught by that person that are or were required or recommended within the last three years;
- within the last three years the institution did not receive more than two notifications of infringement by the instructor; and
- the institution provides informational materials that accurately describe and promote compliance with federal copyright law.[26]

Anti-Circumvention (Section 1201)

Copyright owners sometimes use technological measures (such as encryption or regional lock codes) to prevent unauthorized access to information and unauthorized copying of information. The DMCA prohibits circumventing or overriding these technological measures in most cases, but it treats access controls (for example, region lock that prevents playing a movie made in China from playing on a device made in the United States) differently from copying controls (such as codes that prevent copying a DVD to a hard drive).

The DMCA prohibits producing or selling devices that break through technological barriers to enable unauthorized access or copying. Even if you acquired one of these devices, in almost all instances it is illegal for you to circumvent or override those technological measures. The only exemptions to this prohibition are granted by the Copyright Office.[27] Here are the most recent set of exemptions, in simplified form:[28]

1. You may break through the Content Scrambling System (CSS) on lawfully-purchased DVDs to incorporate small portions of the work for purposes of comment or criticism for educational uses by college professors or media studies students, documentary films, and noncommercial videos.
2. You may break through software that prevents your mobile phones from executing other software applications. This is what legitimates jail-breaking your iPhone and installing software not approved by Apple.
3. You may break software controls that force your phone to connect to only one network. You may also buy an iPhone from one phone company and then move it to another company's network.

---

[26] 17 U.S.C. § 512(e) (2006).
[27] 17 U.S.C. § 1201(a)(1)(C) (2006).
[28] 75 Fed. Reg. 43,825 (July 27, 2010).

4. You may break software controls on computer games to test them for security flaws.
5. You may break through software controls when the dongle (a hardware security device needed to operate some programs) malfunctions, is damaged, or becomes obsolete.
6. You may break through software controls to enable read-aloud or screen readers for e-books when all authorized copies do not permit these features. This allows print-disabled readers to access e-books they purchase.

If you have a legitimate copy of a copyrighted work and can lawfully access it, you can also break through technological barriers to make copies because, according to the Copyright Office, copying may be a fair use.[29] Encryption and scrambling programs are both access and copy protections because they control whether a device will access, play, and copy the content. If you lawfully obtain a DVD that uses a scrambling system, you can only use a program to descramble and access the DVD if you fall under the higher education exemption mentioned above. However, if you can legally break the access controls under this exemption, you can also break the copy protection for copying that is covered by fair use or another copyright exception.

To summarize rules for complying with the DMCA, imagine Moses carrying tablets down from Mount Millennium. They might say:

- Thou shalt not decrypt an encrypted work;
- Thou shalt not descramble a scrambled work;
- If one needest a password to access a digital work, thou shall not override password access;
- Thou shalt not avoid, bypass, remove, or deactivate a technological protective measure that limits access to a protected work without permission;
- Thou shalt not traffic in devices that have a primary purpose of circumvention; and
- Thou shalt not covet thy neighbor's databases.

Congress did toss a tiny bone to the library and educational communities. A non-profit library or educational institution may circumvent technologies that prevent access to a work in order to make a decision whether to acquire it.[30] This provision is largely meaningless, of course, because

---

[29] DMCA SUMMARY, supra note 20, at 3–4.
[30] 17 U.S.C. § 1201(d) (2006).

publishers are delighted to give libraries temporary passwords to sample their products.

Copyright Management Information (Section 1202)

Copyright management information includes the copyright notice, the title of the work and other information that identifies it, identifying information about the author, performer, or director of a work, and the terms and conditions of use. The DMCA makes it illegal to knowingly falsify, alter, or remove any copyright management information with the intention of inducing or enabling infringement.[31] Don't mess with copyright management information. This is only a snapshot of some of the DMCA provisions that may affect libraries. For more information on the DMCA, the U.S. Copyright Office,[32] Association of Research Libraries,[33] and EDUCAUSE[34] are particularly helpful.

---

[31] 17 U.S.C. § 1202 (2006).

[32] DMCA SUMMARY, *supra* note 20.

[33] ASSOCIATION OF RESEARCH LIBRARIES, DIGITAL MILLENNIUM COPYRIGHT ACT: STATUS AND ANALYSIS, *available at* http://www.arl.org/bm~doc/ dmca_band.pdf.

[34] EDUCAUSE, CURRENT ISSUES: THE DIGITAL MILLENNIUM COPYRIGHT ACT, *available at* http://www.educause.edu/node/645/tid/31236?time=1304969776.

Chapter Seven
LICENSING
ಐ‍ೞಊ

The Copyright Act of 1976 was for the most part technologically neutral. For example, in defining the types of works eligible for copyright protection, Congress wrote of "original works of authorship *fixed in any tangible medium of expression, now known or later developed. . . .*"[1] The Pythia— the Oracle of Delphi—could not foresee the digital information revolution, and certainly not the topsy turvy world where accessing information has become more common than *owning* it.

The change from ownership to access through licensing has significant consequences for libraries. Licenses can dilute and even eliminate critical rights for libraries and users, including the first sale doctrine, the library exemption, and fair use. For example, the section 107 fair use exemption permits a library patron, in most circumstances, to copy an article from a journal or a chapter from a book. But a patron may be out of luck if the library subscribes only to a digital version of the journal if the license precludes copying even small parts of articles.

Consider this example: Professor Wagstaff, who will speak at a national conference, wants to share with the other panelists copies of federal statutes and court decisions relevant to the program. The professor finds the documents on a licensed database, and, after removing any proprietary elements from the database, downloads the cases and laws and makes a print copy. By removing any copyrightable elements that had been added by the database vendor, such as annotations, he should be only dealing with public domain material that can be freely copied. But then he

---

[1] 17 U.S.C. § 102(a) (2006) (emphasis added).

discovers that the license agreement permits him to "transfer and store temporarily insubstantial amounts of data."

Under the Copyright Act, works of the federal government are not protected by copyright.[2] Professor Wagstaff certainly may copy selected laws and court decisions from print codes and case reporters that sit on the library's shelves. However, a license to an electronic database may prohibit him from copying that same information, even though it is in the public domain. The license makes all the difference: even if the information is identical, the print copy owned by the library is treated differently than the digital copy that is merely licensed to the library and subject to contractual restrictions.

The Uniform Computer Information Transactions Act (UCITA) shows how unfriendly contracts can be to libraries. Uniform laws like UCITA are drafted by a group of attorneys and legal scholars called the Uniform Law Commission (ULC), or the National Conference of Commissioners on Uniform State Laws. After the ULC proposes a uniform law, each state legislature can choose to enact it into state law. Due to some of UCITA's provisions, especially its imposition of liability on a library for patron license violations, we are not fans of UCITA. We are glad only two states, Virginia and Maryland, have adopted it. Even if your licenses are governed by another state's law, it is always wise to understand basic contract law and carefully read your licenses.

The License under the Microscope

7.1. Licensing Agreement

- Read the contract
- Permanent or temporary access
- No barriers to authorized users
- Preserve Copyright Act rights
- Respect user's privacy and confidentiality
- Hold-harmless clause
- Read the contract again

---

[2] 17 U.S.C. § 105 (2006).

You must be vigilant when you sign a license for digital information products. According to the legislative history of the Copyright Act, "[n]othing in the bill derogates from the rights of parties to contract with each other and to sue for breaches of contract. . . ."[3] You must look out for your library, and for those who use it. This includes *other* libraries, too, because librarians share information through interlibrary lending and document delivery, as permitted by section 108.

One way to examine the good, the bad, and the ugly that you may find in license agreements is to take a look at a license. Let's look at the online subscription agreement for journals from the American Meteorological Society,[4] with our comments added.

American Meteorological Society
Journals Online Subscription Agreement

1. Scope of License.

Institutional Subscriber Use Restrictions. Under this Agreement, Subscribing Institution is granted a nonexclusive, revocable, nontransferable right and license to access and use the subscribed AMS journals made available to Subscribing Institution on the World Wide Web via the Subscribing Institution's Internet protocol addresses (IP addresses) and, in connection with the foregoing, to permit Subscribing Institution's Authorized Users to access the journals and:

> *Comment:* Access via IP address is good. This way users working in your library won't have to manage their own passwords. If your library uses a proxy server—a local computer that serves as an intermediary between off-site users and the subscribed online resources—authorized users can access the resource from any computer, anywhere.

a. make searches of the subscribed journals;

> *Comment:* Essential. Users obviously need to be able to search through the licensed information.

---

[3] H.R. REP. No. 94-1476, at 132.
[4] American Meteorological Society, Journals Online Subscription Agreement, *available at* http://www.ametsoc.org/pubs/subscribe/elicense.pdf. © American Meteorological Society. Reprinted with permission.

b. download search results to hard disk or diskette;

> *Comment:* Also essential. Users will want to be able to download and retain relevant materials for future use. Make sure the license doesn't limit you to a specific technology. Today you may be using discs, tomorrow USB drives, and a few years from now some media that is just now being invented.

c. make one hard copy of the output of any search;

> *Comment:* Very good. This license permits the making of a single print copy with no limitation on the amount (for example, "a small excerpt" or "500 words"). Some databases (especially for electronic books) may impose limits because publishers don't want users to print too much of the content. Watch for limits; be sure your users will be able to make effective use of the licensed database.

d. to share such hard copy with third parties to the same extent as the print edition or to the extent permitted under fair use provisions of the Copyright Act of 1976;

> *Comment:* This language is very desirable for two reasons. First, users' expectations are often based on using print resources, so it is great that the license matches the sharing ability of print. Second, the language acknowledges fair use, and you are not signing away any rights you have under the Copyright Act. The language does not specifically recognize the section 108 library exception. We would like to see that expressly acknowledged in the license. The best language would say "to share hard copy with third parties to the same extent as the print edition or the extent permitted under the Copyright Act of 1976, including but not limited to fair use (section 107) and the library exemption (section 108)."

e. to use, with appropriate credit, figures, tables, and brief excerpts from the journals in scientific and educational works or similar work product of the Authorized User, except those portions thereof that are so noted as in the public domain or are U.S. Government works, for which no permission to copy is required.

> *Comment:* Very good. Fair use permits some quotation, especially for purposes of comment and criticism, but this authorizes further quotation and reuse in the users' own work. The attribution requirement is perfectly appropriate and aligned with professional and scholarly norms. It's also nice that this language acknowledges the public domain status of federal government works.

Except as expressly permitted herein, all other uses of the journals or any portion thereof, including republication, resale, systematic reproduction, or storage in a searchable, machine-readable database, or time-share of the AMS journals database require written permission of the AMS.

> *Comment:* In addition to defining what users can do with licensed content, it is helpful when publishers spell out prohibited uses. You need to make sure none of the prohibited uses are things your patrons will need for their work. If you don't understand the meaning of any of the terms (such as "time-share"), clarify the definitions before you sign.

Authorized Users must be employees, faculty, staff, and students officially affiliated with the Subscribing Institution and patrons of the Subscribing Institution's library facilities. This includes occasional users who access AMS journals through stations physically located on the site and under the control and administration of the Subscribing Institution. Authorized Users also includes persons affiliated with remote sites or campuses of the Subscribing Institution that are administered from the Subscribing Institution's site or campus, but not persons affiliated with remote sites or campuses that have separate administrative staffs.

> *Comment:* This inclusive language addresses virtually every type of user and both on- and off-site access. You may need to clarify the distinction between "persons affiliated with remote sites of campuses" (who can access the database) and "persons affiliated with remote sites of campuses that have separate administrative staffs" (who may not). Many academic institutions have multiple campuses. This vendor wants to separately license databases to each campus, which is pretty typical. You will want to find out if the vendor also offers a multi-site or system-wide license.

This Agreement is enforceable only against and by the parties who have executed it; the Agreement neither creates nor restricts rights to third parties. AMS understands that the Subscribing Institution is unable to practically enforce the terms of the Agreement for third parties. However, AMS asks that the Subscribing Institution agree to make reasonable efforts to take appropriate action should they become aware of any misuse that would violate the terms of the Agreement and that the Subscribing Institution continue to promote an environment that does not allow for abuse of the terms of the Agreement.

Comment: This language requires a reasonable commitment from the library to discourage license violations, but also doesn't ascribe user violations to the library. Library staff should, of course, encourage license compliance, but they cannot police every use of the database.

2. Terms and Fees. The agreement will last through the end of the calendar year in which the subscription first becomes effective. This Agreement will remain in effect thereafter for successive subscription years so long as annual subscription fees are paid, subject to any new terms and/or conditions required by AMS at that time and shared with Subscribing Institution 30 days in advance. Both AMS and Subscribing Institution have the right to terminate this Agreement at the end of a subscription year by written notice given at least 30 days before the end of the subscription year.

Comment: The contract should specify that you are to be informed of new terms and conditions in writing. You don't want new terms conveyed merely via e-mail or a notice on the vendor's Web site. It is too easy for e-mail to get caught in a spam filter, and you shouldn't have to monitor the vendor's Web site for changes. Certified mail is probably overkill, but a paper notice in the mail isn't too much to expect. For planning and budget purposes, you may want sixty or even ninety days' notice.

Upon termination for non-renewal of a subscription, Subscribing Institution may continue to use and access those journals to which it previously subscribed, subject to the terms and conditions contained herein. In the event that AMS determines that it will no longer provide the journals over the World Wide Web, AMS may provide Subscribing Institution with access to said subscribed journals in another searchable media format selected by AMS at its sole option.

Comment: The cup is more than half full. It is great that the vendor offers perpetual access to the materials you subscribed to during the term of the license, even if the license is not renewed. You may want to see the format in which the materials can be accessed in the event the vendor takes the content off the Web.

AMS reserves the right to temporarily suspend access without prior notice, to the AMS journals at the IP address from which any violation of this Agreement originates. In the event that either party believes that the other materially has breached any obligations under this Agreement, or if AMS believes that Subscriber has exceeded the scope of the License, such party shall so notify the breaching party in writing. The breaching party shall have 30 days from the receipt of notice to cure the alleged breach and to notify the non-breaching party in writing that cure has been effected. If the breach is not cured within the 30 days, the non-breaching party shall have the right to terminate the Agreement without further notice.

> *Comment:* You want the vendor to notify you of suspected violations of the contract before they suspend access to the content. You should insist on written notice, and also the right to respond. You may even want to include in the agreement how disputes will be handled, including arbitration, and who will pay the costs of the dispute resolution process.

3. Technical Assistance and Customer Support. Technical assistance solely related to the online technical aspects of the AMS journals database can be obtained by sending an e-mail to amsjol@ametsoc.org or, Monday through Friday, excluding holidays, from 9:00 A.M. to 4:30 P.M. ET, by calling 617-227-2426 exts. 3911/3912/3913/3914. Problems with a subscription can be addressed by sending e-mail to amsjol@ ametsoc.org or, Monday through Friday, excluding holidays, from 9:00 A.M. to 4:30 P.M. ET, by calling 617-227-2426 ext. 3911/3912/3913/ 3914.

> *Comment:* You want and need vendor support. This language details how to contact the vendor through phone and e-mail.

4. Copyright. The Subscribing Institution acknowledges that it has no claim to ownership by reason of its use of or access to the subscribed AMS journals. Except as otherwise provided herein, the journals, their content, and the database are owned by the AMS and are protected by the U.S. Copyright Laws and International Treaty provisions. Downloading or copying of content is permitted to allow Subscribing Institution and its Authorized Users to exercise its rights under this Agreement to the same extent as the print edition of the journal. Other recompiling, copying, publication, or republication of the content, or any portion thereof, in any form or medium whatsoever, may be done only with the specific written permission from AMS.

> *Comment:* No surprises here. The distinction between ownership and licensed access is clear. By paying for the license, the library does not own a copy of the database content, nor any of the copyright privileges relating to the database. Some vendors offer a digital ownership option that lets libraries purchase digital copies of the content. Just as libraries keep past copies of journal issues after a subscription is cancelled, they

can retain digital copies after the license is cancelled. Often these owner-ship options do not include the search functionality of the database, so have a plan in place for making effective use of the content if you cancel the subscription. The language in this agreement does provide for perpe-tual access, which means the vendor will let the library keep accessing some content after contract termination, though the library will not own a copy of the content.

5. Disclaimer of Warranties — Limitation of Liability. THE SUB-SCRIBED JOURNALS ARE PROVIDED "AS IS" WITHOUT ANY WARRANTIES OF ANY KIND, EITHER EXPRESS OR IMPLIED, INCLUDING BUT NOT LIMITED TO, WARRANTIES OF DESIGN, MERCHANTABILITY OR FITNESS FOR A PARTICULAR PUR-POSE, OR ARISING FROM A COURSE OF DEALING, USAGE, OR TRADE PRACTICE.

> *Comment:* No surprise. The vendor will not assume responsibility for the content of the information in the database. Often vendors redistribute con-tent published by other companies, so this generally makes sense.

Further, AMS does not warrant that the Subscribing Institution's or any Authorized User's use of the subscribed journals will be uninterrupted or error free, or that the results obtained will be useful or will satisfy the Sub-scribing Institution's or any Authorized User's requirements.

> *Comment:* We all understand that there may be glitches. The real question is whether they are serious, and how long they last. We have no problem agreeing that the vendor will not be responsible for minor interruptions in service or small data errors. But we do have a problem with sustained or continuous lapses in service.
>
> Sometimes vendors will try to disclaim all warranties, both express and implied. If the vendor will not agree to any express warranties, you at least want the contract not to negate the implied warranties of merchant-ability and fitness for a particular purpose, which can provide important protections in the event that the vendor or the product does not perform as promised or expected. If the database or some part of it cannot be used for the purpose for which it was acquired, the library may want to terminate the contract and have the vendor refund part of the subscription payment.

Subscribing Institution's sole and exclusive remedy for damages and/or loss in any way connected with this License shall be limited to the amount of the License Fee. UNDER NO CIRCUMSTANCES SHALL AMS BE LIABLE TO SUBSCRIBING INSTITUTION OR ANY OTHER PERSON,

INCLUDING BUT NOT LIMITED TO AUTHORIZED USERS, FOR ANY SPECIAL, INCIDENTAL, OR CONSEQUENTIAL DAMAGES OF ANY CHARACTER, INCLUDING WITHOUT LIMITATION, DAMAGES ARISING OUT OF INABILITY TO ACCESS AMS'S JOURNALS OR ERRORS OR INACCURACIES IN THE JOURNAL CONTENT.

> *Comment:* In the event of the vendor's breach or other problems the library's remedy is limited to the monies connected to the license fee. The vendor will credit you for the time you cannot access the service beyond the "minor or occasional interruptions" mentioned earlier. That the vendor will not be liable for special, incidental, or consequential damages is standard fare for license agreements. For example, if an article in the database has erroneous information and a user relies on that information and suffers some harm due to that reliance, the user can't blame or recover consequential damages from the vendor.

Additionally, AMS shall not be liable or deemed to be in default for any delay or failure in performance or interruption resulting directly or indirectly from any cause or circumstance beyond the reasonable control of AMS; equipment or telecommunications failure; labor dispute; or failure of any third party to perform any agreement with AMS that adversely affects AMS's ability to perform its obligations hereunder.

> *Comment:* More standard language that protects the vendor from matters not under its control.

6. General

a. This Agreement constitutes the entire Agreement between the parties hereto and supersedes all prior oral and written and all contemporaneous oral negotiations, commitments, and understandings. The various headings in this Agreement are informational only and do not limit the scope or content of the subject matter contained therein. No waiver, amendment, or modification of this Agreement shall be effective unless it is in writing and signed by the parties hereto.

> *Comment:* This is the entire agreement. It doesn't matter what was said over the phone or via e-mail during contract negotiations. If you don't like the license, change it before you sign it.

b. The Subscribing Institution may not assign or transfer its rights under this Agreement.

Comment: Standard language. You can't transfer the license to another institution.

c. Should any provision of this Agreement be held to be void or unenforceable, the remaining provisions shall remain in full force and effect to read and construed as if the void or unenforceable provisions were originally deleted.

Comment: Also standard. If, for example, the "disclaimer of warranty" language was held to be unenforceable because it violates public policy or is preempted by federal law, the rest of the contract is still valid.

d. The validity, interpretation, and performance of this Agreement shall be governed by the laws of the Commonwealth of Massachusetts, excluding that body of laws dealing with conflict of laws. Venue shall be the courts of competent jurisdiction located in Massachusetts.

Comment: You usually want the contract to be interpreted under the laws of your home state. If your library is publicly funded, your state may have laws requiring that contracts be interpreted under the laws of your home state. Although in most cases this probably is good for the library, it is not always true. For example, if your state enacted UCITA (Virginia and Maryland) you may be better off interpreting the contract under the laws of a state that did not. If you are operating under laws that prohibit a contract from stating that disputes will be governed by laws other than those of your home state, you may want to simply delete the choice of law section of the contract.

The last steps are to sign and date the contract. Both parties should have original signed copies of the contract.

You could look at other licenses for ideas about terms to include or exclude. One of the best sources, LicensingModels.org, suggests model licenses for private libraries, public libraries, single academic institutions, and academic consortia. LicensingModels.org puts in [square brackets] optional language for contracting parties to consider. Below you will find selected portions of LicensingModels.org's "Academic Single User License"[5] and our comments on some of the provisions.

---

[5] http://www.licensingmodels.org/SingleAcademicInstitutionLicense.html. This license has been placed in the public domain by its authors. Its authors are from the United Kingdom, so it follows British spelling conventions.

LicensingModels.org
Academic Single Institution License:
Version 4.0 October 6, 2009

KEY DEFINITIONS

> *Comment:* Clear definitions are critical. Make sure important terms are defined and that you and the vendor have a common understand about the meaning of the words.

Authorized Users. Current members of the faculty and other staff of the Licensee (whether on a permanent, temporary, contract or visiting basis) and individuals who are currently studying at the Licensee's institution, who are permitted to access the Secure Network from within the Library Premises or from such other places where Authorized Users work or study (including but not limited to Authorized Users' offices and homes, halls of residence and student dormitories) and who have been issued by the Licensee with a password or other authentication [together with other persons who are permitted to use the Licensee's library or information service and access the Secure Network but only from computer terminals within the Library Premises].

> *Comment:* Again, pay special attention to who is covered as an authorized user. You want to be sure that every patron that may need the database will have access to it. This model language is very inclusive and appears to cover all types of faculty, staff, and students. Libraries that are open to the public will certainly want to include the bracketed language permitting unaffiliated patrons to use the database on site.

Commercial Use. Use for the purposes of monetary reward (whether by or for the Licensee or an Authorized User) by means of sale, resale, loan, transfer, hire or other form of exploitation of the Licensed Materials. Neither recovery of direct costs by the Licensee from Authorized Users, nor use by the Licensee or by an Authorized User of the Licensed Materials in the course of research funded by a commercial organization, is deemed to be Commercial Use.

> *Comment:* We would prefer that cost recovery include both direct and indirect costs. Charging to cover the costs of staff time, for instance, should not make your use commercial.

Course Packs. A collection or compilation of printed materials (e.g. book chapters, journal articles) assembled by members of staff of the Licensee for use by students in a class for the purposes of instruction.

> *Comment:* If you want to use the database to create course packs, it is good to address and define them in the agreement.

Electronic Reserve. Electronic copies of materials (e.g. book chapters, journal articles) made and stored on the Secure Network by the Licensee for use by students in connection with specific courses of instruction offered by the Licensee to its students.

> *Comment:* This is a fair definition. Electronic reserves are an important function for licensed databases in academic institutions. Watch for limits on how much content can be placed in electronic reserves and how long the content can be retained.

Secure Network. A network (whether a standalone network or a virtual network within the Internet) which is only accessible to Authorized Users approved by the Licensee whose identity is authenticated at the time of log-in and periodically thereafter consistent with current best practice, and whose conduct is subject to regulation by the Licensee.

> *Comment:* Different vendors have different requirements for how access is technologically mediated. Make sure you understand how your institution's systems work or bring your information technology department into the loop for database licenses.

Text Mining. A machine process by which information may be derived by identifying patterns and trends within natural language through text categorization, statistical pattern recognition, concept or sentiment extraction, and the association of natural language with indexing terms.

> *Comment*: Text mining is when computers crunch through large datasets of text to find patterns. For example, a researcher could load a dataset containing multiple years of a major newspaper and search it find out when certain words became popular or what were the top news topics at various times. Or librarians could load a huge set of journal articles into a computer and perform citation analyses to discover how theories spread through a scholarly discipline. Vendors generally want to make special arrangements for text mining projects for at least two reasons. First, these projects generally require having a complete digital copy of a large number of copyright-protected works, many more than a normal researcher would need to access. Second, the automated computer programs that

download such large numbers of documents can overload vendors' servers if they are not given advance warning.

AGREEMENT

The Publisher agrees to grant to the Licensee the non-exclusive and non-transferable right, throughout the world, to give Authorized Users access to the Licensed Materials via a Secure Network [for the purposes of research, teaching and private study], subject to the terms and conditions of this License, and the Licensee agrees to pay the Fee.

> *Comment:* If you can delete the language limiting use to research, teaching and private study, that's great. But including them is not a deal-breaker.

[This License shall commence at the beginning of the Subscription Period, for each of the Licensed Materials as set out in Schedule 1 or in new Schedules to this License that may be added subsequently; and shall automatically terminate at the end of the Subscription Period, unless the parties have previously agreed to renew it.]

> *Comment:* You have some choices: If you want the license to terminate automatically at the end of the term, use this language. If you don't, see below.

or

[This License shall commence on [date] and shall remain in effect [until {date}] [for {three} years from that date, and shall continue thereafter to be in effect unless terminated by either party by six months written notice to the other.]

> *Comment:* With this language, the contract renews automatically unless a party gives six months notice in writing. Six months seems a bit long, two or three months is better. You always want notice in writing. Best option is a print letter and e-mail notice.

USAGE RIGHTS

The Licensee, subject to clause 6 below, may:

[Load the Licensed Materials on the Licensee's server on the Secure Network.]

[Make such back-up copies of the Licensed Materials as are reasonably necessary.]

Comment: Good. No computer system is infallible, and having redundant copies provides greater assurance that content will be accessible whenever it is needed.

Make such [temporary] local electronic copies [by means of caching {or mirrored storage}] of all or part of the Licensed Materials as are necessary solely to ensure efficient use by Authorized Users [and not to make available to Authorized Users duplicate copies of the Licensed Material].

Comment: Making a cache copy provides quicker access to the online data.

Provide single printed or electronic copies of single articles at the request of individual Authorized Users.

Comment: Good. This is consistent with the section 108 exemption that permits libraries to make copies at a patron's request.

Authorized Users may, in accordance with the copyright laws of [jurisdiction] and subject to clause 6 below:

Search, view, retrieve and display the Licensed Materials.

Print a copy or download and save individual articles or items of the Licensed Materials for personal use.

Use individual parts of the Licensed Materials within Learning Objects for the Licensee's teaching, learning or training purposes.

Use Text Mining technologies to derive information from the Licensed Materials.

Comment: This language is good because it allows researchers to make full use of the database with software tools.

Distribute a copy of individual articles or items of the Licensed Materials in print or electronic form to other Authorized Users or to other individual scholars collaborating with Authorized Users but only for the purposes of research and private study [; for the avoidance of doubt, this sub-clause shall include the distribution of a copy for teaching purposes to each individual student Authorized User in a class at the Licensee's institution].

Comment: This allows each student to have a print or digital copy of any articles needed for class or research.

Download a copy of individual articles or items of the Licensed Materials and share the same with Authorized Users or other individual scholars collaborating in a specific research project with such Authorized Users provided that it is held and accessibly within a closed network that is not accessible to any person not directly involved in such collaboration and provided that it is deleted from such network immediately upon completion of the collaboration.

> *Comment:* These uses are expressly permitted under the license. Make sure you read this section carefully. Regarding the last permitted use, you could be more succinct (and a little more encompassing) by using the following language: "Distribute a copy of individual articles or items of the Licensed Materials in any format to other Authorized Users, including copies to students enrolled in a class or those who attend educational programs sponsored by the Licensee's institution."

[Nothing in this License shall in any way exclude, modify or affect any of the Licensee's rights under Copyright Revision Act 1976 as amended subsequently provided that such rights are exercised in accordance with Section 108 of the Act and with the guidelines developed by the National Commission on New Technological Uses of Copyrighted Works (CONTU Guidelines) and published in U.S. Copyright Office Circular 21.]

> *Comment:* This is acceptable, but the language below is better.

or

[Nothing in this License shall in any way exclude, modify or affect any of the Licensee's statutory rights under the copyright laws of {jurisdiction}]

> *Comment:* The first clause above references only the section 108 library exception and the CONTU guidelines. The second clause is broader and better: it encompasses all exemptions in the Copyright Act, including fair use, the library exception, and the public performance exception.

SUPPLY OF COPIES TO OTHER LIBRARIES

[The Licensee may, subject to clause 6 below, supply to an Authorized User of another library {within the same country as the Licensee} (whether by post or fax [or secure transmission, using Ariel or its equivalent, whereby the electronic file is deleted immediately after printing]), for the purposes of research or private study and not for Commercial Use, a single paper copy of an electronic original of an individual document being part of the Licensed Materials.]

> *Comment:* This language is too restrictive and focuses on paper copies. The next option is much better.

or

[The Licensee may, subject to clause 6 below, supply to an Authorized User of another library {within the same country as the Licensee}a copy of an individual document being part of the Licensed Materials by post, fax or electronic transmission via the Internet or otherwise, for the purposes of research or private study and not for Commercial Use.]

> *Comment:* This language is better, because it permits electronic transmission. But who is an "authorized user of another library"? We would remove that line. We would also ideally remove the last clause. We prefer the following language: "Consistent with section 108 of the Copyright Act, the Licensee may provide to another library, in any format and by any mode of communication, a single copy of an individual document that is part of the licensed materials."

or

[Notwithstanding the provisions of Clauses 3.1 and 3.3, it is understood and agreed that neither the Licensee nor Authorized Users may provide, by electronic means, to a user at another library a copy of any part of the Licensed Materials for research or private study or otherwise.]

> *Comment:* Undesirable, but it's not uncommon to find a clause that permits you to only send another library a paper copy.

COURSE PACKS AND ELECTRONIC RESERVE

[The Licensee may, subject to clause 6 below, incorporate parts of the Licensed Materials in printed Course Packs [and Electronic Reserve collections and in Virtual Learning Environments] for the use of Authorized Users in the course of instruction at the Licensee's institution, but not for Commercial Use. Each such item shall carry appropriate acknowledgement of the source, listing title and author of the extract, title and author of the work, and the publisher. Copies of such items shall be deleted by the Licensee when they are no longer used for such purpose. Course packs in non-electronic non-print perceptible form, such as audio or Braille, may also be offered to Authorized Users who, in the reasonable opinion of the Licensee, are visually impaired.]

> *Comment:* Along with specifically authorizing putting content in electronic reserves, it is worthwhile to authorize putting content in your institution's online course management system.

or

[For the avoidance of doubt, the Licensee may not incorporate all or any part of the Licensed Materials in [Course Packs] [and] [Electronic Reserve collections or Virtual Learning Environments] without the prior written permission of the Publisher, which may set out further terms and conditions for such usage.]

> *Comment:* Under this language, permission is required to use database content in course packs and electronic reserves. The first part of this license calls the licensor the "Publisher." However, it's common for the licensor to be an aggregator of others' content. This language presumes that the owners of the content have authorized the aggregator/licensor to grant or deny certain permissions. Since you already paid for the content, and because it's available to students at your institution, you might think that vendors would have no problem including content in course packs, electronic reserves, or course management systems. If this is not permitted in the agreement the vendor sends you, add it.

PROHIBITED USES

Neither the Licensee nor Authorized Users may:

remove or alter the authors' names or the Publisher's copyright notices or other means of identification or disclaimers as they appear in the Licensed Materials;

> *Comment:* No problem. As an ethical matter and to comply with the DMCA, don't mess with copyright management information.

systematically make print or electronic copies of multiple extracts or make multiple copies of any part of the Licensed Materials for any purpose other than expressly permitted by this License;

> *Comment:* Systematic copying is not permitted under section 108(g), so this restriction is probably not a problem. It would be nice is systematic copying were defined.

prepare derivative works or download, mount or distribute any part of the Licensed Material on any electronic system or network, including without limitation the Internet and the World Wide Web, other than the Secure Network, except where expressly permitted by this License under clause 3.2.6;

> *Comment:* Making derivative works is one of the copyright owner's rights, so agreeing not to make them without permission is fine. Since the library doesn't obtain copyright ownership through the license, you cannot distribute the content on the open Internet. Sending links to users that can access the content is fine, though, because you are not making copies.

reverse engineer, decompile, alter, abridge or otherwise modify the Licensed Materials or any part of them for any purpose whatsoever, except as expressly provided in this License.

> *Comment:* This catch-all language means if the license doesn't authorize a use, then it is prohibited. This is why carefully reading the authorized uses language is so important.

The Publisher's explicit written permission must be obtained in order to:

use all or any part of the Licensed Materials for any Commercial Use;

> *Comment:* This does not bother us. "Commercial Use" is defined earlier as selling or transferring the licensed information for money. Presumably you can use the information in support of grants. If you are in a for-profit institution, make sure that "Commercial Use" does not include the day-to-day operations of the enterprise.

systematically distribute the whole or any part of the Licensed Materials to anyone other than Authorized Users;

> *Comment:* No problem.

publish, distribute or make available the Licensed Materials, works based on the Licensed Materials or works which combine them with any other material, other than as permitted in this License;

> *Comment:* We assume "publish, distribute, or make available" means very wide distribution, but those words aren't defined. Even so, we can live with this section.

alter, abridge, adapt or modify the Licensed Materials, except to the extent necessary to make them perceptible on a computer screen to Authorized

Users. For the avoidance of doubt, no alteration of the words or their order is permitted.

> *Comment:* We would delete this. You should be able to "alter, abridge, adapt, or modify" the materials as long as you are not creating a derivative work that requires the copyright owner's permission. This broad prohibition may be more important in Europe, where there has been longstanding protection of authors' moral rights. We can understand an author's concerns about her words being altered such that the intended meaning is lost.

PUBLISHER'S UNDERTAKINGS

The Publisher warrants to the Licensee that the Licensed Materials used as contemplated by this License do not infringe the copyright or any other proprietary or intellectual property rights of any person. The Publisher shall indemnify and hold the Licensee harmless from and against any loss, damage, costs, liability and expenses (including reasonable legal and professional fees) arising out of any legal action taken against the Licensee claiming actual or alleged infringement of such rights. This indemnity shall survive the termination of this License for any reason. This indemnity shall not apply if the Licensee has amended the Licensed Materials in any way not permitted by this License.

> *Comment:* This "hold harmless" clause is important for the licensee. Indemnification means that the licensor will protect or compensate the library if the database contains infringing content.

The Publisher shall:

make the Licensed Materials available to the Licensee from the Server via the Internet access to which is authenticated by [Internet Protocol Address] [Athens] [Shibboleth] as specified in Schedule 1. The Publisher will notify the Licensee at least [ninety (90)] [sixty (60)] days in advance of any anticipated specification change applicable to the Licensed Materials. If the changes render the Licensed Materials less useful in a material respect to the Licensee, the Licensee may within thirty days of such notice treat such changes as a breach of this License under clause 10.1.2 and 10.4.

> *Comment:* This important clause requires the publisher to notify you of changes well in advance, and permits the library to terminate the contract if the changes make the licensed materials less useful. The more notice you have, the better.

use reasonable endeavours to make available the electronic copy of each journal issue in the Licensed Materials [not less than {XX} days before the date] [not later than the day] of publication of the printed version. In the event that for technical reasons this is not possible for any particular journal, as a matter of course, such journal shall be identified at the time of licensing, together with such reasons.

provide the Licensee, within 30 days of the date of this License, with information sufficient to enable the Licensee to access the Licensed Material.

use reasonable endeavours to ensure that the Server has adequate capacity and bandwidth to support the usage of the Licensee at a level commensurate with the standards of availability for information services of similar scope operating via the World Wide Web, as such standards evolve from time to time over the term of this License.

use reasonable endeavours to make the Licensed Materials available to the Licensee and to Authorized Users at all times and on a twenty-four hour basis, save for routine maintenance (which shall be notified to the Licensee in advance wherever possible), and to restore access to the Licensed Materials as soon as possible in the event of an interruption or suspension of the service.

> *Comment:* These are all good terms that help guarantee the library effective access to the database.

[Where the Licensed Materials shall not be available to the Licensee for more than thirty (30) consecutive days, the Publisher shall refund to the Licensee a proportion of the Fee prorated to the period of such unavailability within the Subscription Period to which the Fee relates.]

The Publisher reserves the right at any time to withdraw from the Licensed Materials any item or part of an item for which it no longer retains the right to publish, or which it has reasonable grounds to believe infringes copyright or is defamatory, obscene, unlawful or otherwise objectionable. The Publisher shall give written notice to the Licensee of such withdrawal. If the withdrawal [represents more than ten per cent (10%) of the book, journal or other publication in which it appeared, the Publisher shall refund to the Licensee that part of the Fee that is in proportion to the amount of material withdrawn and the remaining un-expired portion of the Subscription Period] [results in the Licensed Materials being no longer useful to the Licensee, the Licensee may within thirty days of such notice treat such changes as a breach of this License under clause 10.1.2 and 10.4].

> *Comment:* Vendors often do not own the content, but rather license it from other authors or publishers. A vendor may lose permission to publish or distribute the works, and thus must remove the content from the database. This helpful clause provides for refunds to the library for withdrawn materials. The bracketed text, which we like, permits the library to treat withdrawals as a breach if the remainder is "no longer useful."

[The Publisher undertakes to [use reasonable endeavours to] provide or to make arrangements for a third party to provide an archive of the Licensed Materials for the purposes of long term preservation of the Licensed Materials, and to permit Authorized Users to access such archive after termination of this License.]

> *Comment:* This is a helpful clause, but language like "undertakes to provide" or "undertakes to use reasonable endeavours to provide" is not the same as saying "the publisher shall provide."

Collection and analysis of data on the usage of the Licensed Materials will assist both the Publisher and the Licensee to understand the impact of this License. The Publisher shall provide to the Licensee or facilitate the collection and provision to the Licensee and the Publisher by the Licensee of such usage data on the number [of titles] [of abstracts and] of articles downloaded, by journal title, on [a monthly] [a quarterly] [an annual] basis for the Publisher's and the Licensee's private internal use only. Such usage data shall be compiled in a manner consistent with applicable privacy [and data protection] laws [and as may be agreed between the parties from time to time], and the anonymity of individual users and the confidentiality of their searches shall be fully protected. In the case that the Publisher assigns its rights to another party under clause 11.3, the Licensee may at its discretion require the assignee either to keep such usage information confidential or to destroy it.

> *Comment:* Collecting data helps you know how much the database is being used, which will help you determine whether to renew the contract. You may want monthly reports, but quarterly ones should suffice. The license must preserve the privacy of users and comply with applicable laws.

LICENSEE'S UNDERTAKINGS

The Licensee shall:

use reasonable endeavours to ensure that all Authorized Users are aware of the importance of respecting the intellectual property rights in the Licensed Materials and of the terms and conditions of this License, and use reasonable endeavours to notify Authorized Users of the terms and conditions of this License and take steps to protect the Licensed Materials from unauthorized use or other breach of this License;

use reasonable endeavours to monitor compliance and immediately upon becoming aware of any unauthorized use or other breach, inform the Publisher and take all reasonable and appropriate steps, including disciplinary action, both to ensure that such activity ceases and to prevent any recurrence;

> *Comment:* Librarians should monitor the use of licensed materials, but we would not agree to inform the publisher of unauthorized uses. The library should decide the reasonable and appropriate steps it will take, not the vendor.

[{SUBJECT TO APPLICABLE LAW,} THE LICENSEE AGREES TO INDEMNIFY, DEFEND AND HOLD THE PUBLISHER HARMLESS FROM AND AGAINST ANY LOSS, DAMAGE, COSTS, LIABILITY AND EXPENSES (INCLUDING REASONABLE LEGAL AND PROFESSIONAL FEES) ARISING OUT OF ANY CLAIM OR LEGAL ACTION TAKEN AGAINST THE PUBLISHER RELATED TO OR IN ANY WAY CONNECTED WITH ANY USE OF THE LICENSED MATERIALS BY THE LICENSEE OR AUTHORIZED USERS OR ANY FAILURE BY THE LICENSEE TO PERFORM ITS OBLIGATIONS IN RELATION TO THIS LICENSE, PROVIDED THAT] NOTHING IN THIS LICENSE SHALL MAKE THE LICENSEE LIABLE FOR BREACH OF THE TERMS OF THE LICENSE BY ANY AUTHORIZED USER PROVIDED THAT THE LICENSEE DID NOT CAUSE, KNOWINGLY ASSIST OR CONDONE THE CONTINUATION OF SUCH BREACH TO CONTINUE AFTER BECOMING AWARE OF AN ACTUAL BREACH HAVING OCCURRED.

> *Comment:* The library shouldn't agree to indemnify the licensor for breaches by any users. Eliminate anything like this bracketed language.

We do like the language relieving the library of liability for breaches by its users unless the library knowingly assisted or condoned the continuation of the breach.

TERM AND TERMINATION

In addition to automatic termination (unless renewed) under clause 2.2, this License shall be terminated:

if the Licensee wilfully defaults in making payment of the Fee as provided in this License and fails to remedy such default within [thirty (30)] [sixty (60)] days of notification in writing by the Publisher;

> *Comment:* Sixty days is better than thirty, and insist on written notice. Sometimes your parent institution may be a little slow paying its bills.

if the Publisher commits a material or persistent breach of any term of this License and fails to remedy the breach (if capable of remedy) within [thirty (30)] [sixty (60)] days of notification in writing by the Licensee;

> *Comment:* Breaches can go both ways. Make sure you notify the vendor promptly—and repeatedly—of any problems.

if the Licensee commits a wilful material and persistent breach of the Publisher's copyright or other intellectual property rights or of the provisions of clause 3 in respect of usage rights or of clause 6 in respect of prohibited uses;

> *Comment:* Make sure you get written notice of any suspected breaches of the agreement or copyright violations, and time to respond and remedy the problem. Think about how, and who, decides if there has been a wilful material and persistent breach.

if either party becomes insolvent or becomes subject to receivership, liquidation or similar external administration.

> *Comment:* This type of "ipso facto" clause may not be enforceable in bankruptcy.

GENERAL

This License constitutes the entire agreement of the parties and supersedes all prior communications, understandings and agreements relating to the subject matter of this License, whether oral or written.

Alterations to this License and to the Schedules to this License are only valid if they are recorded in writing and signed by both parties.

> *Comment:* This language prevents the vendor from modifying the contract simply by sending the library an e-mail or posting a notice on its website. Changes in the contract should be in writing and signed by both parties.

This License may not be assigned by either party to any other person or organisation, nor may either party sub-contract any of its obligations, except as provided in this License in respect of the management and operation of the Server, without the prior written consent of the other party, which consent shall not unreasonably be withheld.

If rights in all or any part of the Licensed Materials are assigned to another publisher, the Publisher shall [use its best endeavours to] ensure that the terms and conditions of this License are maintained.

> *Comment:* If the vendor assigns rights to another publisher, the assignee should be bound by the agreement. If the new publisher cannot comply with the contractual terms or conditions, the library has a right to renegotiate the contract, or terminate it and get a pro rata refund of the contract price.

Any notices to be served on either of the parties by the other shall be sent by prepaid recorded delivery or registered post to the address of the addressee as set out in this License or to such other address as notified by either party to the other as its address for service of notices. All such notices shall be deemed to have been received within 14 days of posting.

> *Comment:* We're not sure you need registered mail. E-mail and first-class mail for notices is fine.

[This License shall be governed by and construed in accordance with {jurisdiction} law; the parties irrevocably agree that any dispute arising out of or in connection with this License will be subject to and within the jurisdiction of the courts of {jurisdiction}.]

> *Comment:* If you are at a state-funded institution, your procurement office probably will require you to insert your state's name here.

The Bottom Line on Licenses: Read a license carefully, and then read it again. If you do not like what you see, write in the changes (deletions, additions, modifications) and initial them. Send two signed copies to the licensor, and ask the licensor to send back to you with his or her signature.

Licensors sometimes will not send back the amended agreement. Therefore, in your cover letter and on the agreement itself, write that if the licensor provides the product after you mailed the amended agreement, you understand that the licensor has assented to your terms.

Permissions

Up to this point, when we have discussed licenses, we have meant contracts with publishers for journal and database subscriptions. However, "license" is also another name for permission from a copyright owner. If you want to use a work in a way that requires permission, your first job is to contact the right person who can grant permission.

Most copyrighted works have copyright notices identifying the copyright owner. Search online for the copyright owner's contact information. If you find the owner, send them a letter explaining what you want to use and how you plan to use it. We provide a sample permission letter in Appendix I.

If you cannot find the owner mentioned in the copyright notice or she doesn't respond, next try contacting the publisher. The publisher might have current contact information for the author or have the power to grant you permission.

A third option is to check with collective licensing agencies.[6] These are private groups that gather licensing privileges from authors and publishers. They grant permissions on behalf of the copyright owners and distribute royalty payments. Collective licensing agencies provide a more centralized and convenient means of getting permission, but they exist to gather money for their members, so they virtually always charge fees for permission.

Collective licensing agencies tend to be organized by industry. The three major music agencies are ASCAP,[7] BMI,[8] and SESAC.[9] Each

---

[6] A good list of collective licensing agencies is available at http://copyright.columbia.edu/copyright/permissions/collective-licensing-agencies/.

[7] http://www.ascap.com/

[8] http://www.bmi.com/

[9] http://www.sesac.com/

agency has a different portfolio of artists and publishers it represents, so if one agency can't give permission for the song you want to use, check with the others. The Motion Picture Licensing Corporation[10] and Swank Motion Pictures[11] handle permissions for a large number of film and television producers. The Copyright Clearance Center[12] grants licenses for print works, such as books, journals, and newspapers. Collective licensing agencies have the ability to grant permissions for a lot of copyrighted material, but no agency has *everything*, so no guarantees.

Photographs can be even trickier, because there is not a collective licensing agency for photographers. Instead, a number of stock photography companies handle permissions for many images, or photographers manage permissions themselves. Corbis,[13] Getty,[14] and Jupiter Images[15] are major places to check for images that can be licensed.

Tracking copyrights is sometimes complicated. For instance, you might think the publisher is the copyright owner, but it will direct you to another copyright owner or to a collective licensing agency. Give yourself as much time as you can to obtain permission. It's great if the owner replies immediately, but your request may take time to process and will require patience.

Once contacted, some copyright owners will give permission for free, while others will require a fee or seek to impose conditions on your use. Good faith negotiation will probably result in a satisfactory outcome, but some license fees will be too high for you, or the owner simply won't want her work used a particular way. If you can't get permission and no copyright exceptions apply, then you will just have to find an alternative to the material you wanted to use.

---

[10] http://www.mplc.org/index/worldwide
[11] http://swank.com/
[12] http://www.copyright.com/
[13] http://www.corbisimages.com/
[14] http://www.gettyimages.com/
[15] http://www.jupiterimages.com/

Chapter Eight
AUDIOVISUAL WORKS AND
NON-PRINT MEDIA
ଌଓଔ

According to the Copyright Act, audiovisual works "are works that consist of a series of related images which are intrinsically intended to be shown by the use of machines, or devices such as projectors, viewers, or electronic equipment, together with accompanying sounds, if any, regardless of the nature of the material objects, such as films or tapes, in which the works are embodied."[1] In other words, audiovisual works mix visual images and sound, and include items such as films, TV shows, and DVDs.

Permissible uses of audiovisual works under the Copyright Act, like uses of copyrighted works in other formats, are not always clear. In fact, sometimes it can be pretty muddy. This chapter covers copying and showing of audiovisual works in light of the copyright owner's public display and public performance rights.

Recording

It has been over a generation since the U.S. Supreme Court decided *Sony Corp. of America v. Universal City Studios, Inc.*,[2] or the "Betamax" case. In 1984, the Court held that off-air taping of broadcast television programs in one's own home for the non-commercial purpose of time-shifting is not infringing. A few points about the Betamax case: First, the decision applies only to programs broadcast on free network television; pay television

---

[1] 17 U.S.C. § 101 (2006).
[2] 464 U.S. 417 (1984).

channels such as cable, premium channels, and pay-per-view programs are not included. Second, it does not address taping outside the home. Third, it focuses on taping for the purpose of time-shifting, or watching a program subsequent to the original broadcast. What all of this means is that you may record free broadcast shows, such as *Dancing with the Stars*, *Modern Family*, or *The Office* for later viewing.

8.1. Guidelines for Off-Air Taping of Copyrighted Works for Educational Use

- Broadcast programs
- Non-profit educational institutions
- For instruction
- At instructor's request
- Local transmission
- Use for first ten days only
- Thirty-five more days for evaluation, then destroy
- Institutional controls

127 Cong. Rec. 24048–49 (Oct. 14, 1981)

Digital video recorders (DVR) have given viewers more options for recording and time-shifting television programming from cable operators. Thus far, the copyright owners of television shows have not sued over DVRs that store copies of selected shows on a hard drive in the viewer's home.[3] These devices function much like VCRs except they record on hard drives instead of magnetic tape cassettes, and they have generally been treated the same as VCRs.

Entertainment companies did sue a cable operator over "remote storage DVR," a system in which the hard drives containing the recorded programming are kept at a central location owned by the cable company. The recorded shows were then streamed to viewers on demand. The appellate court determined that since the viewer selected and ordered the recording of a show, if any infringement was committed, it was by the viewer, not the cable company. The cable company was found not be infringing directly, and for whatever reason, the entertainment companies

---

[3] Ned Snow, *The TiVo Question: Does Skipping Commercials Violate Copyright Law?*, 56 SYRACUSE L. REV. 27, 29 (2005) (arguing that DVRs' enabling viewers to skip commercials is infringing).

chose not to allege contributory infringement, so remote storage DVR has not yet led to any liability.[4]

Institutional recording in libraries or schools is a very different story. Take, for example, *Encyclopedia Britannica Educational Corp. v. Crooks*,[5] where a federal district court held that extensive and systematic off-air taping of educational programs, even for non-profit educational purposes, was infringing. In this case, a non-profit organization funded by nineteen school districts offered a videotaping service for schools. The Videotape and Instructional Television Service (VITS) had a nine-person staff, and a library holding 4,500 videotaped television programs. VITS was able to produce sixty videotape copies of a single program in a twenty-four-hour period, and they transmitted about 14,000 programs to schools in the 1976–77 academic year. Each school could keep the tapes. Jerry Lee Lewis might have sang that there was a whole lot of tapin' goin' on.

Not surprisingly, the court concluded that this "highly organized and systematic practice of making off-the-air videotapes of plaintiffs' copyrighted works for use in later years and the making of numerous derivative copies of plaintiffs' copyrighted works does not constitute fair use. . . ." Even though the defendant was a non-profit educational organization, the court reached the right decision.

This case does not mean that you can never tape programs for educational purposes. You can find some guidance in the *Guidelines for Off-Air Recording of Copyrighted Works for Educational Use*,[6] which were developed by representatives of content producers, educators, and librarians. The negotiations were coordinated by the House Judiciary Committee and the *Guidelines* were published in the *Congressional Record*. But they were not been enacted by Congress, and are not law.

A few things about the *Guidelines*. First, they apply to non-profit educational institutions. A school or academic library that helps its parent institution meet its instructional needs certainly qualifies. But a for-profit library, such as one in a corporation or law firm, does not come within the *Guidelines*, and neither does a city or county public library unless it is part of an educational institution. Second, the *Guidelines* apply to programs

---

[4] Cartoon Network LP, LLLP v. CSC Holdings, Inc., 536 F.3d 121, 133 (2d Cir. 2008).
[5] 542 F. Supp. 1156 (W.D.N.Y. 1982).
[6] 127 Cong. Rec. 24,048–49 (Oct. 14, 1981) (statement of Rep. Kastenmeier).

broadcast to the general public without charge, not to pay-TV programs. (Today this would include basic cable, but not premium channels such as HBO.) Third, the purpose of the taping must be instructional, rather than for entertainment or recreational purposes. Fourth, requests to tape programs must be made by the instructor, rather than ordered from above by, say, the school system. Here are the details.

- You may tape a program only once at the request of the same teacher.
- You may play a recorded program for students only in the course of teaching, and again for reinforcement, within the first ten consecutive school days after the taping.
- You may retain a recording for up to forty-five days after it is recorded, after which time it must be erased or destroyed. After the first ten school days, the recordings may be used up to the end of the forty-five day period only for teacher evaluation purposes.
- You may use a taped program in classrooms and other places in the institution devoted to instruction (presumably including the library), and also in homes of students receiving formalized home instruction.
- You may make a limited number of copies of each recording to meet the needs of teachers. These copies are subject to the same rules that govern the original recording.
- You need not use a program in its entirety, but you may not alter it from its original content so as to change its meaning.
- You may not physically or electronically combine or merge a recording to create a teaching anthology or compilation.
- You must include on all copies the copyright notice as it appeared on the broadcast program as it was recorded.
- An educational institution must establish control procedures that enable it to comply with the *Guidelines*.

The *Guidelines* provide a safe harbor. Taping within them would certainly be permissible, but some uses outside the *Guidelines* also may be permitted as a fair use.

Example 1
Madison High School teacher Connie Brooks tapes a program to show to her class. Student Walter Denton saw the program in class, and asks to see it again three weeks after the first showing because he is working on a term paper.

Comment: The *Guidelines* provide that after the first ten school days the tape may only be used for teacher evaluation purposes. This is pretty silly. If a student wants to watch the tape again, let him. That sure seems like fair use.

Example 2

Walter (the student) is laid up in a hospital for two weeks and asks to see the tape when he returns to school.

Comment: Technically, the *Guidelines* say no. But they are guidelines, not the law. This also seems like a perfect case of fair use.

Example 3

Miss Brooks tapes a program to show to her class. She holds on to the tape for several weeks, in accordance with the *Guidelines*. She then tells the principal, Mr. Conklin, how good the tape is, and Mr. Conklin tells the school librarian to add the tape to the library's collection.

Comment: Just say no. No matter how much you like the teacher or fear the principal, do not add tapes of recorded television programs to the library's collection. If you want it, buy it.

As noted in Chapter Five, the section 108 library exemption also address copying audiovisual works. But unless it is a news program, copying is limited to the purposes enumerated in subsections (b) and (c).[7] Under section 108(b), a library may copy an *unpublished* audiovisual work it owns for the purpose of preservation and security, or for deposit in another library for research purposes. Section 108(c) permits copying to replace a *published* audiovisual work that has been lost, stolen, or damaged, but only if the library determines that it cannot obtain an unused replacement at a fair price.

What about news programs? Section 108(f)(3) provides that audiovisual news programs may be recorded and lent, subject to the limitations in subsection 108(a): there is no purpose of direct or indirect commercial advantage; the library's collections are open to the public or available to researchers; and the reproduction includes a notice of copyright. Unlike the *Off-Air Recording Guidelines*, section 108 rights are not limited to non-profit educational institutions. The legislative history to the 1976 Act sheds a bit more light on taping news programs.

---

[7] 17 U.S.C. § 108(i) (2006).

The conference committee is aware that an issue has arisen as to the meaning of the phrase "audiovisual news program" in section 108(f)(3). The conferees believe that, under the provision as adopted in the conference substitute, a library or archives qualifying under section 108(a) would be free . . . to reproduce, on videotape or any other medium of fixation or reproduction, local, regional, or network newscasts, interviews concerning current news events, and on-the-spot coverage of news events, and to distribute a limited number of reproductions of such programs on a loan basis.[8]

A word of caution here: Congress referred to straight news, not to documentary, magazine format, nor other public affairs programs. In other words, not *60 Minutes*, *Meet the Press*, or *Face the Nation*. But always remember that some uses may be permitted as a section 107 fair use.

As you may recall, section 117 lets you make an archival copy of a computer program. This does not mean, however, that a library may make a copy of a video recording or a sound recording because of the possibility that the original may deteriorate or be destroyed. A library that purchases CDs or DVDs for its collection may not make a backup copy "just in case." If you need two copies, then buy two copies.

The story is a little different for obsolete formats. Remember that under section 108(c) a library may make a copy if the format in which the work is stored is obsolete and the library cannot obtain an unused replacement at a fair price. In other words, if the library purchased a Beta or VHS version of a continuing education program back in 1982 and cannot locate a DVD version today, then it may copy the old tape onto a DVD. After you do this, you should discard your old copy.

Public Performance and Display

8.2. Public Performance
- A place open to the public
- Where a substantial number of persons gather, or
- Available to the public via a transmission
  - Same or separate places
  - Same or different times

---

[8] H.R. Rep. No. 94-1733, at 73.

Take a deep breath and hold on to the reins; we are off to a Day at the Races. Recall that a copyright owner has several different rights, one of which is the right to perform the copyrighted work publicly. Venues for performing and displaying copyright-protected works have greatly expanded. In addition to cable and satellite television, we now have satellite radio and online media providers like YouTube, Hulu, and Netflix. These new media outlets have made public display and performance rights one of the more volatile parts of copyright law. But before we get to the meat of this discussion, it's important to know that U.S. copyright law does not protect *all* performances, only *public* performances. According to the Copyright Act:

> To perform or display a work "publicly" means—
>
> (1) to perform or display it at a place open to the public or at any place where a substantial number of persons outside of a normal circle of a family and its social acquaintances is gathered; or
>
> (2) to transmit or otherwise communicate a performance or display of the work to a place specified by clause (1) or to the public, by means of any device or process, whether the members of the public capable of receiving the performance or display receive it in the same place or in separate places and at the same time or at different times.[9]

In plain English, a public performance occurs under either of three circumstances: (1) when the place where the work is performed is open to the public; (2) if the performance occurs at a place where a large number of people (exclusive of one's family and friends) may gather; or (3) if there is a transmission that allows the public to see or hear the work.

The public performance right is designed to prevent large numbers of people from seeing the same copy of a copyright-protected work, whether at one time or over a period of time. Determining when public performances take place is not always easy. Consider, for example, what different state attorneys general wrote during the 1980s as to whether state prisons could show purchased or rented videos to inmates.

In 1982 the Attorney General of California ruled that showing a purchased video that had a "For Home Use Only" notice on it was a public performance, and that showing those films to prisoners without a public

---

[9] 17 U.S.C. § 101 (2006).

performance license would be infringing.[10] That same year, Utah's Attorney General wrote that the Utah State Prison could not show videotapes of movies to inmates even if the inmates were limited to groups of twenty or less.[11] The Alaska Attorney General similarly held that their Department of Health and Social Services could not show rented videos to inmates.[12] In 1985, however, the Attorney General of Louisiana ruled that their Department of Corrections *could* show films rented from local stores to groups of between twenty to thirty prisoners, reasoning that those performances were not public.[13] Then, in 1988, the Louisiana Attorney General reaffirmed the 1985 ruling, but held that showing tapes to audiences of two- to three-hundred inmates would be infringing.[14]

Performances are public if a substantial number of people have the *potential* to see or hear a protected work over the course of time, regardless of how many people actually see or hear it at a particular time or place. A few cases illustrate how courts determine when a performance is public.

The first case involved a video store that played tapes rented by their customers in small two- to four-person viewing booths. The U.S. Court of Appeals for the Third Circuit decided that this arrangement was similar to a movie theater with the added feature of privacy, and concluded that such performances were public.[15] Two years later, the same court, ruling in a case with slightly different twist, held that a video store could not rent videotapes and allow the *renters* to play the tapes in small viewing rooms in the store.[16]

A line was drawn in 1989 when the Ninth Circuit Court of Appeals held that a rented hotel room is not a public place, and that a hotel could rent videotapes to their guests for viewing on equipment in their rooms.[17] So a guest could receive Room Service at the Hilton and rent the 1938 Marx Brothers film at the same time.

---

[10] California Op. Att'y Gen. No. 81-503 (Feb. 5, 1982).

[11] Utah Op. Att'y Gen. No. 82-03 (Sept. 22, 1982).

[12] Alaska Op. Att'y Gen. No 366-404-82 (June 11, 1982).

[13] Louisiana Op. Att'y Gen. No. 84-436 (Jan. 10, 1985).

[14] Louisiana Op. Att'y Gen. No. 88-576 (Dec. 19, 1988).

[15] Columbia Pictures Indus., Inc. v. Redd Horne, Inc., 749 F.2d 154 (3d Cir. 1984).

[16] Columbia Pictures Indus., Inc. v. Aveco, Inc., 800 F.2d 59 (3d Cir. 1986).

[17] Columbia Pictures Indus., Inc. v. Professional Real Estate Investors, Inc., 866 F.2d 278 (9th Cir. 1989).

These court decisions illustrate that you should look at the place where the performance occurs as a whole, not just at a particular room or space within a building when determining whether a performance is public. Stores, restaurants, and hotels (though not a particular room, once it is rented) are open to the general public or to a large number of people outside of one's family and friends. They are public places, and performances that take place in these places are public performances.

Now let's discuss libraries. You may contend that some libraries— those in private corporations or trade associations, for example—are not open to the public, and that in any case, performances to groups of employees or to board members are not public performances. You are correct. As noted earlier, the legislative history of the Copyright Act states that "[r]outine meetings of businesses and governmental personnel would be excluded because they do not represent the gathering or a 'substantial number of persons.'"[18]

What about city or county public libraries, and public or private academic libraries? These certainly are places where a substantial number of persons outside of a normal family circle and its friends gather. According to the Act's legislative history, Congress considers performances in these venues to be public performances: "[P]erformances in 'semipublic places' such as clubs, lodges, factories, summer camps, and schools are 'public performances' subject to copyright control."[19]

Two questions come to mind. First, does a copyright owner's public performance right prohibit a public library from showing an audiovisual work to large groups? To this question, we think the answer is yes. Unless otherwise permitted under the Copyright Act (fair use, for example, or under the section 110 exemptions, which are discussed below), a library cannot show audiovisual works to large groups. There is an alternative, of course: a public performance license.

Public performance licenses may be acquired from the copyright owner, or, more likely, from a distributor. Some distributors of educational films offer public performances licenses along with the DVDs. Many content producers also authorize the Motion Picture Licensing Corporation to convey umbrella public performance licenses to for-profit and non-

---

[18] H.R. REP. NO. 94-1476, at 64.
[19] *Id.*

profit organizations. The cost of the license depends on the amount of usage, size of patron base, and number of viewing sites.[20]

As for the second question, which asks whether a patron may watch a film in the library, most entertainment companies would regard those as public performances. Even though libraries have purchased copies of films, they have not also purchased public performance rights, so those rights need to be obtained separately. For example, the Library Video Company, while acknowledging fair use and the section 110(2) exemption, advises customers that "The best way to fully enjoy the benefits and flexibility of the digital age is to secure a license for all of your digital content needs."[21]

A former Attorney General of Ohio shared this view years ago when, in 1987, he wrote that patrons of an Ohio school district public library could not view videotapes in library viewing rooms. The Attorney General reasoned that because the public library was accessible to the public, performances of videotapes on the premises—even in individual viewing rooms—were infringing public performances. He wrote that "it is the public accessibility of the location where the videotape is shown that determines whether the playing of the tape is a public performance of the copyrighted work for the purposes of section 106(4)."[22] But even if this is true, and if a few people watching a film in a small library viewing room is a public performance, there is a strong case for fair use.[23]

Libraries do not always need to acquire public performance licenses when they purchase a film for their collections. If the New York Public Library lends Woody Allen a DVD of the 1940 Marx Brothers' film *Go*

---

[20] *See* the Motion Picture Licensing Corporation's FAQs, *available at* http://www.mplc.org/page/faqs.

[21] http://www.libraryvideo.com/articles/article22.asp. For additional discussions of public performance of audiovisual works in libraries, see Laura Jenemann, Public Performance Rights Management in Academic Libraries, 77th IFLA General Conference and Assembly (Aug. 2011), *available at* http://conference.ifla.org/sites/default/files/files/papers/ifla77/161-jenemann-en.pdf; and Brandon Butler, *Copyfraud and Classroom Performance Rights: Two Common Bogus Copyright Claims*, RESEARCH LIBRARY ISSUES: A BIMONTHLY REPORT FROM ARL, CNI, AND SPARC, NO. 276 (September 2011), at 20, *available at* http://publications.arl.org/rli276/.

[22] Ohio Op. Att'y Gen. No 87-108 (Dec. 29, 1987), Copyright L. Rep. (CCH) ¶ 26,240.

[23] J. Wesley Cochran, *Why Can't I Watch This Video Here? Copyright Confusion and Performance of Videocassettes & Videodiscs in Libraries*, 15 HASTINGS COMM. & ENT. L.J. 837, 877 (1993) (applying statutory factors and arguing that viewing films in libraries for educational purposes is likely a fair use).

West so he can watch it at home while eating take-out Chinese food, why can't he watch it in the library's viewing room? Indeed, watching a library-owned DVD in a small viewing room seems little different from using a library's microform reader to read microfiche, or a library computer to access digital information; the library is merely providing the equipment that enables patrons to use library materials in the library.

What about allowing small groups to view films in the library? This is a bit more problematic, but if a group consisting of one's family or friends may watch a rented film at home, they should be able to watch it in a small viewing room in the library. There are limits to how many people can watch a film without it being a public performance, but there is no magic number. We feel very comfortable with the number four, and quite comfortable with eight.

A few words of caution: you can contract away your fair use or other statutory rights, so review carefully any contracts that come with your purchases. And when your library orders a film, you may want to indicate on the purchase order that the film is being purchased by the library for lending and onsite use by library patrons.

Some libraries may be tempted to establish an account with Netflix or a similar service that provides DVDs for rent or streaming access to movies and television programs. The primary issue for libraries in this situation is not copyright, but the terms of service a library must agree to when signing up for the service. No popular service we are aware of offers an institutional account that would authorize sharing the DVDs or streaming access with patrons. So far it appears no library has gotten in serious trouble yet, but violating the terms of service is a good way to get your service terminated.

Some services, such as YouTube or Hulu, stream audiovisual works online for free. For works that are freely available through them, these services have given permission to view them implicitly or expressly in their terms of service. Although this does not necessarily convey public performance rights, you may permit small groups to view online programs via free streaming, as this shouldn't implicate public performance rights. But playing whole programs or clips to larger groups, like classes, will require permission, relying on TEACH Act exceptions (more on that later), or fair use.

The Bottom Line: A single library patron should be able to watch a library-owned film in a private viewing room in the library. A small group should be able to do the same in a small viewing room under fair use. How many people? Certainly four, but arguably no more than eight. At the end of this chapter are some guidelines for the use of films in libraries. Right now, however, you should know that you need not rely on fair use alone. The Copyright Act also includes a section that specifically permits certain public performances without the need for permission.

8.3. Section 110 Public Performance Exemptions

1. Classroom teaching
2. Education broadcasting
3. Religious services (non-dramatic literary or musical works, or dramatic musical religious works
4. Charitable purposes (non-dramatic literary or musical works)
5. Small business (radio or television transmission)
6. Agricultural or horticultural fairs (non-dramatic musical works)
7. Promote sale of non-dramatic musical works or equipment
8. Blind or otherwise handicapped persons (non-dramatic literary works)
9. Handicapped persons (dramatic literary works less than ten years old)
10. Non-profit veterans or fraternal organizations (non-dramatic literary or musical works)

Section 110 of the Copyright Act sets forth ten situations in which public performances are expressly permitted. The section 110 exemptions include certain classroom performances, some educational instructional broadcasting, and certain performances at religious services, for charitable purposes, in small businesses, at agricultural or horticultural fairs, in music stores, transmissions to handicapped audiences, and fraternal organizations.[24]

---

[24] 17 U.S.C. § 110 (2006).

Remember this: there is no automatic exemption for non-profit public performances. There was such an exemption under the 1909 Copyright Act, but that was changed with the 1976 Copyright Act. A performance in a university library or local public library is not necessarily exempt; the performance must meet the criteria of a section 110 exemption to be covered. Also remember that section 110 rights do not attach if an infringing copy is used.

Videos purchased or rented from commercial vendors are legitimate copies, and generally may be used for section 110 performances. This is true even if the video has a "for home use only" label. That label is not itself a contract. A signed form that places limits on library use of a tape or disc is enforceable, though, so watch out for restrictions in any contracts you sign. Furthermore, when your library orders a DVD, you may want to indicate on the purchase order that the DVD is being purchased by the library for lending and onsite use by library patrons. This is not enough to create a license agreement, but it may help protect your statutory rights.

Performances for Educational Purposes (Section 110(1))

8.4. Section 110(1) Performances and Displays for Teaching

- Any type of work
- Nonprofit educational institution
- Classroom or similar place
- Face-to-face teaching
- Instructors and pupils present
- Non-infringing copy

Most of section 110 is not generally applicable to libraries, but now we will focus on the two section 110 exemptions libraries are likely to use: the section 110(1) face-to-face teaching exemption, and section 110(2), which addresses instructional broadcasting, or what we now call distance education. We begin with section 110(1).

Section 110(1) permits the performance or display of both dramatic and non-dramatic works (including audiovisual works) by instructors or pupils that take place in the course of face-to-face teaching activities of non-profit educational institutions. Sometimes called the "face-to-face teaching exemption," section 110(1) requires that there be an educational purpose to the performance. Showing a video for recreation or entertainment, such as rewarding a class for good behavior, does not qualify for this exemption. What might take place in a law school offers a good example of the educational/entertainment dichotomy.

Example 1

A student group wants to start a "Thursday Night at the Movies" series. The group will use films that are part of the library collection or rent them from Netflix. The films will be shown free of charge.

> *Comment:* Because the showings are solely for entertainment purposes, the film series is outside the 110(1) exemption.

Example 2

The school offers a "Law in Film" course that is taught by an instructor as part of the regular curriculum.

> *Comment:* This educational use is fine. Section 110(1) permits you to show everything from *The Accused* to *Twelve Angry Men*, and even comedies such as *My Cousin Vinny*, so long as you meet the other requirements of that section.

Example 3

Several professors want to have a "Law and Film" series open to any law student who wishes to attend. On the first Tuesday of each month a law-related film will be shown, and a professor will introduce and lead a discussion of the film.

> *Comment:* This too is permitted under section 110(1) because the purpose is educational, rather than entertainment.

Let's look a bit more at this exemption. First, what does "face-to-face teaching activities" mean? According to the legislative history of the Copyright Act, the instructor and students must be in the same general area in the building, but not necessarily in the same room.[25] And although the teacher and students do not have to be within eyesight, they must simultaneously be in the same general place. Although broadcasts or other transmissions from outside locations into classrooms are not allowed, loudspeakers or projectors may be used within the building.[26]

As for who may attend section 110(1) performances and where they can take place, the exemption requires that attendance be limited to pupils, a guest lecturer, or the instructor. Performances permitted under section 110(1) may not be open to others, such as students' friends or the general public. Although performances must take place in a classroom or a similar place devoted to instruction, any room that can function as a classroom, including the library, may be used.

In a perfect world, everyone who is entitled to attend a section 110(1) performance would be able to see and hear it at the time and place it happens, and every performance would take place in a classroom. In other words, every showing would fit literally, and perfectly, within the exemption. But we do not live in a perfect world. What if—

- A student misses the History of Film class where Citizen Kane was shown. The student wants to check out the library-owned DVD and watch it in a library viewing room.
- A student saw the film in class but wants to see it again, this time in a library viewing room, to understand it better.
- The instructor recommends that students see two other films directed by and starring Orson Welles, and a student wants to watch them in a library viewing room.

The American Library Association's Model Policy,[27] discussed earlier, considers the reserve room an extension of the classroom for the purpose of photocopying and distributing materials to students. It is equally fair to view a school or university library as an extension of the classroom for purposes of the section 110(1) exemption, thereby permitting an otherwise qualifying use to take place in a library viewing room.

---

[25] H.R. REP. NO. 94-1476, at 81.
[26] Id.
[27] AMERICAN LIBRARY ASSOCIATION, MODEL POLICY CONCERNING COLLEGE AND UNIVERSITY PHOTOCOPYING FOR CLASSROOM RESEARCH AND LIBRARY RESERVE USE (1982), available at http://old.cni.org/docs/infopols/ALA.html.

The motion picture industry may not agree, and instead argue that the section 110(1) exemption does not apply because the instructor and pupil are not simultaneously in the same building. We disagree, but even if one supports such a narrow interpretation of the face-to-face teaching exemption, we still have fair use. A student who wants to watch a library-owned video in a library viewing room, in support of a school related project, should be able to do so under section 107. If the student could borrow the video from the library and watch it at home, he or she should be able to watch it in a library viewing room.

Performances in For-Profit Institutions

The face-to-face teaching exemption applies only to non-profit educational institutions. Performances of educational or training videotapes in organizations such as for-profit schools or corporations are not permitted under section 110(1). But as noted earlier, the legislative history indicates that routine business meeting showings are not public performances because they do not involve the gathering of a substantial number of people.[28] Consequently, under most circumstances educational or training programs may be performed in commercial business settings, without payment of royalties, if the number of people attending the performances—at one time or over a period of time—is not substantial.

Institutional Liability

What should a library employee do when she has reason to believe that a patron plans to show a library-owned DVD to a large audience? If the following conversation takes place, you may wisely decide not to lend the film.

Student: "I'd like to check out Animal House."

Staff: "Great flick."

Student: "Yeah. I plan to show it at a frat party during homecoming. We have this huge 72" screen. We're going have about 300 people in the house."

Staff: "I think you need to speak to my supervisor."

---

[28] H.R. REP. No. 94-1476, at 64.

You *should* be concerned about the library's possibly being liable as a contributory infringer. The library's policy manual should encourage compliance with the Copyright Act and provide some guidance for the staff. Here, then, are our guidelines for using audiovisual works in libraries.

Guidelines for the Use of Audiovisual Works in Libraries

- Viewing rooms should be small, with seating for no more than eight persons.
- The equipment on which videos are shown should be of the kind typically used in a private home, generally no larger than a 65" diagonal screen.
- Do not charge patrons for loans of videos.
- Make available "play-only" equipment; do not supply equipment that can record.
- Library-owned equipment may be used only within the library.
- Do not lend videos or equipment to a person or organization that you have reason to believe will engage in an unauthorized public performance.
- Affix the following notice to videos: "THIS MATERIAL MAY BE PROTECTED BY UNITED STATES COPYRIGHT LAW. UNAUTHORIZED COPYING OR PUBLIC PERFORMANCES ARE PROHIBITED."
- Affix the following notice to equipment: "WARNING: THE MAKING OF A COPY AND PUBLIC DISTRIBUTION, PERFORMANCES OR DISPLAYS MAY BE SUBJECT TO THE UNITED STATES COPYRIGHT LAW (TITLE 17 UNITED STATES CODE)."
- Large groups (more than eight persons) may not view videos on library premises unless
  o The use meets the criteria of a section 110 exemption; or
  o The library has received permission to publicly perform the work, through a blanket public performance license or a license specific to the work.

Distance Education
(Section 110(2))

> ### 8.5. Section 110(2)
> ### The TEACH Act
> - Mediated instruction
> - Accredited non-profit educational institution
> - Most categories of works
> - Anywhere
> - To students or government employees
> - Prevent re-transmission and retention
> - Institutional policies

As enacted by Congress in 1976, the Copyright Act imposed limits on the types of materials that could be used for distance education, and to whom those materials could be transmitted. This changed with the 2002 enactment of the Technology, Education, and Copyright Harmonization Act, known colloquially as the TEACH Act.[29] The TEACH Act broadened the section 110(2) instructional broadcasting exemption to permit the transmission of more materials to more people in more places.

Section 110(2) permits *performances* of non-dramatic literary or musical works, and also reasonable and limited portions of most other types of works. As for *displays*, the amount of a work is limited to what typically is displayed in the course of a live classroom transmission. Such performances or displays are permitted when:

- the performance or display is made by, at the direction of, or under the supervision of an instructor as an integral part of a class session that is a regular part of systematic mediated instructional activities of a governmental body or accredited nonprofit educational institution.

  Post-secondary schools must be accredited by a regional or national accrediting agency recognized by the Council of Higher Education or the U.S. Department of Education. As for elementary and secondary schools, accreditation refers to those which are recognized by state certification or licensing procedures.

---

[29] Pub. L. No. 107-273, § 13301(b), 116 Stat. 1758, 1910–12 (2002).

In the context of digital transmissions, "mediated instructional activities" refers to activities that use the work as an integral part of the class experience that are controlled by or under the supervision of the instructor, and which are analogous to the type of performance or display that takes place in a live classroom. In other words, if you would not use the work in face-to-face teaching, do not transmit it digitally. Furthermore, you cannot transmit textbooks, course packs, or other materials that are typically purchased or acquired by students.

- The performance or display is directly related to and of material assistance to the teaching.

- The transmission is limited to students enrolled in the course for which the transmission is made, or to governmental employees as part of their official duties or employment.

- The transmitting body (a school, for example) must institute copyright policies that provide some measure of guidance to its faculty, students, and staff that describe and promote compliance with U.S. copyright law. Furthermore, the institution must notify students that the materials transmitted may be subject to copyright protection.

- If a work is transmitted digitally, the institution must apply technological measures that prevent those who receive it from retaining the work beyond the time the class is in session. The institution also must make sure that the work is not further disseminated. In addition, it must not do anything that interferes with technological measures a copyright owner uses to prevent permanent retention or further unauthorized dissemination.

Congress made it clear that there must be some institutional controls. First, materials that are stored on systems or networks cannot be accessible to anyone other than anticipated recipients. Not only must you have a secure network, but you must also ensure that no one other than the intended recipients can access the information transmitted. Second, copies cannot reside on networks any longer than is necessary to facilitate the transmissions.

There are other provisions of the TEACH Act that may be of interest, such as the provisions permitting the making of a temporary ("ephemeral") copy of a work in order to transmit it, and permitting the conversion of a print or other analog work to digital format if a digital version of the work is not available to the institution, or, if a digital version *is* available, it is subject to technological protective measures that prevent it from being used for the section 110(2) exemption.[30]

This is only a taste of the TEACH Act. Many universities have helpful information on their Web sites to help you apply the TEACH Act.[31]

Image Collections

Academic and special libraries often maintain collections of images on slides. Some are purchased, while others were reproduced from photographs or books of photographs. Two questions come to mind. First, may a library copy images from a published source? Second, may a library digitize images from its physical collection?

Because photographs are subject to copyright protection, an educator or librarian needs permission to copy protected images unless the copying is a fair use or otherwise allowed under the Copyright Act. An important exception, however, are non-creative photographs of works in the public domain, which are not copyrightable because they lack originality. We discussed this in Chapter One. You need not seek permission nor pay royalties to copy those works.

A compilation of images also may be copyrighted as a collective work. When this is the case, copying dozens of images from, say, a coffee table book of rock 'n' roll posters also may require permission from whoever has copyright in the compilation. This is true even when the original work is not protected. For example, copying numerous photos from a book that reproduces nineteenth-century artwork may violate copyright in the collective work, even though both the original paintings and the photographs of those paintings are in the public domain.

What about a library or archive's slide collections? To suggest that they must destroy their collections of copied slides would be presumptuous. Such collections have been common practice in libraries and archives for decades. Having a slide collection is different from digitizing them.

---

[30] 17 U.S.C. § 112(f)(2) (2006).

[31] See, for example, pages from Columbia University (http://copyright.columbia.edu/ copyright/special-topics/distance-education/), the University of Minnesota (http://www. lib.umn.edu/copyright/teaching), and North Carolina State University (http://www.provost. ncsu.edu/copyright/toolkit/).

This is an unsettled area of law, so for guidance we will rely on the Visual Resources Association's 2004 *Image Collection Guidelines: The Acquisition and Use of Images in Non-Profit Educational Visual Resources Collections*, which are included in Appendix L.[32] Many colleges and universities have either adopted or adapted the *Guidelines* to help them collect and manage their image collections. For librarians, the most interesting part of the *Guidelines* details the circumstances in which library copying of published images is likely to be fair use. Fair use is likely when:

1. Images of suitable quality are not readily available at a reasonable cost and in a reasonable time from any of the options listed above [purchase, license, donation, inter-library loan, original onsite imaging],
2. Images will not be shared between or among other educational institutions if such use is prohibited by the terms of their acquisition,
3. Images will be used for comment, criticism, review, analysis, discussion, or other similar purpose associated with instruction or scholarship, and
4. Images will be used for purposes that are both nonprofit and educational.

The VRA *Guidelines* seem reasonable, but they are not binding and some institutions add or subtract from them. For example, a library may wisely choose

*   to limit to a reasonable amount the number of images taken from a single published source (say, no more than 10%).
*   to limit access to digital images to students enrolled in the course.
*   not to use images scanned for a particular course in a subsequent course without first checking if it is available for purchase.
*   to post these guidelines on the university's website and where the collections are maintained.

Handling copyright questions relating to images is not much different from other types of works. Is the image under copyright? Does a statutory exemption (fair use, section 108, TEACH Act) permit the use? If not, seek permission.

---

[32] The VRA *Guidelines* are available at http://www.vraweb.org/resources/ipr/guide lines.html. Also see the VRA's *Statement on the Fair Use of Images for Teaching, Research and Study*, at http://www.vraweb.org/organization/pdf/VRAFairUseGuidelines Final.pdf.

Chapter Nine
THE LIBRARY AS PUBLISHER
🙲

So far this book has looked at copyright from the perspective of the consumer of copyrighted works. Most of the time, patrons want to use resources in some way—read a book, copy an article, listen to music, or watch a movie. Libraries also need to reproduce resources to preserve them or to fulfill interlibrary loan requests. But what if a library wants to publish original works or republish existing works in new formats?

Digital technologies have increased libraries' publishing capabilities. Many academic libraries have established digital collections of faculty research called institutional repositories.[1] Some academic libraries have gone further and published original scholarly books. For example, the University of Nebraska-Lincoln's repository has published a major reference work, along with undergraduate projects and doctoral dissertations.[2] The University of Michigan Press and Utah State University Press are actually divisions of their library systems. Online publishing systems, such as Open Journal Systems and Digital Commons, enable libraries to publish digital journals and post copies of faculty scholarship. HathiTrust Digital Library, a collaboration of academic libraries, produces collections of digitized books from library collections and is working to establish a division for publishing original works.[3]

---

[1] The vast literature on institutional repositories is organized in Charles W. Bailey, Jr., INSTITUTIONAL REPOSITORY AND ETD BIBLIOGRAPHY 2011, *available at* http://www.digital-scholarship.org/iretd/iretd.pdf.
[2] Paul Royster, *Publishing Original Content in an Institutional Repository*, 34 SERIALS REVIEW 27 (2008).
[3] http://www.hathitrust.org.

In discussing the library as publishe   r, we need to distinguish between the phenomena of "publishing" and "republishing." "Publishing" means making a work available for the first time, while "republishing" is making available a work that had already been published before. When a library posts an article for first time in a digital journal, it is publishing. When a library posts online a scanned book article, or image, it is republishing.

When acting as a publisher, a library is often both a user and a creator of copyrightable works. One the one hand, you must find out if anyone has copyright interests in works you want to publish. On the other hand, you must determine how you will manage any copyright interests the library will have.

Permissions

Before you publish something, make sure you are not infringing a copyright owner's rights. For works that are being published for the first time, this is relatively easy. If your library publishes a journal and an author submits an article, she wants you to publish it. Just ask her to sign a copyright permission form authorizing you to reproduce and distribute her work in any possible formats, including new formats that arise as technology advances. Many libraries that publish journals have author agreements on their sites you can look to for examples.[4] Columbia University also has a web site that gives examples of good and bad language for publication agreements.[5]

Aside from just knowing that you need explicit permission from an author to publish his or her work, you must get that permission in writing. The Copyright Act requires exclusive licenses be in writing, but non-exclusive licenses can be granted verbally or even implied.[6] However, relying on verbal or implied permission increases the risk of misunderstanding or misremembering the scope of the permission. It is worth the small investment of time and paper to make a thorough but concise copyright permission form that any authors you publish will sign. A sample publication agreement can be found in Appendix N.

---

[4] E.g., http://scholarworks.iu.edu/journals/index.php/ndif/about/submissions#copyrightNotice.
[5] http://www.keepyourcopyrights.org/.
[6] 17 U.S.C. § 204 (2006).

Assuming you aren't in the publishing business to make money, then a non-exclusive license should suffice. This means that the author gives you permission to publish her work, but she keeps the copyright and can exercise all her copyright privileges in the future. If you sell copies, then you might want an exclusive license so you will be the only one selling copies or subscriptions. Even here you may let the exclusive license become non-exclusive after a set period of time or when the work goes out of print. For example, your publication agreement could provide that the license will be exclusive for one or two years and non-exclusive thereafter.

While transferring copyright in the article from the author to the library publisher gives the publisher all rights in the article, it's probably unnecessary, and may be undesirable. Taking a long-term exclusive license or copyright transfer means the library is committing itself to handling any permission requests and making sure the work does not become an orphan. The library shouldn't hoard copyrights, so only take the rights you need and let the author keep the rest.

Republishing works can be a bit more difficult. If you know who owns copyright in the work, then you may need to get their permission (again, getting permissions in writing is wise). But sometimes copyright owners are not easy to track down.

Imagine you have a book on local history you want to republish on your Web site so genealogists anywhere can look at it without wearing out the book. Ideally, you can track down the author and get permission. But suppose the author moved out of town or died and no one knows how to find him. Or perhaps the author transferred copyright to a publisher, but that publisher has gone out of business or been acquired by a larger company that tossed all their old records. You now have an "orphan work"—a work that may still be protected by copyright but whose owner cannot be located. At this point, you need to find out if the book is still under copyright and, if it is, identify your library's statutory rights under the fair use doctrine (discussed in Chapter Four) or the Section 108 exemption (discussed in Chapter Five).

Here are questions and answers that cover some of the common issues libraries encounter when publishing or republishing works.

Question: My library has a photograph of a local building we want to digitize and put online. No one knows who the photographer is. Can I just go ahead and put it online?

Answer: Maybe. The fact that the photographer cannot be located does not affect his or her rights. Do a bit of research about the work and photographer. Any bibliographic information might be helpful. If the photo is old enough, or was not registered or marked with a copyright notice during certain years, it might now be in the public domain (see the copyright duration chart in Appendix P to help determine if the work is still copyrighted). Check the Copyright Office's database of copyright registrations to see if copyright over the photo was registered.[7] Ideally, you want to either find a copyright holder to ask for permission or determine that the work is no longer protected by copyright.

Question: OK, I've done all that, and I still cannot tell if the picture is copyrighted or who would hold the copyright. Now what?

Answer: At this point, you need to make a judgment call. Could your republication be fair use? Go to the four factors. (1) Character and purpose of use—is the use non-commercial, and is the use transformative, using the work in a new context or for a different purpose for which it was created? (2) Nature of the work—is the photo factual and just documenting the building, or is creative, like a piece of art photography? (3) Amount and substantiality of use—are you using the entire photo or just a part of it? (4) Effect on the potential market—does your use diminish the photographer's ability to make money from the photograph? Given that the photo is not being exploited commercially and no copyright owner can be found, this factor would favor fair use in this case.

Dealing with orphan works always involves some risk. Could someone claiming to be the copyright holder come out of the woodwork and sue the library for copyright infringement? Sure. Is it likely? Not at all. We have yet to hear of such a case. How much are you on the hook for? Hard to say, but if the work had not been registered (you did check on that first,

---

[7] Copyright registrations filed after January 1, 1978 are searchable online at http://cocatalog.loc.gov. Pre-1978 registrations have not yet been digitized, though the Copyright Office plans to digitize them in the future. *See* http://www.copyright.gov/digitization/goals.html.

right?), then statutory damages are not available. Since orphan works are, by definition, not being commercially exploited, compensatory damages would be insignificant. Also, if a non-profit, educational library acts on the good faith belief that a use of copyrighted material is covered under fair use, there may be no statutory damages at all.[8] Filing a lawsuit is expensive for the copyright owner, too, so if an owner thinks your library is infringing her copyright, you will probably get a letter about it and have a chance to reach an agreement. She will probably just you to remove the work from your web site, which you will do!

The Copyright Office produced a report on orphan works calling for legislation that would add some certainty to the orphan works mess,[9] but agreement has not yet been reached on what steps libraries would have to take for an adequate search and what kind of liability protections should be given. Until Congress passes a law, libraries are going to have to make risk calculations when deciding what to do with orphan works. Our take is that if you do due diligence in trying to see if the work is copyrighted, tried to locate the copyright owner, and reasonably concluded that your use is a fair use, you should be fine.

Question: I found the copyright owner and asked them for permission, and they said no! Can I put the photo online anyway?

Answer: Again, maybe. Copyright gives authors some control over their works, but hardly complete control. Being denied permission doesn't affect the fair use analysis, so if you think fair use covers your use, it doesn't matter if the owner said no.[10] Of course, the owner now knows what you want to do and might complain, but again, filing a lawsuit is an expensive proposition.

---

[8] 17 U.S.C. § 504 (C) (2) (i) (2006).

[9] REGISTER OF COPYRIGHTS, REPORT ON ORPHAN WORKS (2006), *available at* http://www.copyright.gov/orphan/orphan-report-full.pdf.

[10] Campbell v. Acuff-Rose Music, Inc., 510 U.S. 569, 585 n.18 (1994) ("we reject Acuff-Rose's argument that 2 Live Crew's request for permission to use the original should be weighed against a finding of fair use. Even if good faith were central to fair use, 2 Live Crew's actions do not necessarily suggest that they believed their version was not fair use; the offer may simply have been made in a good-faith effort to avoid this litigation. If the use is otherwise fair, then no permission need be sought or granted. Thus, being denied permission to use a work does not weigh against a finding of fair use.")

Question: A donor gave us her unpublished papers and correspondence. We want to digitize and make it available online. Does copyright let us do this if we own the papers?

Answer: Simply owning a physical copy of a work does not mean you also own the copyright. Most archives ask donors to sign a contract transferring ownership of the papers. Check to see if the donor transfers copyright over the papers to you. If the library or archives owns the copyright, you can do anything you like (assuming the contract does not have any restrictions). Depending on how old or thorough your donor contract is, it may not mention digitization. If this is the case, then you can make three copies for preservation purposes under section 108(b). Those copies cannot be accessible outside the library building. If you want to make the papers publicly available online, you will need to get permission from the donor or her heirs.

Question: A faculty member wants me to post her journal article in our digital repository, but the copyright notice on the article says the publisher is the copyright owner. Can I post the article?

Answer: Sometimes publishers ask authors to assign the copyright in the article to the publisher through a copyright transfer agreement. So the first thing you need to find out is if the author signed one of those forms. If she didn't, or the form she signed didn't transfer her copyright and doesn't otherwise prohibit republication, then you are in the clear.

Even if she did sign a copyright transfer agreement, posting the article may be possible. Many publishers permit online posting by the author's institution as long as proper attribution (e.g., author, journal title, and page number) is given or after an embargo (usually six months to three years). These policies can be found on the copyright form, in the publisher's copyright policy (sometimes called an author rights policy), or by asking the publisher. A very useful resource is SHERPA/RoMEO, a database of publisher copyright policies.[11]

Doing this kind of investigation for each article can get time-consuming, so educating authors about copyright and encouraging them to save their copyright forms can be very helpful. Some institutions also encourage

---

[11] http://www.sherpa.ac.uk/romeo.php.

authors to attach an author rights addendum to any copyright forms they sign.[12] These addenda explicitly state that the author's institution can post the article online. When all is said and done, unless the journal issue or publisher website prohibits posting your faculty's articles, go ahead and do so. If the publisher objects they will just ask you to remove it.

Question: We posted a professor's article online, and now we are getting requests for permission to reprint it. Can we give permission?

Answer: Probably not. Recall that copyright privileges are like a bundle of sticks. Having one stick doesn't mean you have the others. You can have permission to post a work online, but not be able to grant further permissions to others. Check your documentation to see if the copyright owner authorized you to sub-license or give further permissions. If he didn't, then the best you can do is refer the requestor to the copyright owner. If you posted a work on the basis of fair use, then you can't give permission, either. The requestor will have to get permission from the copyright owner or decide to use fair use based on the facts of their situation. Your work is done; it's in her hands now.

Question: We want to include some images of art we found on a museum's Web site for an exhibit on artists from our region. Do we need permission, even if we aren't putting the exhibit online? What if we just want to promote the exhibit online using thumbnail images?

Answer: The first question is whether the artwork is still protected by copyright. If copyright has expired, then exact reproductions also have no copyright protection.[13] If the images have some creative elements or the artwork is still copyrighted, then you will need permission unless your use falls under the fair use doctrine. Many museums require you to sign a license agreement to get permission. Read the agreement carefully; it may limit further uses, even those that would be fair use.[14]

---

[12] An example is at http://www.arl.org/sparc/author/addendum.shtml.
[13] See Bridgeman Art Library, Ltd. v. Corel Corp., 36 F.Supp.2d 191 (S.D.N.Y. 1999), which is discussed in Chapter One.
[14] See Kenneth D. Crews & Melissa A. Brown, Control of Museum Art Images: The Reach and Limits of Copyright and Licensing, *available at* http://ssrn.com/abstract=1542070.

The thumbnails (small, low-resolution images) are probably a fair use; using them to promote an exhibit is transformative—the art was not originally made or imaged to promote an exhibit. They were originally made to be appreciated and viewed as artwork. Thumbnails, or even larger images that are still small, are not high-quality enough to be used as artwork, but they can serve as basic illustrations to promote an exhibit that includes high-quality images. Since thumbnails cannot substitute for original artwork or high-quality images, they are unlikely to harm the copyright owner's ability to make money. Two appellate cases have held that search engines that use thumbnails to illustrate search results were fair use.[15] Your use of thumbnails in this case is similar to these cases.

The ARL takes an aggressive position on a library's right to digitize its special collections and archives in its Code of Best Practices, which is included in Appendix M.

Handling Your Copyrights

We've covered what a library needs to do when reproducing and distributing others' copyrighted works, but what should a library do with copyrights that it owns? Almost all libraries (or their parent institutions) own copyrights. When library employees create works as part of their duties, the work-for-hire doctrine says that the employer owns the copyright. Employee-created works, such as guides, bibliographies, and the like are owned by the employer absent a policy to the contrary. Although it is not necessary, authors publishing with the library can assign their copyrights to the library. When people donate their personal papers to archives, they can also sign a contract to donate the copyrights over the papers so the archives handle any permissions requests. One way or another, your library will own copyrights.

---

[15] Perfect 10, Inc., v. Amazon.com, Inc., 508 F.3d 1146, 1168 (9th Cir. 2007); Kelly v. Arriba Soft Corp., 336 F.3d 811, 822 (9th Cir. 2003).

Permissions and Open Licenses

As a copyright owner, keep in mind the purpose of copyright that we have emphasized throughout this book: the dissemination and promotion of knowledge. Be generous with copyright permissions. Letting others use the works your library publishes will increase the social benefits of your publishing efforts. A good way to grant copyright permissions is through open licenses. Think of these like copyright notices, but for granting permission rather than reserving rights. By using an open license, you grant blanket permission to anyone who wishes to use your works, subject to conditions prescribed by you.

There are number of open licenses, but by far the most well-known are those made by Creative Commons.[16] By attaching a Creative Commons license, you give permission to anyone to reproduce, distribute, perform, display, and make derivative works from your works as long as the conditions in the license are followed. The most common conditions are attribution (giving proper credit to the original author and publisher), non-commercial (not selling or using the work directly for profit), share-alike (licensing any derivative works under the same open license), and no-derivatives (no making derivative works). Some copyright owners grant blanket permission only for educational use, such as course packs or copies for classroom distribution.

For example, a book with a Creative Commons Attribution-NonCommercial-NoDerivatives license permits reproducing and distributing the book as long as proper attribution is given, the use is non-commercial, and a derivative work is not made. This is the most restrictive of the Creative Commons licenses; other varieties permit derivative works or commercial use.

All Creative Commons licenses require attribution, but if an owner wants to waive all copyrights, then she can use Creative Commons' CC0 (as in Creative Commons Zero) Public Domain Dedication. The most common use of CC0 is for data sets that can be aggregated and mixed with other data for scientific analysis.

---

[16] http://www.creativecommons.org.

If you don't mind people copying your work as long as it is non-commercial, then you can use a Creative Commons Attribution-NonCommercial license. Here, only people who want to use the work commercially need permission. This benefits both you and the users by reducing the number of people who have to ask for permission, and to whom you have to reply.

Library Publishing May Require Several Layers of Agreements

Suppose your library wants to publish a journal or other compilation of works. What sorts of license agreements do you need? This might seem like a simple question, but it can actually be rather complex. The most important thing is to have everything in writing. A simple verbal agreement and handshake isn't good enough here. You will also need a couple layers of agreement. What the agreements contain should be negotiated to best meet the library's and authors' long-term needs; remember that these copyrights will outlive you, and maybe even your children!

As an example, imagine a group of editors has approached you about publishing a journal through the library. First, the journal needs a license agreement with each author (recall that copyright automatically vests with the author). Some journals require authors to transfer their entire copyrights to the journals, but most authors should have some flexibility to use their articles for personal and professional purposes. The goodwill of the authors is probably worth whatever control over the articles you have to give up.

The agreement between the author and journal should give the journal the rights it needs to publish and archive the article. Beyond that, the rights should stay with the author. Unless you plan on trying to charge money for individual articles, a non-exclusive or temporary exclusive license (that then becomes non-exclusive one or two years after publication) is probably fine.

Then your library needs an agreement with the editors of the journal. The creative selection and arrangement of collective works—such as articles in a journal issue or chapters in an edited book—can also be copyrighted. In addition to having permission to publish each individual article, you also need permission to publish each journal issue. This agreement should also discuss organizational issues like the level of support the library will supply, and what happens if the editors change or want to move the journal to another publisher.

Finally, you may need to deal with agreements with database aggregators. The agreements with authors and editors should cover any formats you may want to publish in. If your license just gives you permission for print hardcopy issues, and if you later want to republish in a new digital format or add the issues to a database, you would need to go back to the copyright holder for permission, which you do not want to do.[17]

If you want to publish a journal article outside of the journal issue, as a separate reprint or in a database like JSTOR, you need your license to authorize that. It will probably be very difficult to change the agreement between the author and journal once it is signed, so think long-term to provide flexibility for future developments. Make sure there is language authorizing you to publish (and authorize other vendors to distribute) the article in print, digital, and other formats. The sample agreement in Appendix N is a good starting point.

---

[17] Digital rights without express permission can be complicated, especially for collective works, like newspapers and journals that, while copyrighted as compilations, also contain individual copyrighted works. The copyright owner of a collective work, like an issue of a magazine, can digitize the entire issue and distribute the digitized issue as a whole. This is what happened in *Faulkner v. National Geographic Enterprises*, 409 F.3d 26 (2005). *National Geographic* sold a CD with digital images of past issues. The court held that the magazine had the right to do this because it was reproducing the entire magazine. On the other hand, in *New York Times v. Tasini*, 533 U.S. 483 (2001), the Court held that the *Times* had infringed freelance writers' copyrights by digitizing their articles and compiling them in a database that was organized very differently from the original newspaper. If the *Times* had just scanned the pages, they would have had a better case.

CONCLUSION

❧❦

That's it. When we were writing this book we knew it would not provide "yes" or "no" answers to every copyright question you have. American copyright law is much too gray for that. As you have seen, the answer to any question dealing with copyright depends on its facts, and subtle factual differences may lead to different answers. We hope *The Librarian's Copyright Companion, Second Edition* gave you a framework that will help you analyze copyright issues in your institution.

There's a lot of information out there, some better than others. Stanford, the University of Texas at Austin, and Columbia University have good websites on copyright law, with very helpful information. Library organizations like the American Library Association and Association of Research Libraries also offer useful information. Even organizations that represent copyright owners, such as the Copyright Clearance Center and Association of American Publishers, can help you analyze copyright issues. Just remember to take their information with a grain of salt or plenty of aspirin.

The bottom line is that you are not alone in thinking that copyright can be confusing and that there are no easy answers to many questions you may confront. Neither are you alone in trying to answer those questions.

If you're a Marx Brothers fan, you may have noticed that we mentioned every Marx Brothers movie in the text—but we couldn't find a place for *Love Happy* except here.

Appendix A
ONLINE COPYRIGHT RESOURCES
୫୦୦୫

American Library Association
http://www.ala.org/ala/issuesadvocacy/copyright/index.cfm

Artists Rights Society
http://www.arsny.com/index.html

Association of Research Libraries
http://www.arl.org/pp/ppcopyright/

Center for Social Media
http://www.centerforsocialmedia.org/fair-use

Columbia University Copyright Advisory Office
http://copyright.columbia.edu/copyright/

Copyright Clearance Center
http://www.copyright.com/

Cornell University
http://www.copyright.cornell.edu/

Creative Commons
http://creativecommons.org/

Duke University
http://blogs.library.duke.edu/scholcomm/copyright-in-teaching/copyright-duke/

Library Copyright Alliance
http://www.librarycopyrightalliance.org/

Stanford University Libraries
http://fairuse.stanford.edu/

United States Copyright Office
http://copyright.gov/

University of Minnesota Libraries
http://www.lib.umn.edu/copyright

University of Texas Copyright Crash Course
http://copyright.lib.utexas.edu/

Visual Resource Association
http://www.vraweb.org/organization/committees/ipr/ipr_resources.html

Appendix B
COPYRIGHT TEXTS FOR LIBRARIANS: A SELECTIVE BIBLIOGRAPHY
❧❧

Aufderheide, Patricia, and Peter Jaszi. *Reclaiming Fair Use: How to Put Balance Back in Copyright*. Chicago: The University of Chicago Press, 2011.

Bielefield, Arlene, and Lawrence Cheeseman. *Technology and Copyright Law: A Guidebook for the Library, Research, and Teaching Professions*. New York: Neal-Schuman Publishers, 2007.

Butler, Rebecca P. *Copyright for Teachers & Librarians in the 21st Century*. New York: Neal-Schuman Publishers, 2011.

Crews, Kenneth D. *Copyright Law for Librarians and Educators: Creative Strategies and Practical Solutions*. Chicago: American Library Association, 2012.

Fishman, Stephen. *The Public Domain: How to Find & Use Copyright-Free Writings, Music, Art & More*. Berkeley, CA: Nolo, 2012.

Fishman, Stephen. *The Copyright Handbook: How to Protect & Use Written Works*. Berkeley, CA: Nolo, 2006.

Gathegi, John N. *The Digital Librarian's Legal Handbook*. New York: Neal-Schuman Publishers, 2012.

Harris, Lesley Ellen. *Licensing Digital Content: A Practical Guide for Librarians*. Chicago: American Library Association, 2009.

Hoffmann, Gretchen McCord. *Copyright in Cyberspace 2: Questions and Answers for Librarians*. New York: Neal-Schuman Publishers, 2005.

Lipinski, Tomas A. *Copyright Law and the Distance Education Classroom*. Lanham, Md: Scarecrow Press, 2005.

Lipinski, Tomas A. *The Complete Copyright Liability Handbook for Librarians and Educators*. New York: Neal-Schuman Publishers, 2006.

Minow, Mary, and Tomas A. Lipinski. *The Library's Legal Answer Book*. Chicago: American Library Association, 2003.

Russell, Carrie, and Dwayne K. Buttler. *Complete Copyright: An Everyday Guide for Librarians*. Chicago: American Library Association, 2004.

Stim, Richard. *Getting Permission: How to License & Clear Copyrighted Materials, Online & Off*. Berkeley, CA: Nolo, 2010.

Wherry, Timothy Lee. *The Librarian's Guide to Intellectual Property in the Digital Age: Copyrights, Patents, and Trademarks*. Chicago: American Library Association, 2002.

Appendix C
AGREEMENT ON GUIDELINES FOR CLASSROOM COPYING IN NOT-FOR-PROFIT EDUCATIONAL INSTITUTIONS WITH RESPECT TO BOOKS AND PERIODICALS (1976)[*]

ജ‍ഇ

The purpose of the following guidelines is to state the minimum and not the maximum standards of educational fair use under Section 106 of H.R. 2223. The parties agree that the conditions determining the extent of permissible copying the educational purpose may change in the future; that certain types of copying permitted under these guidelines may not be permissible in the future; and conversely that in the future other types of copying not permitted under these guide-lines may be permissible under revised guidelines.

Moreover, the following statement of guidelines is not intended to limit the types of copying permitted under the standards of fair use under judicial decision and which are stated in Section 107 of the Copyright Revision Bill. There may be instances in which copying which does not fall within the guidelines stated below may nonetheless be permitted under the criteria of fair use.

---

[*] Reproduced in U.S. COPYRIGHT OFFICE, CIRCULAR 21: REPRODUCTION OF COPYRIGHTED WORKS BY EDUCATORS AND LIBRARIANS 6, *available at* http://www.copyright.gov/circs/circ21.pdf.

Guidelines

I. Single Copying for Teachers

A single copy may be made of any of the following by or for a teacher at his or her individual request for his or her scholarly research or use in teaching or preparation to teach a class:

A. A chapter from a book;
B. An article from a periodical or newspaper;
C. A short story, short essay, or short poem, whether or not from a collective work;
D. A chart, graph, diagram, drawing, cartoon or picture from a book, periodical, or newspaper.

II. Multiple Copies for Classroom Use

Multiple copies (not to exceed in any event more than one copy per pupil in a course) may be made by or for the teacher giving the course for classroom use or discussion; provided that:

A. The copying meets the tests of brevity and spontaneity as defined below; and,
B. Meets the cumulative effect test as defined below; and,
C. Each copy includes a notice of copyright.

Definitions
Brevity
(i) Poetry: (a) A complete poem if less than 250 words and if printed on not more than two pages or, (b) from a longer poem, an excerpt of not more than 250 words.
(ii) Prose: (a) Either a complete article, story or essay of less than 2,500 words, or (b) an excerpt from any prose work of not more than 1,000 words or 10% of the work, whichever is less, but in any event a minimum of 500 words.
(iii) Illustration: One chart, graph, diagram, drawing, cartoon or picture per book or per periodical issue.
(iv) "Special" works: Certain works in poetry, prose or in "poetic prose" which often combine language with illustrations and which are intended sometimes for children and at other times for a more general audience fall short of 2,500 works in their entirety. Paragraph "ii" above notwithstanding such "special works" may not be reproduced in their entirety; however, an excerpt comprising not more than two of the

published pages of such special work and containing not more than 10% of the works found in the text thereof, may be reproduced.

Spontaneity
(i) The copying is at the instance and inspiration of the individual teacher.
(ii) The inspiration and decision to use the work and the moment of its use for maximum teaching effectiveness are so close in time that it would be unreasonable to expect a timely reply to a request for permission.

Cumulative Effect
(i) The copying of the material is for only one course in the school in which the copies are made.
(ii) Not more than one short poem, article, story, essay or two excerpts may be copies from the same author, nor more than three from the sane collective work or periodical volume during one class term.
(iii) There shall not be more than nine instances of such multiple copying for one course during one class term.

III. Prohibitions as to I and II Above

Notwithstanding any of the above, the following shall be prohibited:

A. Copying shall not be used to create or to replace or substitute for anthologies, compilations or collective works. Such replacement or substitution may occur whether copies of various works or excerpts therefrom are accumulated or reproduced and used separately.
B. There shall be no copying of or from works intended to be "consumable" in the course of study or of teaching. These include workbooks, exercises, standardized tests and test booklets and answer sheets and like consumable material.
C. Copying shall not:
   (a) substitute for the purchase of books, publishers' reprints or periodicals;
   (b) be directed by higher authority;
   (c) be repeated with respect to the same item by the same teacher from term to term.
D. No charge shall be made to the student beyond the actual cost of the photocopying.

Agreed March 19, 1976.

Ad Hoc Committee on Copyright Law Revision by Sheldon Elliott Steinbach.

Author-publisher Group and Authors League of America by Irwin Karp, Counsel.

Association of American Publishers, Inc. by Alexander C. Hoffman, Chairman, Copyright Committee.

Appendix D
MODEL POLICY CONCERNING COLLEGE AND UNIVERSITY PHOTOCOPYING FOR CLASSROOM, RESEARCH, AND LIBRARY RESERVE USE (1982)*

ೞಃೕೞ

This model policy, another in a series of copyright advisory documents developed by the American Library Association (ALA), is intended for the guidance and use of academic librarians, faculty, administrators, and legal counsel in response to implementation of the rights and responsibilities provisions of Public Law 94-553, General Revision of the Copyright Law, which took effect on January 1, 1978.

Prepared by ALA Legal Counsel Mary Hutchings of the law firm Sidley & Austin, with advice and assistance from the Copyright Subcommittee (ad hoc) of ALA's Legislation Committee, Association of College and Research Libraries (ACRL) Copyright Committee, Association of Research Libraries (ARL) and other academic librarians and copyright attorneys, the model policy outlines "fair use" rights in the academic environment for classroom teaching, research activities and library services. Please note that it does not address other library photocopying which may be permitted under other sections of the Copyright Law, e.g., § 108 (Reproduction by Libraries and Archives).

Too often, members of the academic community have been reluctant or hesitant to exercise their rights of fair use under the law for fear of courting an infringement suit. It is important to understand that in U.S. law, copyright is a limited statutory monopoly and the public's right to use materials must be protected. Safeguards have been written into the legislative history accompanying the new copyright law protecting librarians, teachers, researchers and scholars and guaranteeing their rights of access to information as they carry out their responsibilities for educating or conducting research. It is, therefore, important to heed the advice of a former U.S. Register of Copyrights: "If you don't use fair use, you will lose it!"

I. The Copyright Act and Photocopying

From time to time, the faculty and staff of this University [College] may use photocopied materials to supplement research and teaching. In many cases, photocopying can facilitate the University's [College's] mission; that is, the development and transmission of information. However, the photocopying of copyrighted materials is a right granted under the copyright law's doctrine of "fair use" which must not be abused. This report will explain the University's [College's] policy concerning the photocopying of copyrighted materials by faculty and library staff. Please note that this policy does not address other library photocopying which may be permitted under sections of the copyright law, e.g., 17 U.S.C. § 108.

Copyright is a constitutionally conceived property right which is designed to promote the progress of science and the useful arts by securing for an author the benefits of his or her original work of authorship for a limited time. U.S. Constitution, Art. I, Sec. 8. The Copyright statute, 17 U.S.C. § 101 et seq., implements this policy by balancing the author's interest against the public interest in the dissemination of information affecting areas of universal concern, such as art, science, history and business. The grand design of this delicate balance is to foster the creation and dissemination of intellectual works for the general public.

The Copyright Act defines the rights of a copyright holder and how they may be enforced against an infringer. Included within the Copyright Act is the "fair use" doctrine which allows, under certain conditions, the copying of copyrighted material. While the Act lists general factors under the heading of "fair use" it provides little in the way of specific directions for what constitutes fair use.

The law states:

17 U.S.C. § 107. Limitations on exclusive rights: Fair use

Notwithstanding the provisions of section 106, the fair use of a copyrighted work, including such use by reproduction in copies or phonorecords or by any other means specified by that section, for purposes such as criticism, comment, news reporting, teaching (including multiple copies for classroom use), scholarship, or research, is not an infringement of copyright. In determining whether the use made of a work in any particular case is a fair use the factors to be considered shall include—

(1) the purpose and character of the use, including whether such use is of a commercial nature or is for nonprofit educational purposes;

(2) the nature of copyrighted work;

(3) the amount and substantiality of the portion used in relation to the copyrighted work as a whole; and

(4) the effect of the use upon the potential market for or value of the copyrighted work.

The purpose of this report is to provide you, the faculty and staff of this University [College], with an explanation of when the photocopying of copyrighted material in our opinion is permitted under the fair use doctrine. Where possible, common examples of research, classroom, and library reserve photocopying have been included to illustrate what we believe to be the reach and limits of fair use.

Please note that the copyright law applies to all forms of photocopying, whether it is undertaken at a commercial copying center, at the University's [College's] central or departmental copying facilities or at a self-service machine. While you are free to use the services of a commercial establishment, you should be prepared to provide documentation of permission from the publisher (if such permission is necessary under this policy), since many commercial copiers will require such proof.

We hope this report will give you an appreciation of the factors which weight in favor of fair use and those factors which weigh against fair use, but faculty members must determine for themselves which works will be photocopied. This University [College] does not condone a policy of photocopying instead of purchasing copyrighted works where such photocopying would constitute an infringement under the Copyright law, but it does encourage faculty members to exercise good judgment in serving the best interests of students in an efficient manner.

Instructions for securing permission to photocopy copyrighted works when such copying is beyond the limits of fair use appear at the end of this report. It is the policy of this University that the user (faculty, staff or librarian) secure such permission whenever it is legally necessary.

II. Unrestricted Photocopying
A. Uncopyrighted Published Works

Writing published before January 1, 1978 which have never been copyrighted may be photocopied without restriction. Copies of works protected by copyright must bear a copyright notice, which consists of the letter "c" in a circle, or the word "Copyright," or the abbreviation "Copr.", plus the year of first publication, plus the name of the copyright owner. 17 U.S.C. § 401. As to works published before January 1, 1978, in the case of a book, the notice must be placed on the title page or the reverse side of the title page. In the case of a periodical the notice must be placed either on the title page, the first page of text, or in the masthead. A pre-1978 failure to comply with the notice requirements results in the work being injected into the public domain, i.e., unprotected. Copyright notice requirements have been relaxed since 1978, so that the absence of notice on copies of a work published after January 1, 1978 does not necessarily mean the work in the public domain. 17 U.S.C. § 405 (a) and (c). However, you will not be liable for damages for copyright infringement of works published after that date, if, after normal inspection, you photocopy a work on which you cannot find a copyright symbol and you have not received actual notice of the fact the work is copyrighted. 17 U.S.C. § 405(b). However, a copyright owner who found out about your photocopying would have the right to prevent further distribution of the copies if in fact the work were copyrighted and the copies are infringing. 17 U.S.C. § 405(b).

B. Published Works with Expired Copyrights

Writings with expired copyrights may be photocopied without restriction. All copyrights prior to 1906 have expired. 17 U.S.C. § 304(b). Copyrights granted after 1906 may have been renewed; however the writing will probably not contain notice of the renewal. Therefore, it should be assumed all writings dated 1906 or later are covered by a valid copyright, unless information to the contrary is obtained from the owner or the U.S. Copyright Office (see Copyright Office Circular 15t).

Copyright Office Circular R22 explains how to investigate the copyright status of a work. One way is to use the Catalog of Copyright Entries published by the Copyright Office and available in [the University Library] many libraries. Alternatively you may request the Copyright Office to conduct a search of its registration and/or assignment records. The Office charges an hourly fee for this service. You will need to submit as much information as you have concerning the work in which you are interested, such as the title, author, approximate date of publication, the type of work or any available copyright data. The Copyright Office does caution that its searches are not conclusive; for instance, if a work obtained copyright less than 28 years ago, it may be fully protected although there has been no registration or deposit.

C. Unpublished Works
Unpublished works, such as theses and dissertations, may be protected by copyright. If such a work was created before January 1, 1978 and has not been copyrighted or published without copyright notice, the work is protected under the new Act for the life of the author plus fifty years, 17 U.S.C. § 303, but in no case earlier than December 31, 2002. If such a work is published on or before that date, the copyright will not expire before December 31, 2027. Works created after January 1, 1978 and not published enjoy copyright protection for the life of the author plus fifty years. 17 U.S.C. § 302.

D. U.S. Government Publications
All U.S. Government publications with the possible exception of some National Technical Information Service Publications less than five years old may be photocopied without restrictions, except to the extent they contain copyrighted materials from other sources. 17 U.S.C. § 105. U.S. Government publications are documents prepared by an official or employee of the government in an official capacity. 17 U.S.C. § 101. Government publications include the opinions of courts in legal cases, Congressional Reports on proposed bills, testimony offered at Congressional hearings and the works of government employees in their official capacities.

Works prepared by outside authors on contract to the government may or may not be protected by copyright, depending on the specifics of the contract. In the absence of copyright notice on such works, it would be reasonable to assume they are government works in the public domain. It should be noted that state government works may be protected by copyright. See 17 U.S.C. § 105. However, the opinions of state courts are not protected.

III. Permissible Photocopying of Copyrighted Works
The Copyright Act allows anyone to photocopy copyrighted works without securing permission from the copyright owner when the photocopying amounts to a "fair use" of the material. 17 U.S.C. § 107. The guidelines in this report discuss the boundaries for fair use of photocopied material used in research or the classroom or in a library reserve operation. Fair use cannot always be expressed in numbers—either the number of pages copied or the number of copies distributed. Therefore, you should weigh

the various factors listed in the Act and judge whether the intended use of photocopied, copyrighted material is within the spirit of the fair use doctrine. Any serious questions concerning whether a particular photocopying constitutes fair use should be directed to University [College] counsel.

A. Research Uses

At the very least, instructors may make a single copy of any of the following for scholarly research or use in teaching or preparing to teach a class:

1. A chapter from a book;
2. An article from a periodical or newspaper;
3. A short story, short essay, or short poem, whether or not from a collective work; and
4. A chart, diagram, graph, drawing, cartoon or picture from a book, periodical, or newspaper.

These examples reflect the most conservative guidelines for fair use. They do not represent inviolate ceilings for the amount of copyrighted material which can be photocopied within the boundaries of fair use. When exceeding these minimum levels, however, you again should consider the four factors listed in Section 107 of the Copyright Act to make sure that any additional photocopying is justified. The following demonstrate situations where increased levels of photocopying would continue to remain within the ambit of fair use:

1. the inability to obtain another copy of the work because it is not available from another library or source cannot be obtained within your time constraints;
2. the intention to photocopy the material only once and not to distribute the material to others;
3. the ability to keep the amount of material photocopied within a reasonable proportion to the entire work (the larger the work, the greater amount of material which may be photocopied).

Most single-copy photocopying for your personal use in research— even when it involves a substantial portion of a work—may well constitute fair use.

B. Classroom Uses

Primary and secondary school educators have, with publishers, developed the following guidelines, which allow a teacher to distribute photocopied material to students in a class without the publisher's prior permission, under the following conditions:

1. the distribution of the same photocopied material does not occur every semester;
2. only one copy is distributed for each student which copy must become the student's property;
3. the material includes a copyright notice on the first page of the portion of material photocopied;
4. the students are not assessed any fee beyond the actual cost of the photocopying.

The educators also agreed that the amount of material distributed should not exceed certain brevity standards. Under those guidelines, a prose work may be reproduced in its entirety if it is less than 2500 words in length. If the work exceeds such length, the excerpt reproduced may not exceed 1000 words, or 10% of the work, whichever is less. In the case of poetry, 250 words is the maximum permitted.

These minimum standards normally would not be realistic in the University setting. Faculty members needing to exceed these limits for college education should not feel hampered by these guidelines, although they should attempt a "selective and sparing" use of photocopied, copyrighted material.

The photocopying practices of an instructor should not have a significant detrimental impact on the market for the copyrighted work. 17 U.S.C. § 107(4). To guard against this effect, you usually should restrict use of an item of photocopied material to one course and you should not repeatedly photocopy excepts from one periodical or author without the permission of the copyright owner.

C. Library Reserve Uses

At the request of a faculty member, a library may photocopy and place on reserve excerpts from copyrighted works in its collection in accordance with guidelines similar to those governing formal classroom distribution for face-to-face teaching discussed above. This University [College] believes that these guidelines apply to the library reserve shelf to the extent it functions as an extension of classroom readings or reflects an individual student's right to photocopy for his personal scholastic use under the doctrine of fair use. In general, librarians may photocopy materials for reserve room use for the convenience of students both in preparing class assignments and in pursuing informal educational activities which higher education requires, such as advanced independent study and research.

If the request calls for only one copy to be placed on reserve, the library may photocopy an entire article, or an entire chapter from a book, or an entire poem. Requests for multiple copies on reserve should meet the following guidelines:

1. the amount of material should be reasonable in relation to the total amount of material assigned for one term of a course taking into account the nature of the course, its subject matter and level, 17 U.S.C. §§ 107(1) and (3);
2. the number of copies should be reasonable in light of the number of students enrolled, the difficulty and timing of assignments, and the number of other courses which may assign the same material, 17 U.S.C. §§ 107(1) and (3);
3. the material should contain a notice of copyright, see 17 U.S.C. § 401;
4. the effect of photocopying the material should not be detrimental to the market for the work. (In general, the library should own at least one copy of the work.) 17 U.S.C. § 107(4).

For example, a professor may place on reserve as a supplement to the course textbook a reasonable number of copies of articles from academic journals or chapters from trade books. A reasonable number of copies will in most instances be less than six, but factors such as the length or difficulty of the assignment, the number of enrolled students and the length of time allowed for completion of the assignment may permit more in unusual circumstances.

In addition, a faculty member may also request that multiple copies of photocopied, copyrighted material be placed on the reserve shelf if there is insufficient time to obtain permission from the copyright owner. For example, a professor may place on reserve several photocopies of an entire article from a recent issue of Time magazine or the New York Times in lieu of distributing a copy to each member of the class. If you are in doubt as to whether a particular instance of photocopying is fair use in the reserve reading room, you should waive any fee for such a use.

D. Uses of Photocopied Material Requiring Permission

1. Repetitive copying: The classroom or reserve use of photocopied materials in multiple courses or successive years will normally require advance permission from the owner of the copyright, 17 U.S.C. § 107(3).
2. Copying for profit: Faculty should not charge students more than the actual cost of photocopying the material, 17 U.S.C. § 107(1).
3. Consumable works: The duplication of works that are consumed in the classroom, such as standardized tests, exercises, and workbooks, normally requires permission from the copy-right owner, 17 U.S.C. § 107(4).
4. Creation of anthologies as basic text material for a course: Creation of a collective work or anthology by photocopying a number of copyrighted articles and excerpts to be purchased and used together as the basic text for a course will in most instances require the permission of the copy-

righted owners. Such photocopying of a book and thus less likely to be deemed fair use, 17 U.S.C. § 107(4).

E. How to Obtain Permission

When a use of photocopied material requires that you request permission, you should communicate complete and accurate information to the copyright owner. The American Association of Publishers suggests that the following information be included in a permission request letter in order to expedite the process:

1. Title, author and/or editor, and edition of materials to be duplicated.
2. Exact material to be used, giving amount, page numbers, chapters and, if possible, a photocopy of the material.
3. Number of copies to be made.
4. Use to be made of duplicated materials.
5. Form of distribution (classroom, newsletter, etc.).
6. Whether or not the material is to be sold.
7. Type of reprint (ditto, photography, offset, typeset).

The request should be sent, together with a self-addressed return envelope, to the permissions department of the publisher in question. If the address of the publisher does not appear at the front of the material, it may be readily obtained in a publication entitled The Literary Marketplace, published by the R. R. Bowker Company and available in all libraries.

The process of granting permission requires time for the publisher to check the status of the copyright and to evaluate the nature of the request. It is advisable, therefore, to allow enough lead time to obtain permission before the materials are needed. In some instances, the publisher may assess a fee for the permission. It is not inappropriate to pass this fee on to the student who receive copies of the photocopied material.

The Copyright Clearance Center also has the right to grant permission and collect fees for photocopying rights for certain publications. Libraries may copy from any journal which is registered with the CCC and report the copying beyond fair use to CCC and pay the set fee. A list of publications for which the CCC handles fees and permissions is available from CCC, 310 Madison Avenue, New York, N.Y. 10017.

Sample Letter To Copyright Owner (Publisher) Requesting Permission To Copy

March 1, 1982
Material Permissions Department
Hypothetical Book Company

500 East Avenue
Chicago, IL 60601
Dear Sir or Madam:

I would like permission to copy the following for continued use in my classes in future semesters:

> Title: Learning is Good, Second Edition
> Copyright: Hypothetical Book Co., 1965, 1971
> Author: Frank Jones
> Material to be duplicated: Chapters 10, 11 and 14
>   (photocopy enclosed).
> Number of copies: 500
> Distribution: The material will be distributed to students in my classes
>   and they will pay only the cost of the photocopying.
> Type of reprint: Photocopy
> Use: The chapter will be used as supplementary teaching materials.

I have enclosed a self-addressed envelope for your convenience in replying to this request.

Sincerely,
Faculty Member

F. Infringement

Courts and legal scholars alike have commented that the fair use provisions in the Copyright Act are among the most vague and difficult that can be found anywhere in the law. In amending the Copyright Act in 1976, Congress anticipated the problem this would pose for users of copyrighted materials who wished to stay under the umbrella of protection offered by fair use. For this reason, the Copyright Act contains specific provisions which grant additional rights to libraries and insulate employees of a non-profit educational institution, library, or archives from statutory damages for infringement where the infringer believed or had reasonable ground to believe the photocopying was a fair use of the material. 17 U.S.C. § 504(c)(2).

Normally, an infringer is liable to the copyright owner for the actual losses sustained because of the photocopying and any additional profits of the infringer. 17 U.S.C. § 504(a)(1) and (b). Where the monetary losses are nominal, the copyright owner usually will claim statutory damages instead of the actual losses. 17 U.S.C. § 504(a)(2) and (c). The statutory damages may reach as high as $10,000 (or up to $50,000 if the infringement is willful). In addition to suing for money damages, a copyright owner can usually prevent future infringement through a court injunction. 17 U.S.C. § 502.

The Copyright Act specifically exempts from statutory damages any employee of a non-profit educational institution, library, or archives, who "believed and had reasonable grounds for believing that his or her use of the copyrighted work was a fair use under Section 107." 17 U.S.C. § 504(c)(2). While the fair use provisions are admittedly ambiguous, any employee who attempts to stay within the guidelines contained in this report should have an adequate good faith defense in the case of an innocently committed infringement.

If the criteria contained in this report are followed, it is our view that no copyright infringement will occur and that there will be no adverse effect on the market for copyrighted works. [Many educational institutions will provide their employees legal counsel without charge if an infringement suit is brought against the employee for photocopying performed in the course of employment. If so, this should be noted here.]

Appendix E
CONTU GUIDELINES ON PHOTOCOPYING UNDER INTERLIBRARY LOAN ARRANGEMENTS (1978)*

ຂ໐ຕ໌ຮ

The CONTU guidelines were developed to assist librarians and copyright proprietors in understanding the amount of photocopying for use in interlibrary loan arrangements permitted under the copyright law. In the spring of 1976 there was realistic expectation that a new copyright law, under consideration for nearly twenty years, would be enacted during that session of Congress. It had become apparent that the House subcommittee was giving serious consideration to modifying the language concerning "systematic reproduction" by libraries in Section 108(g)(2) of the Senate-passed bill to permit photocopying under interlibrary arrangements, unless such arrangements resulted in the borrowing libraries obtaining "such aggregate quantities as to substitute for a subscription to or purchase of" copyrighted works.

The Commission discussed this proposed amendment to the Senate bill at its meeting on April 2, 1976. Pursuant to a request made at that meeting by the Register of Copyrights, serving in her ex officio role, the Commission agreed that it might aid the House and Senate subcommittees by offering its good offices in bringing the principal parties together to see whether agreement could be reached on a definition of "such aggregate quantities." This offer was accepted by the House and Senate subcommittees and the interested parties, and much of the summer of 1976 was spent by the Commission in working with the parties to secure agreement on "guidelines" interpreting what was to become the proviso in Section

---

* FINAL REPORT OF THE NATIONAL COMMISSION ON NEW TECHNOLOGICAL USE OF COPYRIGHTED WORKS (1978). Available at http://old.cni.org/docs/infopols/CONTU.html.

108(g)(2) relating to "systematic reproduction" by libraries. The pertinent parts of that section, with the proviso added by the House emphasized, follow.

> (g) The rights of reproduction and distribution under this section extend to the isolated and unrelated reproduction or distribution of a single copy or phonorecord of the same material on separate occasions, but do not extend to cases where the library or archives, or its employee . . .

> (2) engages in the systematic reproduction or distribution of single or multiple copies or phonorecords of material described in subsection (d): Provided, That nothing in this clause prevents a library or archives from participating in inter-library arrangements that do not have, as their purpose of effect, that the library or archives receiving such copies or phonorecords for distribution does so in such aggregate quantities as to substitute for a subscription to or purchase of such work.

Before enactment of the new copyright law, the principal library, publisher, and author organizations agreed to the following detailed guidelines defining what "aggregate quantities" would constitute the "systematic reproduction" that would exceed the statutory limitations on a library's photocopying activities.

Photocopying-Interlibrary Arrangements

Introduction

Subsection 108(g) (2) of the bill deals, among other things, with limits on interlibrary arrangements for photocopying. It prohibits systematic photocopying of copyrighted materials but permits interlibrary arrangements "that do not have, as their purpose or effect, that the library or archives receiving such copies or phonorecords for distribution does so in such aggregate quantities as to substitute for a subscription to or purchase of such work."

The National Commission on New Technological Uses of Copyrighted Works offered its good offices to the House and Senate subcommittees in bringing the interested parties together to see if agreement could be reached on what a realistic definition would be of "such aggregate quantities." The Commission consulted with the parties and suggested the interpretation which follows, on which there has been substantial agreement by the principal library, publisher, and author organizations. The Commission considers the guidelines which follow to be a workable and fair interpretation of the intent of the proviso portion of subsection 108(g) (2).

These guidelines are intended to provide guidance in the application of section 108 to the most frequently encountered interlibrary case: a library's obtaining from another library, in lieu of interlibrary loan, copies of articles from relatively recent issues of periodicals—those published within five years prior to the date of the request. The guidelines do not specify what aggregate quantity of copies of an article or articles published in a periodical, the issue date of which is more than five years prior to the date when the request for the copy thereof is made, constitutes a substitute for a subscription to such periodical. The meaning of the proviso to sub-section 108(g)(2) in such case is left to future interpretation.

The point has been made that the present practice on interlibrary loans and use of photocopies in lieu of loans may be supplemented or even largely replaced by a system in which one or more agencies or institutions, public or private, exist for the specific purpose of providing a central source for photocopies. Of course, these guidelines would not apply to such a situation.

Guidelines for the Proviso of Subsection 108(g) (2)

1. As used in the proviso of subsection 108(g) (2), the words "such aggregate quantities as to substitute for a subscription to or purchase of such work" shall mean:

   (a) with respect to any given periodical (as opposed to any given issue of a periodical), filled requests of a library or archives (a "requesting entity") within any calendar year for a total of six or more copies of an article or articles published in such periodical within five years prior to the date of the request. These guidelines specifically shall not apply, directly or indirectly, to any request of a requesting entity for a copy or copies of an article or articles published in any issue of a periodical, the publication date of which is more than five years prior to the date when the request is made. These guidelines do not define the meaning, with respect to such a request, of ". . . such aggregate quantities as to substitute for a subscription to [such periodical]."

   (b) With respect to any other material described in subsection 108(d), including fiction and poetry), filled requests of a requesting entity within any calendar year for a total of six or more copies or phono-records of or from any given work (including a collective work) during the entire period when such material shall be protected by copyright.

2. In the event that a requesting entity:

   (a) shall have in force or shall have entered an order for a subscription to a periodical, or

   (b) has within its collection, or shall have entered an order for, a copy of phonorecord of any other copyrighted work, materials from either category of which it desires to obtain by copy from another library or archives (the "supplying entity"), because the material to be copied is not reasonably available for use by the requesting entity itself, then the fulfillment of such request shall be treated as though the requesting entity made such copy from its own collection. A library or archives may request a copy or phonorecord from a supplying entity only under those circumstances where the requesting entity would have been able, under the other provisos of section 108, to supply such copy from materials in its own collection.

3. No request for a copy or phonorecord of any materials to which these guidelines apply may be fulfilled by the supplying entity unless such request is accompanied by a representation by the requesting entity that the request was made in conformity with these guidelines.

4. The requesting entity shall maintain records of all requests made by it for copies or phonorecords of any materials to which these guidelines apply and shall maintain records of the fulfillment of such requests, which records shall be retained until the end of the third complete calendar year after the end of the calendar year in which the respective request shall have been made.

5. As part of the review provided for in subsection 108(i), these guidelines shall be reviewed not later than five years from the effective date of this bill.

These guidelines were accepted by the Conference Committee and were incorporated into its report on the new act. During the ensuing twenty months, both library and publisher organizations have reported considerable progress toward adapting their practices to conform with the CONTU guidelines.

The guidelines specifically leave the status of periodical articles more than five years old to future determination. Moreover, institutions set up for the specific purpose of supplying photocopies of copyrighted material are excluded from coverage of the guidelines.

Appendix F
FAIR USE GUIDELINES FOR ELECTRONIC RESERVE SYSTEMS (CONFU) (1996)*
ಬಾಂಧ

Authors' note: These guidelines were developed during the Conference on Fair Use, but did not garner consensus support and thus is a not an adopted CONFU Guideline.

Introduction
Many college, university, and school libraries have established reserve operations for readings and other materials that support the instructional requirements of specific courses. Some educational institutions are now providing electronic reserve systems that allow storage of electronic versions of materials that students may retrieve on a computer screen, and from which they may print a copy for their personal study. When materials are included as a matter of fair use, electronic reserve systems should constitute an ad hoc or supplemental source of information for students, beyond a textbook or other materials. If included with permission from the copyright owner, however, the scope and range of materials is potentially unlimited, depending upon the permission granted. Although fair use is determined on a case-by-case basis, the following guidelines identify an understanding of fair use for the reproduction, distribution, display, and performance of materials in the context of creating and using an electronic reserve system.

Making materials accessible through electronic reserve systems raises significant copyright issues. Electronic reserve operations include the making of a digital version of text, the distribution and display of that

---

* *Available at* http://copyright.lib.utexas.edu/rsrvguid.html.

version at workstations, and downloading and printing of copies. The complexities of the electronic environment, and the growing potential for implicating copyright infringements, raise the need for a fresh understanding of fair use. These guidelines are not intended to burden the facilitation of reserves unduly, but instead offer a workable path that educators and librarians may follow in order to exercise a meaningful application of fair use, while also acknowledging and respecting the interests of copyright owners.

These guidelines focus generally on the traditional domain of reserve rooms, particularly copies of journal articles and book chapters, and their accompanying graphics. Nevertheless, they are not meant to apply exclusively to textual materials and may be instructive for the fair use of other media. The guidelines also focus on the use of the complete article or the entire book chapter. Using only brief excerpts from such works would most likely also be fair use, possibly without all of the restrictions or conditions set forth in these guidelines. Operators of reserve systems should also provide safeguards for the integrity of the text and the author's reputation, including verification that the text is correctly scanned.

The guidelines address only those materials protected by copyright and for which the institution has not obtained permission before including them in an electronic reserve system. The limitations and conditions set forth in these guidelines need not apply to materials in the public domain —such as works of the U.S. government or works on which copyright has expired—or to works for which the institution has obtained permission for inclusion in the electronic reserve system. License agreements may govern the uses of some materials. Persons responsible for electronic reserve systems should refer to applicable license terms for guidance. If an instructor arranges for students to acquire a work by some means that includes permission from the copyright owner, the instructor should not include that same work on an electronic reserve system as a matter of fair use.

These guidelines are the outgrowth of negotiations among diverse parties attending the Conference on Fair Use ("CONFU") meetings sponsored by the Information Infrastructure Task Force's Working Group on Intellectual Property Rights. While endorsements of any guidelines by all conference participants is unlikely, these guidelines have been endorsed by the organizations whose names appear at the end. These guidelines are in furtherance of the Working Group's objective of encouraging negotiated guidelines of fair use.

This introduction is an integral part of these guidelines and should be included with the guidelines wherever they may be reprinted or adopted by a library, academic institution, or other organization or association. No copyright protection of these guidelines is claimed by any person or entity, and anyone is free to reproduce and distribute this document without permission.

A. Scope of Material

1. In accordance with fair use (Section 107 of the U.S. Copyright Act), electronic reserve systems may include copyrighted materials at the request of a course instructor.
2. Electronic reserve systems may include short items (such as an article from a journal, a chapter from a book or conference proceedings, or a poem from a collected work) or excerpts from longer items. "Longer items" may include articles, chapters, poems, and other works that are of such length as to constitute a substantial portion of a book, journal, or other work of which they may be a part. "Short items" may include articles, chapters, poems, and other works of a customary length and structure as to be a small part of a book, journal, or other work, even if that work may be marketed individually.
3. Electronic reserve systems should not include any material unless the instructor, the library, or another unit of the educational institution possesses a lawfully obtained copy.
4. The total amount of material included in electronic reserve systems for a specific course as a matter of fair use should be a small proportion of the total assigned reading for a particular course.

B. Notices and Attributions

1. On a preliminary or introductory screen, electronic reserve systems should display a notice, consistent with the notice described in Section 108(f)(1) of the Copyright Act. The notice should include additional language cautioning against further electronic distribution of the digital work
2. If a notice of copyright appears on the copy of a work that is included in an electronic reserve system, the following statement shall appear at some place where users will likely see it in connection with access to the particular work: "The work from which this copy is made includes this notice: [restate the elements of the statutory copyright notice: e.g., Copyright 1996, XXX Corp.]"
3. Materials included in electronic reserve systems should include appropriate citations or attributions to their sources.

C. Access and Use

1. Electronic reserve systems should be structured to limit access to students registered in the course for which the items have been placed on reserve, and to instructors and staff responsible for the course or the electronic system.

2. The appropriate methods for limiting access will depend on available technology. Solely to suggest and not to prescribe options for implementation, possible methods for limiting access may include one or more of the following or other appropriate methods:

   (a) individual password controls or verification of a student's registration status; or

   (b) password system for each class; or

   (c) retrieval of works by course number or instructor name, but not by author or title of the work; or

   (d) access limited to workstations that are ordinarily used by, or are accessible to, only enrolled students or appropriate staff or faculty.

3. Students should not be charged specifically or directly for access to electronic reserve systems.

D. Storage and Reuse

1. Permission from the copyright holder is required if the item is to be reused in a subsequent academic term for the same course offered by the same instructor, or if the item is a standard assigned or optional reading for an individual course taught in multiple sections by many instructors.

2. Material may be retained in electronic form while permission is being sought or until the next academic term in which the material might be used, but in no event for more than three calendar years, including the year in which the materials are last used.

3. Short-term access to materials included on electronic reserve systems in previous academic terms may be provided to students who have not completed the course.

Appendix G
GUIDELINES FOR OFF-AIR RECORDINGS OF BROADCAST PROGRAMMING FOR EDUCATIONAL PURPOSES (1984)[*]

ഇൽൽ

In March 1979, Congressman Robert Kastenmeier, Chairman of the House Subcommittee on Courts, Civil Liberties and Administration of Justice, appointed a Negotiating Committee consisting of representatives of educational organizations, copyright proprietors, and creative guilds and unions. The following guidelines reflect the Negotiating Committee's consensus as to the application of "fair use" to the recording, retention, and use of television broadcast programs for educational purposes. They specify periods of retention and use of such off-air recordings in classrooms and similar places devoted to instruction and for homebound instruction. The purpose of establishing these guidelines is to provide standards for both owners and users of copyrighted television programs.

1. The guidelines were developed to apply only to off-air recording by nonprofit educational institutions.
2. A broadcast program may be recorded off-air simultaneously with broadcast transmission (including simultaneous cable retransmission) and retained by a nonprofit educational institution for a period not to exceed the first forty-five (45) consecutive calendar days after date of recording. Upon conclusion of such retention period, all off-air recordings must be erased or destroyed immediately. "Broadcast programs" are television programs transmitted by television stations for reception by the general public without charge.

---

[*] Reproduced in U.S. COPYRIGHT OFFICE, CIRCULAR 21: REPRODUCTION OF COPYRIGHTED WORKS BY EDUCATORS AND LIBRARIANS 23, *available at* http://www.copyright.gov/circs/circ21.pdf.

3.   Off-air recordings may be used once by individual teachers in the course of relevant teaching activities, and repeated once only when instructional reinforcement is necessary, in class-rooms and similar places devoted to instruction within a single building, cluster or campus, as well as in the homes of students receiving formalized home instruction, during the first ten (10) consecutive school days in the forty-five (45) day calendar day retention period. "School days" are school session days—not counting weekends, holidays, vacations, examination periods, and other scheduled interruptions—within the forty-five (45) calendar day retention period.

4.   Off-air recordings may be made only at the request of and used by individual teachers, and may not be regularly recorded in anticipation of requests. No broadcast program may be re-corded off-air more than once at the request of the same teacher, regardless of the number of times the program may be broadcast.

5.   A limited number of copies may be reproduced from each off-air recording to meet the legitimate needs of teachers under these guidelines. Each such additional copy shall be subject to all provisions governing the original recording.

Appendix H
GUIDELINES FOR EDUCATIONAL
USES OF MUSIC (1976)*
ℬ⌘ℭ₰

The following guidelines were developed and approved in April 1976 by the Music Publishers' Association of the United States, Inc., the National Music Publishers' Association, Inc., the Music Teachers National Association, the Music Educators National Conference, the National Association of Schools of Music, and the Ad Hoc Committee on Copyright Law Revision.

Guidelines for Educational Uses of Music
The purpose of the following guidelines is to state the minimum and not the maximum standards of educational fair use under Section 107 of HR 2223. The parties agree that the conditions determining the extent of permissible copying for educational purposes may change in the future; that certain types of copying permitted under these guidelines may not be permissible in the future, and conversely that in the future other types of copying not permitted under these guide-lines may be permissible under revised guidelines.

Moreover, the following statement of guidelines is not intended to limit the types of copying permitted under the standards of fair use under judicial decision and which are stated in Section 107 of the Copyright Revision Bill. There may be instances in which copying which does not fall within the guidelines stated below may nonetheless be permitted under the criteria of fair use.

---

* Reproduced in U.S. COPYRIGHT OFFICE, CIRCULAR 21: REPRODUCTION OF COPYRIGHTED WORKS BY EDUCATORS AND LIBRARIANS 7, *available at* http://www.copyright.gov/circs/circ21.pdf.

A. Permissible Uses

1. Emergency copying to replace purchased copies which for any reason are not available for an imminent performance provided purchased replacement copies shall be substituted in due course.

2. For academic purposes other than performance, single or multiple copies of excerpts of works may be made, provided that the excerpts do not comprise a part of the whole which would constitute a performable unit such as a section, movement or aria, but in no case more than 10 percent of the whole work. The number of copies shall not exceed one copy per pupil.

3. Printed copies which have been purchased may be edited or simplified provided that the fundamental character of the work is not distorted or the lyrics, if any, altered or lyrics added if none exist.

4. A single copy of recordings of performances by students may be made or evaluation or rehearsal purposes and may be retained by the educational institution or individual teacher.

5. A single copy of a sound recording (such as a tape, disc, or cassette) of copyrighted music may be made from sound recordings owned by an educational institution or an individual teacher for the purpose of constructing aural exercises or examinations and may be retained by the educational institution or individual teacher. (This pertains only to the copyright of the music itself and not to any copyright which may exist in the sound recording.)

B. Prohibitions

1. Copying to create or replace or substitute for anthologies, compilations or collective works.

2. Copying of or from works intended to be "consumable" in the course of study or of teaching such as workbooks, exercises, standardized tests and answer sheets and like material.

3. Copying for the purpose of performance, except as in A(1) above.

4. Copying for the purpose of substituting for the purchase of music, except as in A(1) and A(2) above.

5. Copying without inclusion of the copyright notice which appears on the printed copy.

Appendix I

SAMPLE PERMISSION LETTER
TO COPYRIGHT OWNER

ဆာ၆ဃ

[Date]

[Name and Address]

Dear _____:

I am writing to request permission to use [name of article/chapter from book/ illustration . . .] for use in classes I teach at _____ during the 2012/2013 academic year and in future semesters.

[If a Book]	**[If an Article]**
Title:	Title:
Author:	Author:
Chapter:	Volume Number and Pages:
Copyright Date:	Copyright Date:
ISBN #	ISSN #

The materials will be distributed to students enrolled in my classes, or made available through the library's reserve operations or electronically. If the materials are placed on reserve, we will make no more than five copies. If the materials are made available electronically, they will be distributed only to students enrolled in the class on a secure website, and we will implement control procedures that restrict further distribution.

I greatly appreciate your supporting my students and their coursework. I hope you will agree to this non-profit academic use of your materials by returning this letter, with your signature, in the self-addressed envelope that I have enclosed for your convenience. Alternatively, you may e-mail your permission to me at [   ].

Again, many thanks,

Name:_____

Title:_____

School Name/Address:_____

Phone Number/Fax Number/E-mail address: _____

Permission to Use the Materials Listed Above is Granted

Name:_____

Title:_____

Date:_____

Appendix J
AMERICAN ASSOCIATION OF LAW LIBRARIES GUIDELINES ON THE FAIR USE OF COPYRIGHTED WORKS BY LAW LIBRARIES (2001)[*]
৪৩৫

May 1997, Revised January 2001
Approved by the Copyright Committee, January 2001.[1]

1. Introduction

1.1. Preamble
The Copyright Act[2] sets out the rights of copyright ownership,[3] as well as the limits to those exclusive rights.[4] Two of the most important limits for law libraries are fair use (Section 107 of the Copyright Act) and the library exemption (Section 108 of the Copyright Act). The purpose of these Guidelines is to provide guidance to law librarians on copying by the

---

[*] © 2001 by the American Association of Law Libraries, reprinted with permission from the American Association of Law Libraries. *Available at* http://www.aallnet.org/main-menu/Advocacy/recommended guidelines/policy-fair.html.
[1] The American Association of Law Libraries encourages the free reproduction and distribution of the AALL Guidelines on the Fair Use of Copyrighted Works by Law Libraries without permission. Because digital technology is in a dynamic phase, there may come a time when it is necessary to revise the Guidelines. All institutions should review their own policies to ensure compliance with all applicable laws.
[2] Title 17 of the United States Code.
[3] 17 U.S.C. § 106.
[4] 17 U.S.C. §§ 107–122.

library and by users under fair use and the library exemption, rather than by authorization from the copyright owners.

These Guidelines describe conditions under which fair use and the library exemption should generally apply. A particular use that exceeds these Guidelines may or may not be a fair use, but the more one exceeds the Guidelines, the greater the risk that fair use does not apply. The American Association of Law Libraries believes that operation within these Guidelines provides a safe harbor, although only the courts can determine authoritatively whether a particular use is a fair use.

The limitations and conditions set forth in these Guidelines do not apply to works in the public domain for which there are no restrictions (such as facts, U.S. government works, or works in which copyright has expired), or to works for which the institution has obtained permission for the particular use. License agreements or contracts may govern the uses of some works, in particular, electronic information products; users should refer to the applicable license or contract terms for guidance on the use of those works.

These Guidelines represent the American Association of Law Libraries' collective understanding of fair use in law libraries. This Preamble is an integral part of these Guidelines and should be included whenever the Guidelines are reprinted or adopted by libraries or their parent organizations and institutions.

1.2. Background and Intent

The AALL Electronic Fair Use Committee was appointed in 1994 to develop Guidelines on the fair use of legal materials by U.S. law libraries. The AALL 2000–2001 Copyright Committee felt it important to update the 1997 Guidelines due to subsequent federal legislation and case law.

These Guidelines represent recommendations for "best practices" in all types of law libraries. Because of differences in types of institutions and different uses made of copyrighted works, and because certain exemptions apply only to nonprofit educational institutions, some Guidelines relate only to one type of library. Government libraries, such as court, county and agency libraries, and bar association and other membership libraries, are nonprofit libraries and generally fall somewhere between non-profit law school and for-profit law firm libraries in these Guidelines.

These Guidelines cover the reproduction, distribution, transmission, and display of copyrighted works, or substantial portions thereof, whether published in print or available in digital format. Further, the copying may be analog (i.e., photocopying or microform) or electronic (i.e., scanning or transmission). The Guidelines assume that the library's "original" copy is a legal copy.

1.3. Fair Use (Section 107)

Fair use is a legal principle that limits the exclusive rights[5] of copyright owners. There is no simple test to determine what is fair use. Section 107 of the Copyright Act[6] lists four factors that must be considered to determine whether a use is a "fair use;" other factors may also be considered based on the particular facts of a given case.[7] Section 107 states:

> Notwithstanding the provisions of sections 106 and 106A, the fair use of a copyrighted work, including such use by reproduction in copies or phonorecords or by any other means specified by that section, for purposes such as criticism, comment, news reporting, teaching (including multiple copies for classroom use), scholarship, or research, is not an infringement of copyright. In determining whether the use made of a work in any particular case is a fair use the factors to be considered shall include—
>
> > the purpose and character of the use, including whether such use is of a commercial nature or is for nonprofit educational purposes;
> >
> > the nature of the copyrighted work;
> >
> > the amount and substantiality of the portion used in relation to the copyrighted work as a whole; and
> >
> > the effect of the use upon the potential market for or value of the copyrighted work.

The fact that a work is unpublished shall not itself bar a finding of fair use if such finding is made upon consideration of all the above factors.[8]

1.4. The Library Exemption (Section 108)

Much of the copying covered by these Guidelines is permitted under § 108 of the Copyright Act.[9] The exemptions provided in § 108 are available to all types of libraries that meet the requirements of § 108(a). To qualify for the § 108 exemptions, copying must not be for direct or indirect commercial advantage, each copy reproduced must include the notice of copyright that appears on the original work or a legend if no such notice appears on

---

[5] *See* 17 U.S.C. § 106.
[6] The Copyright Act of 1976, as amended, is codified at 17 U.S.C. §§ 101 et seq.
[7] Campbell v. Acuff-Rose Music, Inc., 510 U.S. 569 (1994).
[8] 17 U.S.C. § 107.
[9] 17 U.S.C. §§ 109, 110, and 117 may also be relevant to these Guidelines.

the work (see 1.4.1 for additional detail), and the collection must be open to the public or available to researchers doing research in a specialized field. A library that makes its collection available to others by interlibrary loan or otherwise meets the "open and available" requirement.[10]

Section 108(d) provides that a library which meets the § 108(a) requirements may, at the request of a user, reproduce one copy of an article from a periodical issue or other contribution to a collective work either from material the library owns or from material owned by another library. The copy must become the property of the user. The library must post the warning prescribed in 37 C.F.R. § 201.14 at the place where the orders are placed, and must include it on the order form.[11] Further, the library should have no notice that the user will use the copy for other than fair use purposes.

Under § 108(d), libraries that qualify for the Library Exemption may provide a single copy to an external user upon request from that user. (See 2.1 below.) The copy provided may be either a photocopy or an electronic copy. Consistent with § 108(a)(1), the library may charge a reasonable fee for making the copy as long as the charge does not exceed reasonable cost recovery.

1.4.1. Notice of Copyright Under Section 108

A notice of copyright should appear on each print and electronic copy reproduced.

Under § 108, copies should include the notice of copyright that appears on the copy being reproduced. Absent such notice, the copy should include a legend such as "This work may be protected by copyright; further reproduction and distribution in violation of United States copyright law is prohibited."[12]

---

[10] H.R. REP. NO. 1476, 94th Cong., 2d Sess. (1976), *reprinted in* OMNIBUS COPYRIGHT REVISION LEGISLATION 75 (1977).

[11] Notice Warning Concerning Copyright Restrictions

The Copyright law of the United States (title 17, United States Code) governs the making of photocopies or other reproductions of copyrighted material.

Under certain conditions specified in the law, libraries and archives are authorized to furnish a photocopy or other reproduction. One of these specific conditions is that the photocopy or reproduction is not to be "used for any purpose other than private study, scholarship, or research." If a user makes a request for, or later uses, a photocopy or reproduction for purposes in excess of "fair use," that user may be liable for copyright infringement.

This institution reserves the right to refuse to accept a copying order if, in its judgment, fulfillment of the order would involve violation of copyright law.

37 C.F.R. § 201.14(b).

[12] The Digital Millennium Copyright Act amended Section 108(a)(3) to require that a library copy include the notice of copyright that appears on the work. It is not clear from the language of the statute or the legislative history whether this requirement applies to copying

2. Reproducing Single Copies within the Firm, School, Court, or Other Institutions

2.1. Copying from the Library's Own Collection

Fair Use: Purposes for copying from the library's collection include teaching, scholarship, or research, such as preparation in teaching, background research for drafting a court opinion, a client letter, a brief or a memorandum of law, and writing an article or book. Attorneys may offer reproductions of court opinions, statutes, articles, and sections of treatises into evidence in court proceedings. This also includes reproducing and distributing copies as required for administrative proceedings.

Library Exemption

A library which meets the § 108(a) requirements may, at the request of a user, reproduce one copy of an article from a periodical issue or other contribution to a collective work either from material the library owns or from material owned by another library.[13] The copy must become the property of the user; it may not be added to the library's collection. The library must post the warning prescribed by the Copyright Office at the place where the orders are placed, and must include it on the order form.[14] Further, the library should have no notice that the user will use the copy for other than fair use purposes.

For-Profit Library Copying for External Users

Libraries in the for-profit sector may provide a single copy of an article, a chapter, or a portion of another copyrighted work to clients to support work done for the client. The copy provided may be either a photocopy or an electronic copy, provided it includes the appropriate notice (see 1.4.1 above).

For-Profit Library Copying for Internal Users

Law firm and other law libraries in the for-profit sector should be aware that the *Texaco* decision[15] may apply to them. The AALL Model Law Firm Copyright Policy cautions against copying and distributing articles for later (rather than current) use and creating personal libraries. Libraries are also cautioned against systematically routing journals with knowledge

---

the copyright notice in front matter of the volume when copying independently authored articles from a journal or compilation.

[13] 17 U.S.C. § 108(d).

[14] *See supra* note 11.

[15] American Geophysical Union v. Texaco, 60 F.3d 913 (2d Cir. 1994).

or reason to believe that recipients will copy the articles for later (rather than current) use and creating personal libraries. Libraries may copy tables of contents, but should not solicit requests for copies of articles that would constitute systematic copying.[16]

2.1.1. Printed Copies of Printed Works
To satisfy a user's request, a library may make a photocopy or other printed copy of a printed work such as an article, a chapter or portions of other copyrighted works.

2.1.2. Electronic Copies of Printed Works
To satisfy a user's request, a library may scan an article from a periodical issue, a chapter, or portions of other copyrighted works and provide an electronic copy to the user in lieu of a photocopy. Because the copy must become the property of the user, the library may not retain the scanned image. A copy may be faxed or otherwise transmitted electronically to the user, but the library should destroy any temporary copy made incidental to the transmission. In other words, an incidental copy made to facilitate transmission is a fair use, as long as that copy is not retained.

2.1.3. Printed Copies of Digital Works
Unless prohibited or otherwise restricted by the terms of a valid license agreement, a library may print a copy of an article, a chapter, or portions of other copyrighted works at the request of a user.

2.1.4. Electronic Copies of Digital Works
Unless prohibited or otherwise restricted by the terms of a valid license agreement, a library may download a copy of an article, a chapter, or portions of other copyrighted works at the request of a user and forward it electronically to the user.

2.2. Obtaining Copies from Another Library

2.2.1 Interlibrary Loan Copies
A library may request single copies of articles, book chapters, or portions of other copyrighted works from the collection of another library to satisfy user requests as described above. The receiving library may deliver the copy to the user in print or electronic format. Neither the borrowing nor lending library may retain the print or digital image. Libraries may request print or electronic copies of works through interlibrary loan, but borrowing

---

[16] AALL MODEL LAW FIRM COPYRIGHT POLICY, *available at* http://www.aallnet.org.

libraries of all types should be aware of the CONTU suggestion of five.[17] The more a library exceeds the suggestion of five, the less likely it is that the interlibrary loan request is fair use.

2.2.2. Access to Digital Works by External Users[18]
Terms of a valid license agreement may prohibit access to or reproduction of digital works for external users, including interlibrary loan, or may limit the external constituencies to which a law library may supply either print or electronic copies of digital works. If the license agreement is silent on providing copies to external users, then the library may make either printed or digital copies for external users.

3. Multiple Copying of Copyrighted Works

3.1. Multiple Copying in General
Multiple copying is limited under the Copyright Act and under these Guidelines. Section 108 of the Act (the Library Exemption) is restricted to single copies. There are, however, instances in which multiple copying might be considered fair use under § 107.

3.1.1. Academic Law Libraries
Under the Classroom Guidelines,[19] nonprofit educational institutions may, under certain circumstances, make multiple copies of articles, book chapters, and portions of other copyrighted works for classroom use. The Classroom Guidelines restrict use to one term, and also impose tests such as brevity, spontaneity and cumulative effects. Scholars, librarians, and publishers agree that uses within the terms of the Classroom Guidelines are fair.

The Classroom Guidelines were designed to cover uses in primary and secondary schools. In higher education, including nonprofit law school-sponsored continuing legal education programs, however, fair use should encompass copying beyond that which is permitted in the Classroom Guidelines. The word limitations in the Classroom Guidelines are especially problematic for legal education due to the length of most copyrightable legal documents and scholarship.

---

[17] The suggestion of five permits libraries to copy five articles from the most recent five years of a single title without paying a royalty. All copying of articles more than five years old is considered permissible without paying a royalty. Records are maintained by the requesting entity. H.R. REP. NO. 1733, 94th Cong., 2d Sess. (1976), *reprinted in* OMNIBUS COPYRIGHT REVISION LEGISLATION 72–74 (1977).

[18] For example, secondary users not affiliated with the institution.

[19] H.R. REP. NO. 1476, 94th Cong., 2d Sess. (1976), *reprinted in* OMNIBUS COPYRIGHT REVISION LEGISLATION 68–70 (1977).

Academic libraries may make a limited number of copies of articles, chapters, and portions of other copyrighted works for library reserve collections as an extension of the classroom. The ALA Model Policy suggests that no more than six copies be made for reserve for any one class.[20] The copies may be print or electronic. In the case of electronic copies, access should be limited to no more than six simultaneous users. For electronic reserves, the institution should take reasonable steps to ensure copies are only accessible to enrolled students.

3.1.2. Other Law Libraries

Multiple simultaneous copying generally is not permitted under the library exemption. There may be instances, however, where such copying would be permitted under fair use. The library should apply the four fair use factors to determine whether making the copies qualifies for the fair use exemption.

3.2. Preservation

A library may make three copies of either a published or unpublished work for preservation purposes under specified conditions.[21] Such copies may be in analog or digital formats, but digital copies may not be used outside the premises of the library nor sent to other libraries.

3.2.1. Obsolete Devices

A library may make three copies of a published work when the format in which the work is stored has become obsolete. A format is obsolete if the equipment or device necessary to perceive the work is no longer manufactured or not reasonably available in the commercial marketplace.[22]

3.2.2. Unpublished Works

A library that has a copy of an unpublished work in its collection may make a copy of that work for deposit in another library that qualifies for the Library Exemption [see 1.4 above]. Such copies may only be in analog format.

---

[20] Model Policy Concerning College and University Photocopying for Classroom, Research and Library Reserve Use, American Library Association, Washington Office, Washington, DC (Mar. 1982).
[21] 17 U.S.C. §§ 108(b)–(c).
[22] 17 U.S.C. § 108(c).

3.3. Copying Newsletters

Libraries generally may reproduce only small portions of copyrighted newsletters. All types of libraries should avoid multiple copying of newsletters or routing newsletters if they have knowledge or reason to believe that recipients will reproduce the newsletter or articles therein for a later use or create personal libraries.

4. Copying Database Search Results

4.1. Signed License Agreements

Most libraries sign license agreements to obtain access to legal and other databases. Because libraries must comply with the terms of a valid license agreement, they should review the terms of all licenses closely.

4.2. Redistribution of Results—Single Copy to a User

Distribution of database search results to a single user clearly is permitted under fair use unless prohibited by a valid license agreement. This includes providing a copy of search results to any library patron, including a faculty member, student, judge, or law firm client. Public domain information is not subject to any of these limitations.

4.3. Redistribution of Results—Multiple Users

Absent a license agreement that restricts redistribution of non-public domain research results, redistribution to multiple users may be permitted. Libraries should seek permission for multiple distributions of research results, whether by print or via electronic means, if that use exceeds these Guidelines.

Appendix K
AMERICAN ASSOCIATION OF LAW LIBRARIES MODEL LAW FIRM COPYRIGHT POLICY (2007)*

ဢၯဢ

Approved October 1996
Revised January 2001, July 2007, and August 2007
Last approved by the Copyright Committee in August 2007

INTRODUCTORY STATEMENT: Reproducing copyrighted materials is governed by the Copyright Act of 1976, subsequent legislation,[1] and interpretive case law. AALL reaffirms the application of the fair use provision (17 U.S.C. - 107) and the library exemption (17 U.S.C. - 108) in the law firm environment.[2] This Policy is intended solely for the consideration of law firm libraries as suggested procedures in complying with copyright law. Firm-wide implementation should be done with the input and advice of firm management.

FIRM STATEMENT: [FIRM] does not condone the unauthorized reproduction of copyrighted materials, in any format. Unauthorized reproduction includes copying done beyond that which is permitted under the Copyright Act, if it is done without permission and/or payment of royalties.

---

* © 2007 by the American Association of Law Libraries, reprinted with permission from the American Association of Law Libraries. Available at http://www.aallnet.org/main-menu/Advocacy/recommendedguidelines/model-law.html.
[1] Title 17 of the United States Code includes the Copyright Act of 1976 and subsequent legislation.
[2] For an expanded discussion of what constitutes fair use, see the AALL Guidelines on the Fair Use of Copyrighted Works by Law Libraries (revised, January 2001) [hereinafter AALL Fair Use Guidelines], at http://www.aallnet.org/about/policy_fair.asp.

RESPONSIBILITY STATEMENT: Compliance with the Copyright Act is the individual responsibility of every employee, including partners, associates, paralegals, other staff members, and independent contractors working at or for the firm.

SOURCES OF COPIES: Under this Policy, sources of copies should be the lawfully obtained original copyrighted work, whether found in the library, obtained through inter-library loan from a lending library, or retrieved from an online service or document delivery service that receives permission from or pays royalties to the copyright owner.

DEFINITIONS:
1. **Copy:** For purposes of this Policy, a copy is either 1) a photoreproduction of text or images via a copier; 2) transmission or downloading of text or images from a computer, or 3) any other replication of text or images by way of electronic means, or other form of transcription.
2. **Reproduction equipment:** Reproduction equipment includes photocopiers, printers, scanners, facsimile machines, microform reader/printers, networked workstations and other electronic transmission devices. It is not intended that copyright notices be posted on individual computer workstations throughout the firm.
3. **Reproduction centers:** Reproduction centers include areas of the firm staffed by personnel, either employed by the firm or by a third party, who have the primary responsibility for attending to copiers and other reproduction equipment. It should be noted that reproduction centers that are staffed by third party vendors may not be able to take advantage of the Section 108 library exemption to the same extent as reproduction centers staffed by firm employees.

SIGNAGE: NOTICE ON EQUIPMENT: The firm should post the following signs on all reproduction equipment: "THE MAKING OF A COPY MAY BE SUBJECT TO THE UNITED STATES COPYRIGHT LAW (Title 17 United States Code)." Alternatively, the firm may elect to use the following notice recommended by the American Library Association – "THE COPYRIGHT LAW OF THE UNITED STATES (Title 17 U.S. Code) GOVERNS THE MAKING OF PHOTOCOPIES OR OTHER REPRODUCTIONS OF COPYRIGHTED MATERIAL. THE PERSON USING THIS EQUIPMENT IS LIABLE FOR ANY INFRINGEMENT."
SIGNAGE: NOTICE ON COPIES: The notice of copyright that appears on the original work should be reproduced and affixed to the copy. If no such notice appears on the original work, the printed copy should include

the following notice stamped on or affixed to the first page of every copyrighted item reproduced by the library or reproduction center: "THIS MATERIAL IS SUBJECT TO THE UNITED STATES COPYRIGHT LAW; FURTHER REPRODUCTION IN VIOLATION OF THAT LAW IS PROHIBITED."

SIGNAGE: NOTICE WHERE ORDERS ARE PLACED AND ON REQUEST FORM: The Library or reproduction center should display the following sign where copying orders are placed, and should include this notice on the actual copying request form:

NOTICE
WARNING CONCERNING
COPYRIGHT RESTRICTIONS

The copyright law of the United States (Title 17, United States Code) governs the making of photocopies or other reproduction of copyrighted material.

Under certain conditions specified in the law, libraries and archives are authorized to furnish a photocopy or other reproduction. One of these specified conditions is that the photocopy or reproduction is not to be "used for any purpose other than private study, scholarship or research." If a user makes a request for, or later uses, a photocopy or reproduction for purposes in excess of "fair use", that user may be liable for copyright infringement.

This institution reserves the right to refuse to accept a copying order if, in its judgment, fulfillment of the order would involve violation of copyright law.

ROUTING AND LIBRARY REPRODUCTION: The Library may route originals and/or copies of tables of contents. When the length of the routing list becomes excessive, the firm should purchase additional copies of a copyrighted work. Libraries are cautioned against systematically routing journals with knowledge or reason to believe that recipients will reproduce the articles for later (rather than current) use and to create personal libraries.

The library or reproduction center may make one copy of an article in response to a specific request from an employee or partner for individual scholarship, research or educational use. Recipients are cautioned against systematic reproduction of articles for later (rather than current) use and creating personal libraries. Although in most instances making subsequent copies from the original copy requires permission, circumstances may exist—such as making a single copy for one client or co-counsel, or for submission to a court[3]—where the copying may be a fair use.[4]

The Library or reproduction center should not, nor should individuals, make multiple copies of articles, or cover-to-cover copies of newsletters, periodical issues or volumes. This practice should be observed for both standard library materials and materials obtained from online services. NOTE: Because of the typically short length of newsletters, the library or reproduction center, as a general rule, may reproduce only small portions of copyrighted newsletters. Libraries may reproduce tables of contents, but should not solicit requests for copies of articles that would constitute systematic reproduction.

INTERLIBRARY LENDING/DOCUMENT DELIVERY: The library typically may borrow or lend only lawfully obtained original copies of copyrighted materials, or the original copyrighted work.

Lending: In response to requests from other libraries, the library may make one copy of an article so long as the requester attests, and the library reasonably believes, that the request complies with the Copyright Act or the CONTU guidelines.[5]

Borrowing: In requesting materials from other libraries, the library may request a single copy of an article or brief excerpts from a book, so long as the request complies with the Copyright Act or the CONTU guidelines. (CONTU suggests that a library subscribe to a journal title if it requests photocopies of articles published in the periodical within five years prior to the date of the request more than five times within a given year).

COMPUTER PROGRAMS: According to Section 117 of the Copyright Act, the firm may make one archival copy of software it has purchased, and may also adapt purchased software so that it can be used on firm equipment. Firm personnel should not load any unauthorized copy of any computer program, or portion thereof, onto any computer, file server, or other magnetic or electronic media storage device belonging to the firm. License agreements should be strictly followed with regard to the use of all authorized copies of software programs. The general rule for software use

---

[3] See Nimmer on Copyright - 13.05[D][2] (2007).
[4] For additional examples of what constitutes fair use, see AALL Fair Use Guidelines, at http://www.aallnet.org/about/policy_fair.asp.
[5] National Commission on New Technological Uses of Copyrighted Works (CONTU) (1976); the CONTU Guidelines are available online at http://www.cni.org/docs/infopols/CONTU.html.

in law firms is that each copy is for a single computer. A site license should be considered for multiple copies on multiple computers, or for access by multiple simultaneous users.

PERMISSIONS AND ROYALTIES: This Policy expresses minimum standards of fair use.[6] Circumstances may exist where copying beyond this Policy is permitted under the Copyright Act. However, reproducing materials beyond that which is permitted by this Policy generally will require permission, and, when necessary, payment of royalties. Royalties may be made directly to the copyright owner or its agent.

QUESTIONS/FOR MORE INFORMATION: Please direct any copyright concerns to [LIBRARIAN AND/OR INTELLECTUAL PROPERTY ATTORNEY].

REVIEW AND IMPLEMENTATION: Firm management should review the copyright law—particularly 17 U.S.C. - 106–109—as well as firm-wide copying and other copyright related activities before implementing a copyright policy. At a minimum, this review should include examining Copyright Office Circular 21: Reproduction of Copyrighted Words by Educators and Librarians (http://www.copyright.gov/circs/ circ21.pdf). Other recommended resources are; James S. Heller, *The Librarian's Copyright Handbook* (Wm. S. Hein & Co., 2004); Richard Stim, *Getting Permission: How to License & Clear Copyrighted Materials Online & Off* (Nolo Press, 2004); and Arlene Bielefield, *Technology and Copyright Law* (2d ed., Neal-Schuman, 2007).

Management should review carefully all firm-wide online database, CD-ROM and software contracts.

---

[6] For an expanded discussion of what constitutes fair use, see AALL Fair Use Guidelines, at http://www.aallnet.org/about/policy_fair.asp.

Appendix L
VISUAL RESOURCES ASSOCIATION IMAGE COLLECTION GUIDELINES: THE ACQUISITION AND USE OF IMAGES IN NON-PROFIT EDUCATIONAL VISUAL RESOURCES COLLECTIONS (2004)[*]

ೞೋೞ

As published by the VRA Committee on Intellectual Property Rights

Many educational disciplines are dependent upon the use of illustrative images for teaching purposes. Visual resources collections which support those disciplines strive to assemble the best resources in terms of technical quality, fidelity to the underlying work, accuracy of basic identifying information, and flexibility of access and utilization. The development and use of these resources should be guided by the following principles in regard to acquisition, attribution, display and responsibility.

The acquisition and use of image resources, as with any intellectual property, is governed by legal conditions, as well as by practical, technical, and scholarly considerations. Intellectual property law, including the concept of Copyright, attempts to balance the sometimes competing interests of those who produce or provide such resources, and those who use them. It is the intent of this Guide to enable the visual resources professional to acquire image resources for educational, non-profit use in a manner that

---

[*] Reprinted with permission from the Visual Resources Association Intellectual Property Rights Committee. *Available at* http://www.vraweb.org/resources/ipr/guidelines.html

respects the rights and concerns of providers, while acknowledging public domain rights and educational exemptions such as Fair Use.

Although these guidelines have been reviewed by legal counsel, the content represents the consensus of visual resources curators and does not constitute a legal document. For further guidance on acquisition, attribution, display, and responsibility, individual visual resources curators should consult the legal counsel of their respective educational institutions.

A. ACQUISITION

Acquisition of visual resources falls into several categories: purchase and license, donation, and copystand photography.

1. Purchase, license, or otherwise legally acquire, the following in developing permanent archives of images:
   a) slides or digital files from museums, galleries or other such institutions
   b) slides or digital files from vendors and image providers
   c) original on-site photography produced for sale by professional or highly skilled photographers.
   d) slides or digital files distributed on a free-use basis through recognized educational or professional institutions, organizations and consortia.

2. Gifts and donations are considered legitimate forms of acquisition, even though they may be subject to restrictions or requirements by the donors. It is recommended that donors of original photographic images in whatever form be encouraged to grant in writing to the recipient institution discretionary rights over extended use, as well as physical custody, of the photographic materials.

3. Images created by copystand photography and scanning from published materials for inclusion in the permanent archive are subject to the following considerations:
   a) images of suitable quality are not readily available at a reasonable cost and in a reasonable time from any of the options listed above
   b) images will not be shared between or among other educational institutions if such use is prohibited by the terms of their acquisition.
   c) images will be used for comment, criticism, review, analysis, discussion, or other similar purpose associated with instruction or scholarship

d) images will be used for purposes that are both nonprofit and educational.

If these conditions can be met, it is likely that making images and digital files from published materials will be within "fair use" as outlined in the Copyright Act of 1976.

Uses outside the understood parameters described above, such as use on an unrestricted website or in print publications, including scholarly publications, are not covered in this document. Such uses to be considered fair must be judged independently and individually, using the four-factor analysis described in Section 107 of the Copyright Act of 1976. The four factors to be considered in determining if a use is a fair use are: (1) purpose and character of the use; (2) nature of the copyrighted work; (3) amount and substantiality of the material used; and (4) the effect on the market.

4. Public Domain images (those in which neither the underlying work of art documented nor the photographic reproduction itself is subject to copyright) may be safely acquired by any appropriate means, including copystand photography or scanning. Use of such images is unrestricted. (**see VRA Copy Photography Computator)

B. ATTRIBUTION

To the extent that such information is available, it is recommended that all images acquired for the permanent archive of an educational institution should be identified with the following:

1) source of image
2) year of acquisition
3) in the case of a purchased or licensed image, the provider's inventory or identifying number or code.

C. DISPLAY

While the traditional means of display for such image archives have been through projection, or otherwise viewing the physical surrogate (photograph, slide, video, film), the introduction of new technologies, specifically the digital environment of the Internet and the World Wide Web has expanded the display options. There is little in the way of legal precedent, code, or case law which addresses the issues particular to educational image archives. However, it seems reasonable to expect that digital materials should be available to the same user group that the analog collection serves, for the same purposes.

Analog materials acquired as outlined above may be used in digital format as follows:

1) Images purchased or licensed are subject to the conditions specified at the time of purchase or according to license agreement.
2) Gifts and donations are subject to restrictions made at the time of contribution. In addition, a gift of images purchased by the donor may be subject to the conditions of the original purchase.
3) Images made by copystand photography may be digitized and used digitally according to the same criteria under which they were originally acquired for analog use.

D. RESPONSIBILITY

The educational institution holding such an archive should have a designated overseer who is responsible for carrying out the principles outlined above. A budget sufficient to make purchases described above should be allocated. Information on source data should be available to the collection users.

Under the law, liability may be held by both the institution and the individual; however, individual liability may depend on the institution's policies. Usually, although not always, individuals who adhere to institutional policies will be indemnified by their institutions against all the costs they may suffer if they are sued. Following institutional policy is a good way for individuals to stay within the protections of a good-faith fair use defense. It is recommended that the designated overseer discuss institutional policies with the institution's legal counsel.

Appendix M
CODE OF BEST PRACTICES IN FAIR USE FOR ACADEMIC AND RESEARCH LIBRARIES (2012)[*]

ℰℐℭℬ

Coordinated by the Association of Research Libraries, the Center for Social Media at American University's School of Communication, and the Program on Information Justice and Intellectual Property at American University's Washington College of Law.

Endorsed by the American Library Association and the Association of College and Research Librarians.

INTRODUCTION

The mission of academic and research librarians is to enable teaching, learning, and research.[1] Along with serving current faculty, researchers, and students (especially graduate students), these librarians also serve the general public, to whom academic and research libraries are often open. Finally, academic and research librarians are committed to faculty, researchers, and students of the future, who depend on the responsible collection, curation, and preservation of materials over time.

Copyright law affects the work of academic and research librarians pervasively and in complex ways, because the great bulk of these librarians' work deals with accessing, storing, exhibiting, or providing access to

---

* Available at http://www.arl.org/bm~doc/code-of-best-practices-fair-use.pdf.

[1] This code was developed by and for academic and research librarians. While some of the ideas and principles in the code may be helpful to librarians in other contexts, any reference to "librarians" in this document refers to academic and research librarians, not to all librarians.

241

copyrighted material. The rights of copyright holders create incentives for the publication of important work that forms the core of library collections, while at the same time constraining academic and research librarians in the exercise of their mission. Similarly, limitations on and exceptions to copyright rights enable academic and research librarians to use copyrighted materials in important ways, but impose limits and responsibilities of their own.

In addition to specific exceptions for libraries and educators, academic and research librarians use the important general exemption of fair use to accomplish their mission. Fair use is the right to use copyrighted material without permission or payment under some circumstances, especially when the cultural or social benefits of the use are predominant. It is a general right that applies even—and especially—in situations where the law provides no specific statutory authorization for the use in question. Consequently, the fair use doctrine is described only generally in the law, and it is not tailored to the mission of any particular community. Ultimately, determining whether any use is likely to be considered "fair" requires a thoughtful evaluation of the facts, the law, and the norms of the relevant community.

HOW THIS DOCUMENT WAS CREATED

The first step in creating this code was to conduct an in-depth survey, using long form interviews, with 65 librarians at a diverse array of academic and research institutions in the United States, from Ivy League colleges to rural satellite campuses. The results demonstrated clearly both that fair use is an essential component of copyright exemptions for librarians, and also that they lacked a clear sense of what they and their peers might agree to as appropriate employment of fair use in recurrent situations.[2] As a result, librarians frequently did not use their fair use rights when they could have, and they overestimated the level of conflict between the strictures of copyright law on the one hand and their respective libraries' missions on the other. The cost of this uncertainty was amplified because many research and academic librarians routinely act as the de facto arbiters of copyright practice for their institutions and the constituencies they serve.

Working librarians with many different institutional roles at a wide range of institutions then gathered together in a series of small group discussions about fair use held in five cities between October 2010 and

---

[2] See Association of Research Libraries et al., Fair Use Challenges in Academic and Research Libraries (2010), http://www.arl.org/bm~doc/arl_csm_fairusereport.pdf.

August 2011. In each conversation, participants were asked to discuss a series of brief hypothetical examples designed to raise questions about fair use and its limitations. Conversations revealed that members of this community understand that their mission depends on copyright, both the protection it provides for those who have already produced knowledge and the important rights it creates for those who need access to copyrighted material to enable learning, scholarship, and creativity. Their understanding of fair use, represented below, is grounded in this understanding of copyright balance. To ensure that the applications of fair use represented by the principles fall within the bounds of reason, an outside panel of distinguished copyright experts reviewed this document.

However, this document is not intended and should not be construed as representing their legal advice. With this information in hand, each institution can undertake its own legal and risk analysis in light of its own specific facts and circumstances.

WHAT THIS IS

This is a code of best practices in fair use devised specifically by and for the academic and research library community. It enhances the ability of librarians to rely on fair use by documenting the considered views of the library community about best practices in fair use, drawn from the actual practices and experience of the library community itself.

It identifies eight situations that represent the library community's current consensus about acceptable practices for the fair use of copyrighted materials and describes a carefully derived consensus within the library community about how those rights should apply in certain recurrent situations. These are the issues around which a clear consensus emerged over more than a year of discussions. The groups also talked about other issues; on some, there seemed not to be a consensus, and group members found others to be less urgent. The community may wish to revisit this process in the future to deliberate on emerging and evolving issues and uses.

WHAT THIS ISN'T

This code of best practices was not negotiated with rights holders. This code is the work of the academic and research library community and arises from that community's values and mission. It presents a clear and conscientious articulation of the values of that community, not a compromise between those values and the competing interests of other parties.

This code of best practices does not exhaust the application of fair use rights when copyrighted material is concerned. The objective of this code is not to constrain librarians' reliance on fair use, but to enable it. The principle of fair use can and does operate in a wide diversity of contexts, along with the ones specifically addressed below.

Although the code incorporates consensus-based community standards relating to commonly experienced conflicts between library practice and perceived copyright constraints, it is not a comprehensive or exhaustive guide to all possible applications of fair use in and around libraries—even in the recurrent situations detailed below.

Institutions may be able to make persuasive arguments for fair use that go beyond the shared norms expressed here. Likewise, institutions engaging in their own "risk management" may choose policies that do not take full advantage of these consensus principles.

This dynamic legal doctrine will no doubt continue to evolve along with educational, scholarly, and artistic practice. One area in which further developments certainly can be expected is that of so-called "orphan works"— texts (or images or music) that can no longer be reliably traced to a known copyright owner, and therefore cannot be licensed for use. Although the principles below address this problem obliquely, they do not by any means exhaust the range of possible solutions—including those based in the application of fair use.

This code is not a guide to using material that people give the public permission to use, such as works covered by Creative Commons licenses. While fair use applies to such works, anyone may use those works in ways their owners authorize in addition to ways permitted by the fair use doctrine. Similarly, it is not a guide to the use of works that are in the public domain; those works may be used without any copyright limitation whatever, including uses that otherwise would far exceed the bounds of fair use.

Copyright law is "territorial," which means that fair use applies to uses of copyrighted material in the United States, regardless of where in the world it originates. Hence, the principles in this code also apply regardless of a work's origin, so long as the use takes place in the U.S. By the same token, these principles will not necessarily apply to uses outside the U.S., where fair use may have little or no legal status.[3]

---

[3] At this time, the issue of "choice of laws" in copyright disputes that cross national boundaries is unclear, whether or not those disputes involve the Internet. See Peter K. Yu, "Conflicts of Laws Issues in International Copyright Cases" (2001), http://www.peteryu. com/gigalaw0401.pdf.

Under some circumstances, fair use rights can be overridden by contractual restrictions. Thus, these principles may not apply if a library has agreed, in a license agreement, donor agreement, or other contract, to forgo the exercise of fair use with respect to some set of collection materials. If fair use rights are to be preserved, library personnel in charge of acquisitions and procurement should be vigilant as they negotiate and enter into contracts related to collections materials.

COPYRIGHT AND FAIR USE

The goal of copyright law and policy is to foster the progress of science, the creation of culture, and the dissemination of ideas. Its best-known feature is protection of owners' rights. But copying, quoting, and generally reusing existing cultural and scientific material can be a critically important part of generating new research and culture and promoting intellectual exchange. In fact, the value of these practices is so well established that it is written into the social bargain at the heart of copyright law.

We as a society give limited property rights to creators to encourage them to produce science and culture; at the same time, we guarantee that all works eventually will become part of the public domain and, in the meantime, we give other creators and speakers the opportunity to use copyrighted material without permission or payment in some circumstances. Without the second half of the bargain, we could all lose important new work and impoverish public discourse.

Fair use is widely and vigorously employed in many professional communities. For example, historians regularly quote both other historians' writings and primary sources; filmmakers and visual artists use, reinterpret, and critique copyrighted material; scholars illustrate cultural commentary with textual, visual, and musical examples. Fair use is also healthy and vigorous in broadcast news and other commercial media, where references to popular films, classic TV programs, archival images, and popular songs are frequently unlicensed. Trade and academic publishers regularly rely on fair use to justify the incorporation of third-party material into books they produce. Librarians likewise need fair use to execute their mission on a daily basis.

No group of institutions, no matter how important their cultural function, is immune from the operation of copyright law. Academic and research libraries are not-for-profit institutions, but they still must build collections by buying books and subscribing to journals and databases. Likewise, they get no "free pass" simply because their function is to support education. That said, the United States Copyright Act is particularly solicitous of educational and academic uses in many circumstances. That solicitude is reflected in several structural features that benefit users of copyrighted material in and around the academic or research library. These include the specific exceptions contained in Sections 108, 110, and 121 of the Copyright Act and the special protections granted by Section 504(c)(2). Even when, as is often the case, specific exceptions don't literally reach the proposed library activities, the policies behind them may help to guide the interpretation of fair use as it applies to schools and libraries.[4]

As legislative history makes clear, these provisions were designed to complement rather than to supplant fair use, which has been part of copyright law for 170 years and remains the most fundamental of such structural features.[5] Section 107 of the Act, which codified the fair use doctrine in 1976, specifically includes references in its preamble to a number of activities associated with the academic and research library mission, including "criticism, comment…, teaching…, scholarship, [and] research."

Fair use is a user's right. In fact, the Supreme Court has pointed out that it is fair use that keeps copyright from violating the First Amendment; without fair use and related exceptions, copyright would create an unconstitutional constraint on free expression. Creators, scholars, and other users face new challenges as copyright protects more works for longer periods, with increasingly draconian punishments and narrow, outdated specific exceptions. As a result, fair use is more important today than ever before.

Because copyright law does not specify exactly how to apply fair use, the fair use doctrine has a useful flexibility that allows the law to adjust to evolving circumstances and works to the advantage of society as a whole. Needs and practices differ with the field, with technology, and with time. Rather than following a prescriptive formula, lawyers and judges decide whether a particular use of copyrighted material is "fair" according to an "equitable rule of reason." In effect, this amounts to taking all the facts and circumstances into account to decide whether an unlicensed use of copy-

---

[4] See Jonathan Band, "The Gravitational Pull of Specific Exceptions on Fair Use" (Sept. 1, 2011), unpublished manuscript, http://papers.ssrn.com/sol3/papers.cfm?abstract_id= 1966593.

[5] See, e.g., 17 U.S.C. § 108(f)(4), ("[Nothing in this section] in any way affects the right of fair use as provided by section 107…"); U.S. Copyright Office, The Section 108 Study Group Report 22 (2008), ("[S]ection 108 was not intended to affect fair use. Certain preservation activities fall within the scope of fair use, regardless of whether they would be permitted by section 108"); memorandum from Randolph D. Moss, acting assistant attorney general to the general counsel, Department of Commerce (April 30, 1999), ("Section 108 of the 1976 Act does not narrow the protection for fair use provided by the common law doctrine codified in section 107"), http://www.justice.gov/olc/pincusfinal430.htm.

righted material generates social or cultural benefits that are greater than the costs it imposes on the copyright owner.

This flexibility in the law can lead to uncertainty among librarians (as in other practice communities) about whether specific uses are fair. However, fair use is flexible, not unreliable. Like any exercise of expressive freedom, taking advantage of fair use in education and libraries depends on the application of general principles to specific situations. One way of easing this application is to document the considered attitudes and best practices of the library community as it works to apply the rules.

In weighing the balance at the heart of fair use analysis, judges generally refer to four types of considerations mentioned in Section 107 of the Copyright Act: the nature of the use, the nature of the work used, the extent of the use, and its economic effect (the so-called "four factors"). Over the years, attempts have been made to promulgate so-called "fair use guidelines," with the goal of reducing uncertainty about the application of this formula—even at a cost to flexibility. Unfortunately, the processes by which most guidelines have been developed are suspect, and the results are almost universally over-restrictive.[6] In fact, "bright line" tests and even "rules of thumb" are simply not appropriate to fair use analysis, which requires case-by-case determinations made through reasoning about how and why a new use repurposes or recontextualizes existing material.

How judges have interpreted fair use affects the community's ability to employ fair use. There are very few cases specifically involving libraries.[7] However, we know that for any particular field of activity, lawyers and judges consider expectations and practice in assessing what is "fair"

---

[6] See Kenneth Crews, "The Law of Fair Use and the Illusion of Fair-Use Guidelines," 62 Ohio State Law Journal 602 (2001).

[7] At the time of this writing, there are no judicial opinions describing in any detail the scope of fair use in a nonprofit educational context. Courts have examined unlicensed copying in for-profit copy shops, but those cases have explicitly distinguished commercial enterprises from nonprofit ones (see, e.g., Princeton University Press v. Michigan Document Svces, 99 F. 3d 1381, 1389 (6th Cir. 1996), ("We need not decide [the status of nonprofit uses], however, for the fact is that the copying complained of here was performed on a profit-making basis by a commercial enterprise"). Several cases involving fair use were filed against universities in the last year or two. Of these, one has been dismissed without a clear finding on the issue of fair use (AIME et al. v. Regents of Univ. of Cal. et al., No. CV 10-9378 (C.D. Cal. Oct. 10, 2011)). (AIME subsequently filed an amended complaint, which is pending at the time of this writing, while two others await decision.) See Cambridge U.P. v. Patton, No. 08-1425 (N.D. Ga. filed April 15, 2008); Authors' Guild, Inc. v. HathiTrust, No. 11-6351 (S.D.N.Y. filed Sept. 12, 2011). The path of litigation is typically long and unpredictable, and even a final decision in one case may not provide clear guidance to users in other judicial districts or whose uses may differ in important ways.

within that field. Moreover, the history of fair use litigation of all kinds shows that judges return again and again to two key analytical questions:[8]

- Did the use "transform" the material taken from the copyrighted work by using it for a broadly beneficial purpose different from that of the original, or did it just repeat the work for the same intent and value as the original?
- Was the material taken appropriate in kind and amount, considering the nature of the copyrighted work and of the use?

These two questions effectively collapse the "four factors." The first addresses the first two factors, and the second rephrases the third factor. Both key questions touch on the so-called "fourth factor," whether the use will cause excessive economic harm to the copyright owner. If the answers to these two questions are "yes," a court is likely to find a use fair—even if the work is used in its entirety. Because that is true, the risk of a challenge to such a use is dramatically reduced.

Fair use ensures that copyright owners do not have a monopoly over transformative uses of their works. The converse is also true. When a use merely supplants a copyright owner's core market rather than having a transformative purpose, it is unlikely to be fair. Thus, for example, a library clearly cannot acquire current books for its collection simply by photocopying or scanning published editions.

In cases decided since the early 1990s, the courts have made it clear that in order for a use to be considered "transformative," it need not be one that modifies or literally revises copyrighted material. In fact, uses that repurpose or recontextualize copyrighted content in order to present it to a new audience for a new purpose can qualify as well. The courts also have taught that the more coherent an account the user can give of how and why the material was borrowed, the more likely the use is to be considered transformative.[9]

A final consideration influencing judges' decisions historically has been whether the user acted reasonably and in good faith in light of standards of accepted practice in his or her particular field. Among the eight other communities of practice that established codes of best practices

---

[8] See Neil Netanel, "Making Sense of Fair Use," 15 Lewis & Clark L. Rev. 715, 768 (2011), surveying data about fair use cases decided between 1978 and 2011 and concluding that "the key question" is whether the use is transformative, and, if so, whether the amount taken is appropriate to the transformative purpose.

[9] Courts also have applied and will continue to apply the fair use doctrine to uses that do not fall neatly into the "transformative" rubric, but are nevertheless important aspects of users' rights. Examples include the transient digital copies that are incidental to valid uses, as well as time- and space-shifting for personal uses.

in fair use for themselves between 2005 and 2012, all have benefited from establishing a community understanding of how to employ their fair use rights. Documentary filmmakers, for example, changed business practice in their field; errors-and-omissions insurers, whose insurance is essential to distribution, now accept fair use claims routinely, as a direct result of the creation of such a code. Groups that followed in creating codes include K-12 teachers, open educational resources providers, dance archivists, film and communications scholars, and poets. No community has suffered a legal challenge for creating a code of best practices in fair use. Nor have members of any community with a code been sued successfully for actions taken within its scope.[10]

Exercising fair use is a right, not an obligation. There will always be situations in which those entitled to employ fair use may forgo use or obtain permission instead; people may, for instance, choose easy licensing or a continued low-friction business relationship over employing their fair use rights. Seeking selected permissions from known, reasonable, and responsive rights holders may be an appropriate risk management strategy for large-scale digitization or web archiving projects, for example, even when the fair use analysis seems favorable. But the choice to seek a license or ask permission should be an informed one.

Some librarians express concern that employing one's fair use rights in good faith may inadvertently make material available for potential misuse by others. But—just as they must now—all future users will have to engage in fair use analysis for themselves and in their own context. Libraries should of course be prepared to assist students and others who have questions about how to exercise their own rights with regard to library materials, but the ultimate responsibility will lie with the user, not the library. But—just as they do now—libraries that employ fair use responsibly to make material available to students, to researchers, or even to public view are unlikely to have legal liability for uninvited and inappropriate downstream uses.

Perfect safety and absolute certainty are extremely rare in copyright law, as in many areas of law, and of life. Rather than sit idle until risk is reduced to zero, institutions often employ "risk management," a healthy approach to policy making that seeks to enable important projects to go

---

[10] Documentary filmmakers won a high-profile dispute with Yoko Ono and EMI records over a parodic use of John Lennon's "Imagine." Fair use experts collaborated with the filmmakers to vet the film, and ultimately prevailed in a precedent-setting order that held the filmmakers had made a fair use of the song. Ono and EMI dropped their suit in light of the court's findings on fair use. See Lennon v. Premise Media, 2008 U.S. Dist. LEXIS 42489 (S.D.N.Y. June 2, 2008).

forward despite inevitable uncertainty by identifying possible risks (legal and otherwise) and reducing them to acceptable levels. This code of best practices should be of great assistance in arriving at rational risk management strategies, as it provides a more accurate picture of the risk (or lack thereof) associated with exercising legitimate fair use rights. Indeed, simply by articulating their consensus on this subject, academic and research librarians have already lowered the risk associated with these activities.[11]

CODE OF BEST PRACTICES IN FAIR USE FOR ACADEMIC AND RESEARCH LIBRARIES

GENERAL POINTS ABOUT THE PRINCIPLES

This code of best practices identifies eight sets of common current practices in the use of copyrighted materials in and around academic and research libraries, to which the doctrine of fair use can be applied. It articulates principles describing generally how and why fair use applies to each such practice or situation. Each principle is accompanied by a list of considerations that the library community believes should inform or qualify it: limitations that should be observed to assure that the case for fair use is strong, and enhancements that could further strengthen that case. Please note that enhancements represent what the community believes are additional practices that demonstrate "above and beyond" efforts to add value to existing material or accommodate the interests of other stakeholders; such measures are laudable when they will not cause undue hardship but are not prerequisite to support a strong fair use rationale.

Some of the limitations and suggested enhancements involve the use of technical protection measures (TPMs) to help ensure that material intended for a particular institutional audience is confined to that audience. In some circumstances, the use of TPMs may be a meaningful demonstration of "good faith" on the part of the library in question. However, TPMs come in many varieties; for a library's purposes, less obtrusive ones (password protection or watermarking) may be as or more appropriate than, for example, encryption.

---

[11] The law bars statutory damages for unauthorized reproduction of copyrighted works where employees of nonprofit educational institutions or libraries have "reasonable grounds for belief " that their use was fair, even if the court ultimately decides the use was not fair. See 17 U.S.C. 504(c)(2).

Because, in the opinion of some courts, fair use is sensitive to whether a use is undertaken in good faith, some of the principles include limitations or enhancements that address broader ethical concerns. While issues such as respecting privacy and including proper attribution may seem unrelated to copyright at first, they show good faith and serve the same overarching goals of responsible stewardship of library collections. These values are central to academic and research libraries, of course, but it is worth noting that by doing what comes naturally, libraries are also strengthening their fair use case.

In addition, the code refers at several points to providing copyright holders an opportunity to register concerns or complaints about a library's decision to employ fair use. The library community believes that engaging in such a process should not necessarily lead to automatic removal of content. Rather, it would trigger a conversation between the library and the rights holder, which would inform the institution's decision about whether to remove or maintain the material. Welcoming this interaction with a rights holder shows the library's good faith and provides an opportunity to develop voluntary arrangements that benefit all parties.

The fair use doctrine draws no blanket distinctions among different media or among different formats. Librarians felt strongly that except in narrow, specific instances, all kinds of content (e.g., text, image, audio-visual, music) should be subject to the same principles. Likewise, they did not distinguish generally between uses in various media. So, except as otherwise indicated, a digital copy should be considered on the same footing as an analog one for purposes of fair use.

The situations below concern the fair use of copyrighted materials, not the way the user acquires the copy from which she works. When a user's copy was obtained illegally or in bad faith, that fact may negatively affect fair use analysis; similarly, special contractual restrictions (such as conditions on the use of donated material) may circumscribe fair use. The principles therefore assume the library or user has obtained a copy in good faith and that it is not subject to conflicting license or contract restrictions.

While the principles address separate situations, in practice these areas are sure to overlap from time to time; some special collections will need digitizing for both scholarly access and preservation, for example, implicating both the third and fourth principles. Libraries should feel free to consult multiple principles to determine the best fair use rationale to apply to their specific situations.

ONE: SUPPORTING TEACHING AND LEARNING WITH ACCESS TO LIBRARY MATERIALS VIA DIGITAL TECHNOLOGIES

DESCRIPTION:

Academic and research libraries have a long, and largely noncontroversial, history of supporting classroom instruction by providing students with access to reading materials, especially via physical on-site reserves. Teachers, in turn, have depended on libraries to provide this important service. Today, students and teachers alike strongly prefer electronic equivalents (e-reserves for text, streaming for audio and video) to the old-media approaches to course support. Section 110(2) of the Copyright Act provides specific protection for some streaming and other uses, but it does not cover the entire variety of digital uses that are becoming increasingly important to twenty-first-century instruction. Over time, a set of practices has grown up around the related but distinct practice of providing students with physical "course packs," which typically occurs outside the library setting. The following principle is not intended to address that activity, but rather to focus on emerging digital uses in the library context. Fair use will play an important role in making these uses possible.

There are multiple bases on which these library uses can be considered fair ones. These modes of course support occur in a nonprofit educational environment, can be persuasively analogized to activities specifically authorized by Congress in Section 110 of the Copyright Act, may be supported by a "place-shifting" argument,[12] and are susceptible to a compelling transformativeness rationale. Most of the information objects made available to students, in whatever format, are not originally intended for educational use. For example, works intended for consumption as popular entertainment present a case for transformative repurposing when an instructor uses them (or excerpts from them) as the objects of commentary and criticism, or for purposes of illustration. Amounts of material used for online course support should be tailored to the educational purpose, though it will not infrequently be the case that access to the entire work (e.g., an illustrative song in a class on the history of popular music) will be necessary to fulfill the instructor's pedagogical purpose. It is also reasonable for works to be posted repeatedly from semester to semester to the extent that they are the most appropriate, relevant, and still timely materials for the course.

---

[12] Space-shifting is a theory of fair use often employed in the context of new technological uses of media. See, e.g., David Hansen, "Why Can't I Digitize My (Institution's) Library?," Scholarly Communications @ Duke, July 27, 2011, http://blogs.library.duke.edu/scholcomm/2011/07/27/whycan't-i-digitize-my-institution's-library.

PRINCIPLE:
It is fair use to make appropriately tailored course-related content available to enrolled students via digital networks.

LIMITATIONS:
- Closer scrutiny should be applied to uses of content created and marketed primarily for use in courses such as the one at issue (e.g., a textbook, workbook, or anthology designed for the course). Use of more than a brief excerpt from such works on digital networks is unlikely to be transformative and therefore unlikely to be a fair use.
- The availability of materials should be coextensive with the duration of the course or other time-limited use (e.g., a research project) for which they have been made available at an instructor's direction.
- Only eligible students and other qualified persons (e.g., professors' graduate assistants) should have access to materials.
- Materials should be made available only when, and only to the extent that, there is a clear articulable nexus between the instructor's pedagogical purpose and the kind and amount of content involved.
- Libraries should provide instructors with useful information about the nature and the scope of fair use, in order to help them make informed requests.
- When appropriate, the number of students with simultaneous access to online materials may be limited.
- Students should also be given information about their rights and responsibilities regarding their own use of course materials.
- Full attribution, in a form satisfactory to scholars in the field, should be provided for each work included or excerpted.

ENHANCEMENTS:
- The case for fair use is enhanced when libraries prompt instructors, who are most likely to understand the educational purpose and transformative nature of the use, to indicate briefly in writing why particular material is requested, and why the amount requested is appropriate to that pedagogical purpose. An instructor's justification can be expressed via standardized forms that provide a balanced menu of common or recurring fair use rationales.
- In order to assure the continuing relevance of those materials to course content, libraries should require instructors of recurrently offered courses to review posted materials and make updates as appropriate.

TWO: USING SELECTIONS FROM COLLECTION MATERIALS TO PUBLICIZE A LIBRARY'S ACTIVITIES, OR TO CREATE PHYSICAL AND VIRTUAL EXHIBITIONS

DESCRIPTION:

Academic and research libraries have always sought publicity of a certain kind—in order to introduce themselves, their services, and their valuable holdings to potential students, scholars, and others, as well as to attract donors of materials and to assure administrators and funders of their fidelity to mission. Just as libraries have chosen in the past to display their holdings through on-site exhibitions, or through in-house publications ranging from simple newsletters to glossy magazines, they now use the Internet as a tool for making themselves known. Library websites have become extremely important modes of access for library patrons, and most temporary physical exhibitions now have permanent virtual counterparts. While the lawfulness of past practices has been widely (and correctly) assumed, the use of new technology adds a new dimension to the issue. The wider audience that online exhibits reach, and the possibility of down-stream misuse, could lead librarians to avoid online uses, but in fact these uses can be just as fair as their physical counterparts.

Section 109(c) of the Copyright Act provides a safe harbor for certain on-site exhibits. However, exhibition and related illustrative uses, whether physical or virtual, can also be transformative. They highlight and public-ize library collections and stimulate interest in the individual original works of which they are comprised. Exhibits place original works in a new context to convey information and illustrate themes and ideas that can be quite different from those of the single work. Curation, in-line commen-tary, and juxtaposition add to the transformative nature of exhibits, dis-plays, and other illustrative uses.

PRINCIPLE:

It is fair use for a library to use appropriate selections from collection materials to increase public awareness and engagement with these collec-tions and to promote new scholarship drawing on them.

LIMITATIONS:

- Full attribution, in a form satisfactory to scholars in the field, should be provided for each work included or excerpted in an exhibit, to the extent it can be determined with reasonable effort.
- The amount of any particular work used and the format in which it is displayed should be appropriate to the illustrative purpose, i.e., tailored to support the goals of the exhibit or other illustrative project. The use of a

work (other than a single image) in its entirety is likely to require a special level of justification. Similarly, larger-scale, high-resolution images should be displayed only when appropriate to the pedagogical or illustrative purpose of the exhibit.

- This principle does not apply to the sale of souvenirs and other nonprint merchandise in connection with an exhibit.

ENHANCEMENTS:

- For publications such as catalogs of exhibitions, the case for fair use will be stronger when the material is offered to the public without charge, or on a cost recovery basis.
- Where library websites are concerned, fair use claims will be enhanced when libraries take technological steps, reasonable in light of both the nature of the material and of institutional capabilities, to discourage downloading.
- Fair use claims will be further enhanced when libraries provide copyright owners a simple tool for registering objections to use of copyrighted works, such as an e-mail address associated with a full-time employee.
- Fair use arguments will be enhanced when curation is overt and visible rather than implicit—for instance, when commentary is being provided on the illustrative objects, whether by means of express written or spoken commentary by critics or curators, through selection and juxtaposition of works in a larger context, or both. For example, when exhibited works and excerpts are viewable online in isolation from the larger exhibit or display, it may be helpful to use graphical cues or navigational elements to ensure that visitors who find the item via a deep link can perceive and easily move to the larger exhibit of which the item is a part.

THREE: DIGITIZING TO PRESERVE AT-RISK ITEMS

DESCRIPTION:

Preservation is a core function of academic and research libraries. It involves not only rescuing items from physical decay, but also coping with the rapid pace of change in media formats and reading technologies. Even when libraries retain the originals of preserved items, digital surrogates can spare the original items the wear and tear that access necessarily inflicts. Section 108 of the Copyright Act authorizes some preservation activities, but does not address some of today's most pressing needs: the preemptive preservation of physical materials that have not yet begun to deteriorate but are critically at risk of doing so, and the transfer to new formats of materials whose original formats (such as VHS magnetic tape) are not yet obsolete (as the term is narrowly defined in section 108(c)) but have become increasingly difficult for contemporary users to consult.

The primary purpose of preservation is indubitably beneficial and arguably strongly transformative: ensuring access to aspects of our cultural heritage for future generations, well past the limited term of copyright protection. Furthermore, responsible preservation is a necessary precursor for future scholarly use in a variety of transformative contexts, including criticism, commentary, and teaching. A broader, four-factor analysis further supports digital preservation: Its purpose is noncommercial and educational, the amount of the work used is appropriate to the purpose (preserving only parts of works would be unsatisfactory), the nature of the works will in many cases be scholarly nonfiction (although this may be less likely in the case of VHS tapes), and preservation in the absence of a suitable replacement copy has no negative effect on the potential market of the preserved work (indeed, preserving the work for posterity should have a positive effect, if any).

To justify the effort and expense of digital preservation, the works preserved will typically be unique, rare, or, in any event, out-of-commerce, and the library's activities therefore will not be mere substitutes for acquisition of a new digital copy of the work. Works in obscure, near-obsolete formats present access challenges as well as preservation ones, but the same fair use rationales will apply. Works trapped in decaying and increasingly obscure formats will disappear completely without diligent work from librarians to migrate them to usable formats.

PRINCIPLE:
It is fair use to make digital copies of collection items that are likely to deteriorate, or that exist only in difficult-to-access formats, for purposes of preservation, and to make those copies available as surrogates for fragile or otherwise inaccessible materials.

LIMITATIONS:
- Preservation copies should not be made when a fully equivalent digital copy is commercially available at a reasonable cost.
- Libraries should not provide access to or circulate original and preservation copies simultaneously.
- Off-premises access to preservation copies circulated as substitutes for original copies should be limited to authenticated members of a library's patron community, e.g., students, faculty, staff, affiliated scholars, and other accredited users.
- Full attribution, in a form satisfactory to scholars in the field, should be provided for all items made available online, to the extent it can be determined with reasonable effort.

ENHANCEMENTS:

- Fair use claims will be enhanced when libraries take technological steps to limit further redistribution of digital surrogates, e.g., by streaming audiovisual media, using appropriately lower-resolution versions, or using watermarks on textual materials and images.
- Fair use claims will be further enhanced when libraries provide copyright owners a simple tool for registering objections to use of digital surrogates, such as an e-mail address associated with a full-time employee.

FOUR: CREATING DIGITAL COLLECTIONS OF ARCHIVAL AND SPECIAL COLLECTIONS MATERIALS

DESCRIPTION:
Many libraries hold special collections and archives of rare or unusual text and nontext materials (published and unpublished) that do not circulate on the same terms as the general collection. The copyright status of materials in these collections is often unclear. Despite the investments that have been made in acquiring and preserving such collections, they frequently are of limited general utility because they typically can be consulted only on-site, and in some cases using only limited analog research aids. The research value of these collections typically resides not only in the individual items they contain (although such items are often unique in themselves), but also in the unique assemblage or aggregation they represent. Special collections can have a shared provenance or be organized around a key topic, era, or theme.

Libraries and their patrons would benefit significantly from digitization and off-site availability of these valuable collections. While institutions must abide by any donor restrictions applicable to their donated collections, and they will inevitably consider practical and political concerns such as maintaining good relations with donor communities, librarians will benefit significantly from knowing their rights under fair use.

Presenting these unique collections as a digital aggregate, especially with commentary, criticism, and other curation, can be highly transformative. Works held in these collections and archives will serve a host of transformative scholarly and educational purposes relative to their typically narrower original purposes.

Materials in special collections typically include significant amounts of primary sources and artifacts (correspondence, institutional records, annotated volumes, ephemeral popular entertainment) whose value as historical objects for scholarly research is significantly different from their original purpose. The new value created by aggregating related documents in a single, well-curated collection is also significant. In addition to access for scholarly purposes, digitization facilitates novel transformative uses of the collection as a whole—see principle seven below regarding digitization for search and other nonconsumptive uses.

PRINCIPLE:
It is fair use to create digital versions of a library's special collections and archives and to make these versions electronically accessible in appropriate contexts.

LIMITATIONS:
- Providing access to published works that are available in unused copies on the commercial market at reasonable prices should be undertaken only with careful consideration, if at all. To the extent that the copy of such a work in a particular collection is unique (e.g., contains marginalia or other unique markings or characteristics), access to unique aspects of the copy will be supportable under fair use. The presence of non-unique copies in a special collection can be indicated by descriptive entries without implicating copyright.
- Where digitized special collections are posted online, reasonable steps should be taken to limit access to material likely to contain damaging or sensitive private information.
- Full attribution, in a form satisfactory to scholars in the field, should be provided for all special collection items made available online, to the extent it is reasonably possible to do so.

ENHANCEMENTS:
- The fair use case will be even stronger where items to be digitized consist largely of works, such as personal photographs, correspondence, or ephemera, whose owners are not exploiting the material commercially and likely could not be located to seek permission for new uses.
- Libraries should consider taking technological steps, reasonable in light of both the nature of the material and of institutional capabilities, to prevent downloading of digital files by users, or else to limit the quality of files to what is appropriate to the use.
- Libraries should also provide copyright owners with a simple tool for registering objections to online use, and respond to such objections promptly.
- Subject to the considerations outlined above, a special collection should be digitized in its entirety, and presented as a cohesive collection whenever possible.
- Adding criticism, commentary, rich metadata, and other additional value and context to the collection will strengthen the fair use case.

- The fair use case will be stronger when the availability of the material is appropriately publicized to scholars in the field and other persons likely to be especially interested.

FIVE: REPRODUCING MATERIAL FOR USE BY DISABLED STUDENTS, FACULTY, STAFF, AND OTHER APPROPRIATE USERS

DESCRIPTION:

Print-disabled academic and research library patrons require access to readable text in order to function as full members of an academic community; likewise, hearing disabled patrons require captioned audiovisual materials, while those with physical disabilities may require the electronic delivery of materials outside the library setting.

Relatively new electronic technologies make these kinds of accommodations possible at relatively low cost. True accommodation for these patrons means access to any materials in the library's collection for any reason the patron may have (required reading, voluntary study, or recreation), i.e., access that is equivalent to the access afforded to students without disabilities. In addition to moral and mission-related imperatives to serve all patrons, there are also legal obligations to accommodate scholars and researchers with diverse needs. Although Section 121 of the Copyright Act authorizes the reproduction of copyrighted materials to meet these needs under some circumstances, there is continued controversy over its exact scope. Some stakeholders insist, however unreasonably, that Section 121 does not cover academic libraries' efforts to provide accessible materials to print-disabled members of a college or university community. No specific exception to copyright even arguably addresses the needs of patrons with disabilities related to media other than print.

Making library materials accessible serves the goals of copyright, not to mention the goals of a just and inclusive society, and has no negative consequence for rights holders who have not entered the market to serve these users. Such uses add value to a work by making it available to communities that would otherwise be excluded, presenting the work in a format the rights holder has not provided and to an audience that the rights holder is not serving. Making this material available to disabled patrons, furthermore, should not penalize other potential constituents, for instance, by removing the original copy for the time that the version for the disabled is available.

PRINCIPLE:
When fully accessible copies are not readily available from commercial sources, it is fair use for a library to (1) reproduce materials in its collection in accessible formats for the disabled upon request, and (2) retain those reproductions for use in meeting subsequent requests from qualified patrons.

LIMITATIONS:
- Libraries should provide patrons with information about their own rights and responsibilities regarding works provided to them in this way.
- When appropriate (taking into consideration the needs of the disabled patron), the requester's use of the materials should be time-limited by analogy to the limits the library imposes on use by other persons.
- Libraries should coordinate their response to requests with the university's disability services office, or the equivalent, and observe standard conventions on the identification of individuals entitled to service.

ENHANCEMENTS:
- Claims for fair use may well be further reinforced if technological protection measures are applied to assure that limitations on the use of accessible copies are observed.
- The fair use case will be enhanced by programs that are well publicized to the affected communities together with policies that are widely and consistently applied.

SIX: MAINTAINING THE INTEGRITY OF WORKS DEPOSITED IN INSTITUTIONAL REPOSITORIES

DESCRIPTION:
Many libraries that serve postsecondary institutions are developing digital institutional repositories (or IRs) that house and provide access to a variety of different kinds of material directly related to their institutions' activities, including scholarship of faculty and graduate students as well as documentation of institutional histories. The collection and maintenance of electronic theses and dissertations (ETDs) is a related issue. Access to ETDs and other material in IRs may be restricted to individuals with institutional affiliations, but many libraries aspire to make their contents available to the general public. Many deposited works quote or incorporate third-party material in ways that represent appropriate fair use by the faculty member or student in question. Librarians can and should respect the integrity of deposited materials that include selections from copyright works incorporated in reliance on fair use.

Use of quotations, still frames, illustrative excerpts, and the like is common practice in scholarly writing, and is at the heart of fair use. Libraries respect the authors' fair use rights when they accept these materials intact into the IR and make them available unchanged to the public. Libraries that operate IRs can and should respect and maintain the integrity of materials they accept for deposit, rather than insisting on unnecessary permissions or requiring unnecessary deletions. Fair use makes this possible. Many institutions use vendors to host and maintain ETDs and IRs, and libraries should work to ensure that vendors also respect authors' fair use rights.

PRINCIPLE:
It is fair use for a library to receive material for its institutional repository, and make deposited works publicly available in unredacted form, including items that contain copyrighted material that is included on the basis of fair use.

LIMITATIONS:
- In the case of publicly accessible IRs, libraries should provide copyright owners outside the institution with a simple tool for registering objections to the use of materials in the IR, and respond to such objections promptly.
- Libraries and their parent institutions should provide depositing authors with useful information about the nature and the scope of fair use, and the proper forms of attribution for incorporated materials, in order to help them make informed uses in their own work. This information should specifically address the fact that fair use is context-specific, and that what is fair use within the academy may not be fair use when a work is more broadly distributed.
- Full attribution, in a form satisfactory to scholars in the field, should be provided for all incorporated third-party materials included in works deposited to the IR, to the extent it is reasonably possible to do so.

ENHANCEMENTS:
- The fair use case will be stronger when institutions have developed or adopted a clear institutional policy about appropriate use of quotations, illustrations, etc., in faculty and student scholarship.
- Likewise, libraries may consider providing individualized advice on the appropriate use of copyrighted material in scholarship to members of the community upon request.

SEVEN: CREATING DATABASES TO FACILITATE NON CONSUMPTIVE RESEARCH USES (INCLUDING SEARCH)

DESCRIPTION:
In addition to making specific collection items available to patrons for intensive study, librarians have always played an important role in conducting and supporting scholarship in disciplines that examine trends and changes across broad swaths of information, e.g., information science, linguistics, bibliography, and history of science. Developing indexing systems and finding aids is also a core part of the library mission. Digital technology offers new possibilities where both of these traditional functions are concerned. Libraries can offer scholars digital databases of collection items on which to perform computerized analyses, and they themselves can employ such databases to develop new and powerful reference tools. Because they do not involve ordinary reading or viewing of the processed works, these uses are often referred to as nonconsumptive.

Nonconsumptive uses are highly transformative. Digitizing and indexing works for purposes such as statistical meta-analysis and search creates a powerful new scholarly resource that is not at all a mere substitute for the original work. The analyses facilitated by scanning for nonconsumptive use do not use the works for their original intended purposes; no person ever "reads" the underlying work or works. Instead, this kind of analysis focuses on the underlying facts about a collection of works (how many times a word appears across an author's body of work, how frequently scientists used a particular species of mouse as test subject, and so on) rather than the protected expression of any single work. Courts have found search engines, which copy millions of web pages into their indexed databases in order to help users find relevant sites, to be fair uses for precisely this reason.

Nonconsumptive uses are an emerging phenomenon at many libraries, and despite their obvious transformative character, there is a risk that the opportunity to make use of these techniques will be lost due to overly restrictive licensing provisions. If librarians agree to licensing restrictions that prohibit such uses, they lose their ability to exercise or permit others to exercise their fair use rights. Librarians should be mindful of this as they negotiate license agreements and should work to preserve their patrons' rights to conduct nonconsumptive research across licensed database materials.

PRINCIPLE:
It is fair use for libraries to develop and facilitate the development of digital databases of collection items to enable nonconsumptive analysis across the collection for both scholarly and reference purposes.

LIMITATION:
- Items in copyright digitized for nonconsumptive uses should not be employed in other ways (e.g., to provide digital access for ordinary reading) without independent justification, either by a license from the rights holder or pursuant to a statutory exception. Search access to database materials should be limited to portions appropriate to the nonconsumptive research purpose.

ENHANCEMENTS:
- The case for fair use will be at its strongest when the database includes information such as rich metadata that augments the research or reference value of its contents.
- Assertions of fair use will be particularly persuasive when libraries cooperate with other institutions to build collective databases that enable more extensive scholarship or reference searching.

EIGHT: COLLECTING MATERIAL POSTED ON THE WORLD WIDE WEB AND MAKING IT AVAILABLE

DESCRIPTION:
Gathering impressions of ephemeral Internet material such as web pages, online video, and the like is a growth area in academic and research library collection building, with activities typically focusing on areas in which the institution has an established specialty, or on sites specific to its local area. Such collections represent a unique contribution to knowledge and pose no significant risks for owners of either the sites in question or third-party material to which those sites refer. In the absence of such collections, important information is likely to be lost to scholarship.

Selecting and collecting material from the Internet in this way is highly transformative. The collecting library takes a historical snapshot of a dynamic and ephemeral object and places the collected impression of the site into a new context: a curated historical archive. Material posted to the Internet typically serves a time-limited purpose and targets a distinct network of users, while its library held counterpart will document the site for a wide variety of patrons over time. A scholar perusing a collection of archived web pages on the Free Tibet movement, or examining the evolution of educational information on a communicable disease, seeks and encounters that material for a very different purpose than the creators originally intended. Preserving such work can also be considered strongly transformative in itself, separate from any way that future patrons may access it.

Authors of online materials often have a specific objective and a particular audience in mind; libraries that collect this material serve a different and broader purpose and a different and broader network of users. Libraries collect not only for a wide range of purposes today, but also for unanticipated uses by future researchers.

PRINCIPLE:
It is fair use to create topically based collections of websites and other material from the Internet and to make them available for scholarly use.

LIMITATIONS:
- Captured material should be represented as it was captured, with appropriate information on mode of harvesting and date.
- To the extent reasonably possible, the legal proprietors of the sites in question should be identified according to the prevailing conventions of attribution.
- Libraries should provide copyright owners with a simple tool for registering objections to making items from such a collection available online, and respond to such objections promptly.

ENHANCEMENTS:
- Claims of fair use relating to material posted with "bot exclusion" headers to ward off automatic harvesting may be stronger when the institution has adopted and follows a consistent policy on this issue, taking into account the possible rationales for collecting Internet material and the nature of the material in question.
- The more comprehensive a collection of web impressions in a given topic area is, the more persuasively the inclusion of any given item can be characterized as fair use.

COORDINATING ORGANIZATIONS:

The Association of Research Libraries (ARL) is a nonprofit organization of 126 research libraries at comprehensive, research-extensive institutions in the U.S. and Canada that share similar research missions, aspirations, and achievements. The association's importance and distinction is born from its membership and the nature of the institutions represented. ARL member libraries make up a large portion of the academic and research library marketplace, spending more than $1 billion every year on library materials.

The Program on Information Justice and Intellectual Property (PIJIP), cofounded by Prof. Peter Jaszi, promotes social justice in law governing information dissemination and intellectual property through research, scholarship, public events, advocacy, and provision of legal and consulting services. The program is a project of the Washington College of Law at American University in Washington, D.C.

The Center for Social Media (CSM), founded and led by Prof. Patricia Aufderheide, has run the Fair Use and Free Speech project in coordination with PIJIP and Prof. Jaszi since 2004. The center is a project of the School of Communication at American University in Washington, D.C.

CO-FACILITATORS:

Prudence S. Adler, Associate Executive Director, Federal Relations and Information Policy, Association of Research Libraries

Patricia Aufderheide, University Professor, American University School of Communication

Brandon Butler, Director of Public Policy Initiatives, Association of Research Libraries

Peter Jaszi, Professor of Law, American University Washington College of Law

ENDORSERS:

The American Library Association
The Association of College and Research Librarians

LEGAL ADVISORY BOARD:

Jamie B. Bischoff, Partner, Ballard Spahr LLP

William W. Fisher III, Hale and Dorr Professor of Intellectual Property Law, Harvard University

Michael J. Madison, Professor of Law, University of Pittsburgh School of Law

Steven J. McDonald, General Counsel, Rhode Island School of Design

Kevin L. Smith, Director of Scholarly Communications, Duke University Libraries

Special thanks to Carrie Russell and Kara Malenfant for their help with outreach to the librarian community; to Jonathan Band, Sharon Farb, and Peter Hirtle for their conscientious counsel; and to all the librarians and library directors who gave so generously of their time and insight in interviews and discussion sessions over the last two years.

FUNDED BY:

The Andrew W. Mellon Foundation

Appendix N
SAMPLE LAW JOURNAL
AUTHOR AGREEMENT (2011)*
ঔোঙ

The following is an agreement (this "Agreement") between _____, referred to as the "Author," and the _____, referred to as the "Journal," and pertains to the article entitled "[TITLE]," referred to as the "Work." In consideration of their promises, the Author and the Journal agree as follows:

1. **Author's Grant of Rights**
a. Except as provided in Paragraphs 1(c) and 2(b), the Author grants to the Journal a license to reproduce and distribute the Work in the Journal, in facsimile reprints or microforms, as a contribution to a collection of works published by the Journal, by means of an Internet or Intranet site over which the Journal exercises effective control, and by means of a third-party online legal information provider, such as, but not limited to, LEXIS-NEXIS, Westlaw, JSTOR, HEIN Online, the NELLCO Scholarship Repository, the Washington & Lee Law School Journal Database, and the Journal's official Website.
b. The Journal's license provided in Paragraph 1(a) shall be (i) exclusive for a period beginning when this Agreement is executed and ending on the earlier of one (1) year after publication of the Work in the Journal or eighteen (18) months after execution of this Agreement, and (ii) nonexclusive thereafter.

---

* This sample agreement is from Michael N. Widener, *Safeguarding "The Precious": Counsel on Law Journal Publication Agreements in Digital Times*, 28 J. MARSHALL J. COMPUTER & INFO. L. 217, 247 (2010), *available at* http://ssrn.com/abstract=1674162, and is reproduced here with the author's permission. It is written for an academic law journal, but covers the important contractual issues for most publications. Footnotes omitted.

c.   The Journal's license to reproduce the Work includes the right to prepare a translation in any language or to authorize the preparation of such a translation, but such right is subject to the Author's approval of the translation, which is not to be unreasonably withheld or delayed.

d.   After the Work has been published in the Journal, the Journal shall have a non-exclusive license to authorize another party to reproduce and distribute the Work in the forms specified in Paragraph 1(a).

e.   The Author grants this license to the Journal without claim of royalties or any other compensation.

2. Author's Ownership of Copyright and Reservation of Rights

a.   The copyright in the Work shall remain with the Author.

b.   The Author retains the rights:

i.   In any format, to reproduce and distribute the Work, and to authorize others to reproduce and distribute the Work, to students for educational purposes;

ii.   To include the Work, in whole or part, in another work of which the Author is an author or editor, provided that in either circumstance the Author may not submit a work for publication that is substantially the same as the Work to another periodical, without the permission of the Journal, earlier than one (1) year after publication of the Work or eighteen (18) months after execution of this Agreement, whichever first shall occur, and provided further that the subsequent work identifies the Author, the Journal, the volume, the number of the first page, and the year of the Work's publication in the Journal.

iii. To post the Work, in whole or in part, on an Internet or Intranet site (a) over which the Author has effective control (such as a personal Website with digitized images), or (b) on a site maintained for individual authors such as those established by www. bepress.com/ir/ [Digital Commons] or SSRN), or (c) on a site (such as the repository of a law school in the manner of "Legal Studies/Research Paper Series") specific to the Author's academic or research institution; provided, that in any such event, such posting of the Work shall identify the Author, the Journal, the volume, the number of the first page, and the year of the Work's first publication in the Journal.

iv.   To incorporate or embed the Work, in whole or part, within any future Internet architecture facilitating public dissemination of content for "open access," so long as that architecture does not compete for revenue-generation with a for-profit content provider with whom the Journal currently contracts for replication and content-provision of written works like the Work.

3. Publication by Others

The Journal shall have the non-exclusive license to authorize another party to reproduce and distribute the Work in a form besides those specified in Paragraph 1(a), provided that (i) such reproduction identifies the Author, the Journal, the volume, the number of the Work's first page, and the year of the Work's publication in the Journal, (ii) the Author has been notified in writing by the Journal of its intent to authorize such reproduction and distribution not less than thirty (30) days prior to the grant of such authorization and (iii) the Author has not, within thirty (30) days after actual receipt of Journal's notice, notified the Journal of the Author's objection to the reproduction and distribution referenced in the notice.

4. Author's Warranties and Undertakings

a. The Author warrants that to the best of the Author's knowledge:
   i. The Author is the sole author of the Work and has the power to convey the rights granted in this Agreement;
   ii. The Work has not previously been published, in whole or in part, except that it has been posted (and may be re-posted) on [the Social Science Research Network Website (http://ssrn.com/)] [or the Berkeley Electronic Press Digital Commons Website (http://www.bepress.com/ir)];
   iii. The Work does not infringe the copyright or property right of another; and
   iv. The Work does not contain content that (a) is defamatory, or (b) violates the rights of privacy and of publicity or other legal right of another, or (c) is contrary to any law or public policy of the State.
b. If the Work reproduces any textual or graphic material that is the property of another for which permission is required, the Author shall, if requested by the Journal, obtain written consent to such reproduction.

5. Litigation

a. If a claim is asserted against the Journal as a result of the Author's alleged breach of this Agreement or his warranties, the Author shall be promptly notified. The Author shall have the right to participate in the Journal's response to and defenses against any claim, and the Journal shall not settle such claim without the Author's approval. If a settlement requires the Journal to make a money payment, or a money judgment is rendered against the Journal, the Author shall reimburse the

Journal for the amount of such payment or judgment, and shall pay the costs and expenses reasonably incurred by the Journal in responding the claim.

b. The Journal shall have the power, after giving notice to the Author, to initiate legal proceedings against persons or entities believed to be infringing the licensed rights hereby granted by the Author to the Journal. The Author agrees to cooperate reasonably in the institution and maintenance of such proceedings. Damages recovered in such proceedings shall first reimburse the Journal's costs and expenses actually incurred in the proceedings, and the balance (if any) shall first reimburse the Author's costs and expenses in assisting the Journal in the prosecution of the Journal's claim.

6. Editing and Printing

a. The Author authorizes the Journal to edit and revise the Work prior to publication in the Journal, but the Work shall not be published by the Journal unless it is acceptable in its final form to each of the Author and the Journal. After its print publication, the Journal shall not alter the Work's substance without the prior written consent of the Author in each instance.

b. The Author agrees to harmonize all citations in the Work (to the best of his ability with the aid of the Journal's editors) to the rules found in the most recent edition of The Bluebook: A Uniform System of Citation; and the parties mutually agree to use commercially reasonable efforts to create a timely, first-class quality, publishable work.

c. Promptly upon any print publication, the Journal shall give the Author, without charge, 25 offprint copies of the printed Work and, if requested by the Author, additional copies at a per-copy cost to be determined by the Journal in its reasonable discretion. Promptly upon publication in any non-print medium, the Journal shall afford the Author cost-free access to the medium (by affording access codes or security passwords or "keys") such that the Work can be downloaded and then "uploaded" to the Author's personal archives or institutional-affiliate repository, as the case may be.

7. Sole Agreement, Modifications, Time Essential & Governing Law

This Agreement constitutes the sole agreement between the Author and the Journal with respect to the publication and copyright of the Work. Any modifications of or additions to the terms of this Agreement shall be in writing and signed by the parties. Time is of the essence in respect to each term of this Agreement. This Agreement shall be governed in its interpretation and enforcement by the laws of the State of _____.

Author's Signature: _____

Author's Printed Name: _____

Date: _____, 201_

Journal Representative's Signature: _____

Representative's Printed Name: _____

Date: _____, 201_

Appendix O
SELECTED PROVISIONS FROM THE U.S. COPYRIGHT ACT (TITLE 17, UNITED STATES CODE)

ВЭСЯ

§ 101. Definitions
Except as otherwise provided in this title, as used in this title, the following terms and their variant forms mean the following:

***

"Audiovisual works" are works that consist of a series of related images which are intrinsically intended to be shown by the use of machines, or devices such as projectors, viewers, or electronic equipment, together with accompanying sounds, if any, regardless of the nature of the material objects, such as films or tapes, in which the works are embodied.

The "Berne Convention" is the Convention for the Protection of Literary and Artistic Works, signed at Berne, Switzerland, on September 9, 1886, and all acts, protocols, and revisions thereto.

***

A "collective work" is a work, such as a periodical issue, anthology, or encyclopedia, in which a number of contributions, constituting separate and independent works in themselves, are assembled into a collective whole.

A "compilation" is a work formed by the collection and assembling of preexisting materials or of data that are selected, coordinated, or arranged in such a way that the resulting work as a whole constitutes an original work of authorship. The term "compilation" includes collective works.

A "computer program" is a set of statements or instructions to be used directly or indirectly in a computer in order to bring about a certain result.

"Copies" are material objects, other than phonorecords, in which a work is fixed by any method now known or later developed, and from which the work can be perceived, reproduced, or otherwise communicated, either directly or with the aid of a machine or device. The term "copies" includes the material object, other than a phonorecord, in which the work is first fixed.

***

"Copyright owner", with respect to any one of the exclusive rights comprised in a copyright, refers to the owner of that particular right.

A work is "created" when it is fixed in a copy or phonorecord for the first time; where a work is prepared over a period of time, the portion of it that has been fixed at any particular time constitutes the work as of that time, and where the work has been prepared in different versions, each version constitutes a separate work.

A "derivative work" is a work based upon one or more preexisting works, such as a translation, musical arrangement, dramatization, fictionalization, motion picture version, sound recording, art reproduction, abridgment, condensation, or any other form in which a work may be recast, transformed, or adapted. A work consisting of editorial revisions, annotations, elaborations, or other modifications which, as a whole, represent an original work of authorship, is a "derivative work".

***

To "display" a work means to show a copy of it, either directly or by means of a film, slide, television image, or any other device or process or, in the case of a motion picture or other audiovisual work, to show individual images nonsequentially.

***

A work is "fixed" in a tangible medium of expression when its embodiment in a copy or phonorecord, by or under the authority of the author, is sufficiently permanent or stable to permit it to be perceived, reproduced, or otherwise communicated for a period of more than transitory duration. A work consisting of sounds, images, or both, that are being transmitted, is "fixed" for purposes of this title if a fixation of the work is being made simultaneously with its transmission.

***

To "perform" a work means to recite, render, play, dance, or act it, either directly or by means of any device or process or, in the case of a motion picture or other audiovisual work, to show its images in any sequence or to make the sounds accompanying it audible.

***

"Publication" is the distribution of copies or phonorecords of a work to the public by sale or other transfer of ownership, or by rental, lease, or lending. The offering to distribute copies or phonorecords to a group of persons for purposes of further distribution, public performance, or public display, constitutes publication. A public performance or display of a work does not of itself constitute publication.

To perform or display a work "publicly" means—
(1) to perform or display it at a place open to the public or at any place where a substantial number of persons outside of a normal circle of a family and its social acquaintances is gathered; or
(2) to transmit or otherwise communicate a performance or display of the work to a place specified by clause (1) or to the public, by means of any device or process, whether the members of the public capable of receiving the performance or display receive it in the same place or in separate places and at the same time or at different times.

***

A "transfer of copyright ownership" is an assignment, mortgage, exclusive license, or any other conveyance, alienation, or hypothecation of a copyright or of any of the exclusive rights comprised in a copyright, whether or not it is limited in time or place of effect, but not including a nonexclusive license.

***

A "work made for hire" is—
(1) a work prepared by an employee within the scope of his or her employment; or
(2) a work specially ordered or commissioned for use as a contribution to a collective work, as a part of a motion picture or other audiovisual work, as a translation, as a supplementary work, as a compilation, as

an instructional text, as a test, as answer material for a test, or as an atlas, if the parties expressly agree in a written instrument signed by them that the work shall be considered a work made for hire. For the purpose of the foregoing sentence, a "supplementary work" is a work prepared for publication as a secondary adjunct to a work by another author for the purpose of introducing, concluding, illustrating, explaining, revising, commenting upon, or assisting in the use of the other work, such as forewords, afterwords, pictorial illustrations, maps, charts, tables, editorial notes, musical arrangements, answer material for tests, bibliographies, appendixes, and indexes, and an "instructional text" is a literary, pictorial, or graphic work prepared for publication and with the purpose of use in systematic instructional activities [...]

***

§ 102. Subject Matter of Copyright: In General

(a) Copyright protection subsists, in accordance with this title, in original works of authorship fixed in any tangible medium of expression, now known or later developed, from which they can be perceived, reproduced, or otherwise communicated, either directly or with the aid of a machine or device. Works of authorship include the following categories:

(1) literary works;

(2) musical works, including any accompanying words;

(3) dramatic works, including any accompanying music;

(4) pantomimes and choreographic works;

(5) pictorial, graphic, and sculptural works;

(6) motion pictures and other audiovisual works;

(7) sound recordings; and

(8) architectural works.

(b) In no case does copyright protection for an original work of authorship extend to any idea, procedure, process, system, method of operation, concept, principle, or discovery, regardless of the form in which it is described, explained, illustrated, or embodied in such work.

§ 103. Subject Matter of Copyright: Compilations and Derivative Works

(a) The subject matter of copyright as specified by section 102 includes compilations and derivative works, but protection for a work employing preexisting material in which copyright subsists does not extend to any part of the work in which such material has been used unlawfully.

(b) The copyright in a compilation or derivative work extends only to the material contributed by the author of such work, as distinguished from the preexisting material employed in the work, and does not imply any exclusive right in the preexisting material. The copyright in such work is independent of, and does not affect or enlarge the scope, duration, ownership, or subsistence of, any copyright protection in the pre-existing material.

§ 104. Subject Matter of Copyright: National Origin

(a) Unpublished Works.— The works specified by sections 102 and 103, while unpublished, are subject to protection under this title without regard to the nationality or domicile of the author.

(b) Published Works.— The works specified by sections 102 and 103, when published, are subject to protection under this title if—

    (1) on the date of first publication, one or more of the authors is a national or domiciliary of the United States, or is a national, domiciliary, or sovereign authority of a treaty party, or is a stateless person, wherever that person may be domiciled; or

    (2) the work is first published in the United States or in a foreign nation that, on the date of first publication, is a treaty party; or

    (3) the work is a sound recording that was first fixed in a treaty party; or

    (4) the work is a pictorial, graphic, or sculptural work that is incorporated in a building or other structure, or an architectural work that is embodied in a building and the building or structure is located in the United States or a treaty party; or

    (5) the work is first published by the United Nations or any of its specialized agencies, or by the Organization of American States; or

    (6) the work comes within the scope of a Presidential proclamation. Whenever the President finds that a particular foreign nation extends, to works by authors who are nationals or domiciliaries of the United States or to works that are first published in the United States, copyright protection on substantially the same basis as that on which the foreign nation extends protection to works of its own nationals and domiciliaries and works first published in that nation, the President may by proclamation extend protection under this title to works of which one or more of the authors is, on the date of first publication, a national, domiciliary, or sovereign

authority of that nation, or which was first published in that nation. The President may revise, suspend, or revoke any such proclamation or impose any conditions or limitations on protection under a proclamation.

For purposes of paragraph (2), a work that is published in the United States or a treaty party within 30 days after publication in a foreign nation that is not a treaty party shall be considered to be first published in the United States or such treaty party, as the case may be.

(c) Effect of Berne Convention.— No right or interest in a work eligible for protection under this title may be claimed by virtue of, or in reliance upon, the provisions of the Berne Convention, or the adherence of the United States thereto. Any rights in a work eligible for protection under this title that derive from this title, other Federal or State statutes, or the common law, shall not be expanded or reduced by virtue of, or in reliance upon, the provisions of the Berne Convention, or the adherence of the United States thereto.

(d) Effect of Phonograms Treaties.— Notwithstanding the provisions of subsection (b), no works other than sound recordings shall be eligible for protection under this title solely by virtue of the adherence of the United States to the Geneva Phonograms Convention or the WIPO Performances and Phonograms Treaty.

§ 105. Subject Matter of Copyright: United States Government Works

Copyright protection under this title is not available for any work of the United States Government, but the United States Government is not precluded from receiving and holding copyrights transferred to it by assignment, bequest, or otherwise.

§ 106. Exclusive Rights in Copyrighted Works

Subject to sections 107 through 122, the owner of copyright under this title has the exclusive rights to do and to authorize any of the following:

(1) to reproduce the copyrighted work in copies or phonorecords;

(2) to prepare derivative works based upon the copyrighted work;

(3) to distribute copies or phonorecords of the copyrighted work to the public by sale or other transfer of ownership, or by rental, lease, or lending;

(4) in the case of literary, musical, dramatic, and choreographic works, pantomimes, and motion pictures and other audiovisual works, to perform the copyrighted work publicly;

(5) in the case of literary, musical, dramatic, and choreographic works, pantomimes, and pictorial, graphic, or sculptural works, including the individual images of a motion picture or other audiovisual work, to display the copyrighted work publicly; and

(6) in the case of sound recordings, to perform the copyrighted work publicly by means of a digital audio transmission.

§ 107. Limitations on Exclusive Rights: Fair Use

Notwithstanding the provisions of sections 106 and 106A, the fair use of a copyrighted work, including such use by reproduction in copies or phonorecords or by any other means specified by that section, for purposes such as criticism, comment, news reporting, teaching (including multiple copies for classroom use), scholarship, or research, is not an infringement of copyright. In determining whether the use made of a work in any particular case is a fair use the factors to be considered shall include—

(1) the purpose and character of the use, including whether such use is of a commercial nature or is for nonprofit educational purposes;

(2) the nature of the copyrighted work;

(3) the amount and substantiality of the portion used in relation to the copyrighted work as a whole; and

(4) the effect of the use upon the potential market for or value of the copyrighted work.

The fact that a work is unpublished shall not itself bar a finding of fair use if such finding is made upon consideration of all the above factors.

§ 108. Limitations on Exclusive Rights: Reproduction by Libraries and Archives

(a) Except as otherwise provided in this title and notwithstanding the provisions of section 106, it is not an infringement of copyright for a library or archives, or any of its employees acting within the scope of their employment, to reproduce no more than one copy or phonorecord of a work, except as provided in subsections (b) and (c), or to distribute such copy or phonorecord, under the conditions specified by this section, if—

(1) the reproduction or distribution is made without any purpose of direct or indirect commercial advantage;

(2) the collections of the library or archives are (i) open to the public, or (ii) available not only to researchers affiliated with the library or archives or with the institution of which it is a part, but also to other persons doing research in a specialized field; and

(3) the reproduction or distribution of the work includes a notice of copyright that appears on the copy or phonorecord that is reproduced under the provisions of this section, or includes a legend stating that the work may be protected by copyright if no such notice can be found on the copy or phonorecord that is reproduced under the provisions of this section.

(b) The rights of reproduction and distribution under this section apply to three copies or phonorecords of an unpublished work duplicated solely for purposes of preservation and security or for deposit for research use in another library or archives of the type described by clause (2) of subsection (a), if—

(1) the copy or phonorecord reproduced is currently in the collections of the library or archives; and

(2) any such copy or phonorecord that is reproduced in digital format is not otherwise distributed in that format and is not made available to the public in that format outside the premises of the library or archives.

(c) The right of reproduction under this section applies to three copies or phonorecords of a published work duplicated solely for the purpose of replacement of a copy or phonorecord that is damaged, deteriorating, lost, or stolen, or if the existing format in which the work is stored has become obsolete, if—

(1) the library or archives has, after a reasonable effort, determined that an unused replacement cannot be obtained at a fair price; and

(2) any such copy or phonorecord that is reproduced in digital format is not made available to the public in that format outside the premises of the library or archives in lawful possession of such copy.

For purposes of this subsection, a format shall be considered obsolete if the machine or device necessary to render perceptible a work stored in that format is no longer manufactured or is no longer reasonably available in the commercial marketplace.

(d) The rights of reproduction and distribution under this section apply to a copy, made from the collection of a library or archives where the user makes his or her request or from that of another library or archives, of no more than one article or other contribution to a copyrighted collection or periodical issue, or to a copy or phonorecord of a small part of any other copyrighted work, if—

(1) the copy or phonorecord becomes the property of the user, and the library or archives has had no notice that the copy or phonorecord would be used for any purpose other than private study, scholarship, or research; and

(2) the library or archives displays prominently, at the place where orders are accepted, and includes on its order form, a warning of copyright in accordance with requirements that the Register of Copyrights shall prescribe by regulation.

(e) The rights of reproduction and distribution under this section apply to the entire work, or to a substantial part of it, made from the collection of a library or archives where the user makes his or her request or from that of another library or archives, if the library or archives has first determined, on the basis of a reasonable investigation, that a copy or phonorecord of the copyrighted work cannot be obtained at a fair price, if—

(1) the copy or phonorecord becomes the property of the user, and the library or archives has had no notice that the copy or phonorecord would be used for any purpose other than private study, scholarship, or research; and

(2) the library or archives displays prominently, at the place where orders are accepted, and includes on its order form, a warning of copyright in accordance with requirements that the Register of Copyrights shall prescribe by regulation.

(f) Nothing in this section—

(1) shall be construed to impose liability for copyright infringement upon a library or archives or its employees for the unsupervised use of reproducing equipment located on its premises: Provided, That such equipment displays a notice that the making of a copy may be subject to the copyright law;

(2) excuses a person who uses such reproducing equipment or who requests a copy or phonorecord under subsection (d) from liability for copyright infringement for any such act, or for any later use of such copy or phonorecord, if it exceeds fair use as provided by section 107;

(3) shall be construed to limit the reproduction and distribution by lending of a limited number of copies and excerpts by a library or archives of an audiovisual news program, subject to clauses (1), (2), and (3) of subsection (a); or

(4) in any way affects the right of fair use as provided by section 107, or any contractual obligations assumed at any time by the library or archives when it obtained a copy or phonorecord of a work in its collections.

(g) The rights of reproduction and distribution under this section extend to the isolated and unrelated reproduction or distribution of a single copy or phonorecord of the same material on separate occasions, but do not extend to cases where the library or archives, or its employee—

  (1) is aware or has substantial reason to believe that it is engaging in the related or concerted reproduction or distribution of multiple copies or phonorecords of the same material, whether made on one occasion or over a period of time, and whether intended for aggregate use by one or more individuals or for separate use by the individual members of a group; or

  (2) engages in the systematic reproduction or distribution of single or multiple copies or phonorecords of material described in subsection (d): Provided, That nothing in this clause prevents a library or archives from participating in interlibrary arrangements that do not have, as their purpose or effect, that the library or archives receiving such copies or phonorecords for distribution does so in such aggregate quantities as to substitute for a subscription to or purchase of such work.

(h) (1) For purposes of this section, during the last 20 years of any term of copyright of a published work, a library or archives, including a nonprofit educational institution that functions as such, may reproduce, distribute, display, or perform in facsimile or digital form a copy or phonorecord of such work, or portions thereof, for purposes of preservation, scholarship, or research, if such library or archives has first determined, on the basis of a reasonable investigation, that none of the conditions set forth in subparagraphs (A), (B), and (C) of paragraph (2) apply.

  (2) No reproduction, distribution, display, or performance is authorized under this subsection if—

  (A) the work is subject to normal commercial exploitation;

  (B) a copy or phonorecord of the work can be obtained at a reasonable price; or

  (C) the copyright owner or its agent provides notice pursuant to regulations promulgated by the Register of Copyrights that either of the conditions set forth in subparagraphs (A) and (B) applies.

  (3) The exemption provided in this subsection does not apply to any subsequent uses by users other than such library or archives.

  (i) The rights of reproduction and distribution under this section do not apply to a musical work, a pictorial, graphic or sculptural work, or a motion picture or other audiovisual work other than an audiovisual work dealing with news, except that no such limitation shall apply with respect to rights granted by subsections (b), (c), and (h), or with respect to pictorial or graphic works published as illustrations, diagrams, or similar adjuncts to works of which copies are reproduced or distributed in accordance with subsections (d) and (e).

§ 109. Limitations on Exclusive Rights: Effect of Transfer of Particular Copy or Phonorecord

(a) Notwithstanding the provisions of section 106 (3), the owner of a particular copy or phonorecord lawfully made under this title, or any person authorized by such owner, is entitled, without the authority of the copyright owner, to sell or otherwise dispose of the possession of that copy or phonorecord. Notwithstanding the preceding sentence, copies or phonorecords of works subject to restored copyright under section 104A that are manufactured before the date of restoration of copyright or, with respect to reliance parties, before publication or service of notice under section 104A (e), may be sold or otherwise disposed of without the authorization of the owner of the restored copyright for purposes of direct or indirect commercial advantage only during the 12-month period beginning on—

   (1) the date of the publication in the Federal Register of the notice of intent filed with the Copyright Office under section 104A (d)(2)(A), or

   (2) the date of the receipt of actual notice served under section 104A (d)(2)(B),

   whichever occurs first.

(b) (1) (A) Notwithstanding the provisions of subsection (a), unless authorized by the owners of copyright in the sound recording or the owner of copyright in a computer program (including any tape, disk, or other medium embodying such program), and in the case of a sound recording in the musical works embodied therein, neither the owner of a particular phonorecord nor any person in possession of a particular copy of a computer program (including any tape, disk, or other medium embodying such program), may, for the purposes of direct or indirect commercial advantage, dispose of, or authorize the disposal of, the possession of that phonorecord or computer program (including any tape, disk, or other medium embodying such program) by rental, lease, or lending, or by any other act or practice in the nature of rental, lease, or lending. Nothing in the preceding sentence shall apply to the rental, lease, or lending of a phonorecord for nonprofit purposes by a nonprofit library or nonprofit educational institution. The transfer of possession of a lawfully made copy of a computer program by a nonprofit educational institution to another nonprofit educational institution or to faculty, staff, and students does not constitute rental, lease, or lending for direct or indirect commercial purposes under this subsection.

(B) This subsection does not apply to—

    (i) a computer program which is embodied in a machine or product and which cannot be copied during the ordinary operation or use of the machine or product; or

    (ii) a computer program embodied in or used in conjunction with a limited purpose computer that is designed for playing video games and may be designed for other purposes.

(C) Nothing in this subsection affects any provision of chapter 9 of this title.

(2) (A) Nothing in this subsection shall apply to the lending of a computer program for nonprofit purposes by a nonprofit library, if each copy of a computer program which is lent by such library has affixed to the packaging containing the program a warning of copyright in accordance with requirements that the Register of Copyrights shall prescribe by regulation.

***

(4) Any person who distributes a phonorecord or a copy of a computer program (including any tape, disk, or other medium embodying such program) in violation of paragraph (1) is an infringer of copyright under section 501 of this title and is subject to the remedies set forth in sections 502, 503, 504, and 505. Such violation shall not be a criminal offense under section 506 or cause such person to be subject to the criminal penalties set forth in section 2319 of title 18.

(c) Notwithstanding the provisions of section 106 (5), the owner of a particular copy lawfully made under this title, or any person authorized by such owner, is entitled, without the authority of the copyright owner, to display that copy publicly, either directly or by the projection of no more than one image at a time, to viewers present at the place where the copy is located.

(d) The privileges prescribed by subsections (a) and (c) do not, unless authorized by the copyright owner, extend to any person who has acquired possession of the copy or phonorecord from the copyright owner, by rental, lease, loan, or otherwise, without acquiring ownership of it.

***

§ 110. Limitations on Exclusive Rights: Exemption of Certain Performances and Displays

Notwithstanding the provisions of section 106, the following are not infringements of copyright:

(1) performance or display of a work by instructors or pupils in the course of face-to-face teaching activities of a nonprofit educational institution, in a classroom or similar place devoted to instruction, unless, in the case of a motion picture or other audiovisual work, the performance, or the display of individual images, is given by means of a copy that was not lawfully made under this title, and that the person responsible for the performance knew or had reason to believe was not lawfully made;

(2) except with respect to a work produced or marketed primarily for performance or display as part of mediated instructional activities transmitted via digital networks, or a performance or display that is given by means of a copy or phonorecord that is not lawfully made and acquired under this title, and the transmitting government body or accredited nonprofit educational institution knew or had reason to believe was not lawfully made and acquired, the performance of a nondramatic literary or musical work or reasonable and limited portions of any other work, or display of a work in an amount comparable to that which is typically displayed in the course of a live classroom session, by or in the course of a transmission, if—

(A) the performance or display is made by, at the direction of, or under the actual supervision of an instructor as an integral part of a class session offered as a regular part of the systematic mediated instructional activities of a governmental body or an accredited nonprofit educational institution;

(B) the performance or display is directly related and of material assistance to the teaching content of the transmission;

(C) the transmission is made solely for, and, to the extent technologically feasible, the reception of such transmission is limited to—

(i) students officially enrolled in the course for which the transmission is made; or

(ii) officers or employees of governmental bodies as a part of their official duties or employment; and

(D) the transmitting body or institution—

(i) institutes policies regarding copyright, provides informational materials to faculty, students, and relevant staff members that accurately describe, and promote compliance with, the laws of the United States relating to copyright, and provides notice to students that materials used in connection with the course may be subject to copyright protection; and

    (ii) in the case of digital transmissions—

        (I) applies technological measures that reasonably prevent—

            (aa) retention of the work in accessible form by recipients of the transmission from the transmitting body or institution for longer than the class session; and

            (bb) unauthorized further dissemination of the work in accessible form by such recipients to others; and

        (II) does not engage in conduct that could reasonably be expected to interfere with technological measures used by copyright owners to prevent such retention or unauthorized further dissemination;

(3) performance of a nondramatic literary or musical work or of a dramatico-musical work of a religious nature, or display of a work, in the course of services at a place of worship or other religious assembly;

(4) performance of a nondramatic literary or musical work otherwise than in a transmission to the public, without any purpose of direct or indirect commercial advantage and without payment of any fee or other compensation for the performance to any of its performers, promoters, or organizers, if—

(A) there is no direct or indirect admission charge; or

(B) the proceeds, after deducting the reasonable costs of producing the performance, are used exclusively for educational, religious, or charitable purposes and not for private financial gain, except where the copyright owner has served notice of objection to the performance under the following conditions:

    (i) the notice shall be in writing and signed by the copyright owner or such owner's duly authorized agent; and

    (ii) the notice shall be served on the person responsible for the performance at least seven days before the date of the performance, and shall state the reasons for the objection; and

    (iii) the notice shall comply, in form, content, and manner of service, with requirements that the Register of Copyrights shall prescribe by regulation;

(5) (A) except as provided in subparagraph (B), communication of a transmission embodying a performance or display of a work by the public reception of the transmission on a single receiving apparatus of a kind commonly used in private homes, unless—

(i) a direct charge is made to see or hear the transmission; or

(ii) the transmission thus received is further transmitted to the public;

(B) communication by an establishment of a transmission or retransmission embodying a performance or display of a nondramatic musical work intended to be received by the general public, originated by a radio or television broadcast station licensed as such by the Federal Communications Commission, or, if an audiovisual transmission, by a cable system or satellite carrier, if—

(i) in the case of an establishment other than a food service or drinking establishment, either the establishment in which the communication occurs has less than 2,000 gross square feet of space (excluding space used for customer parking and for no other purpose), or the establishment in which the communication occurs has 2,000 or more gross square feet of space (excluding space used for customer parking and for no other purpose) and—

(I) if the performance is by audio means only, the performance is communicated by means of a total of not more than 6 loudspeakers, of which not more than 4 loudspeakers are located in any 1 room or adjoining outdoor space; or

(II) if the performance or display is by audiovisual means, any visual portion of the performance or display is communicated by means of a total of not more than 4 audiovisual devices, of which not more than 1 audiovisual device is located in any 1 room, and no such audiovisual device has a diagonal screen size greater than 55 inches, and any audio portion of the performance or display is communicated by means of a total of not more than 6 loudspeakers, of which not more than 4 loudspeakers are located in any 1 room or adjoining outdoor space;

(ii) in the case of a food service or drinking establishment, either the establishment in which the communication occurs has less than 3,750 gross square feet of space (excluding space used for customer parking and for no other purpose), or the establishment in which the communication occurs has 3,750 gross square feet of space or more (excluding space used for customer parking and for no other purpose) and—

(I) if the performance is by audio means only, the performance is communicated by means of a total of not more than 6 loudspeakers, of which not more than 4 loudspeakers are located in any 1 room or adjoining outdoor space; or

(II) if the performance or display is by audiovisual means, any visual portion of the performance or display is communicated by means of a total of not more than 4 audiovisual devices, of which not more than one audiovisual device is located in any 1 room, and no such audiovisual device has a diagonal screen size greater than 55 inches, and any audio portion of the performance or display is communicated by means of a total of not more than 6 loudspeakers, of which not more than 4 loudspeakers are located in any 1 room or adjoining outdoor space;

(iii) no direct charge is made to see or hear the transmission or retransmission;

(iv) the transmission or retransmission is not further transmitted beyond the establishment where it is received; and

(v) the transmission or retransmission is licensed by the copyright owner of the work so publicly performed or displayed;

(6) performance of a nondramatic musical work by a governmental body or a nonprofit agricultural or horticultural organization, in the course of an annual agricultural or horticultural fair or exhibition conducted by such body or organization; the exemption provided by this clause shall extend to any liability for copyright infringement that would otherwise be imposed on such body or organization, under doctrines of vicarious liability or related infringement, for a performance by a concessionnaire, business establishment, or other person at such fair or exhibition, but shall not excuse any such person from liability for the performance;

(7) performance of a nondramatic musical work by a vending establishment open to the public at large without any direct or indirect admission charge, where the sole purpose of the performance is to promote the retail sale of copies or phonorecords of the work, or of the audiovisual or other devices utilized in such performance, and the performance is not transmitted beyond the place where the establishment is located and is within the immediate area where the sale is occurring;

(8) performance of a nondramatic literary work, by or in the course of a transmission specifically designed for and primarily directed to blind or other handicapped persons who are unable to read normal printed material as a result of their handicap, or deaf or other handicapped persons who are unable to hear the aural signals accompanying a transmission of visual signals, if the performance is made without any purpose of direct or indirect commercial advantage and its transmis-

sion is made through the facilities of: (i) a governmental body; or (ii) a noncommercial educational broadcast station (as defined in section 397 of title 47); or (iii) a radio subcarrier authorization (as defined in 47 CFR 73.293–73.295 and 73.593–73.595); or (iv) a cable system (as defined in section 111 (f));

(9) performance on a single occasion of a dramatic literary work published at least ten years before the date of the performance, by or in the course of a transmission specifically designed for and primarily directed to blind or other handicapped persons who are unable to read normal printed material as a result of their handicap, if the performance is made without any purpose of direct or indirect commercial advantage and its transmission is made through the facilities of a radio subcarrier authorization referred to in clause (8)(iii), Provided, That the provisions of this clause shall not be applicable to more than one performance of the same work by the same performers or under the auspices of the same organization;

(10) notwithstanding paragraph (4), the following is not an infringement of copyright: performance of a nondramatic literary or musical work in the course of a social function which is organized and promoted by a nonprofit veterans' organization or a nonprofit fraternal organization to which the general public is not invited, but not including the invitees of the organizations, if the proceeds from the performance, after deducting the reasonable costs of producing the performance, are used exclusively for charitable purposes and not for financial gain. For purposes of this section the social functions of any college or university fraternity or sorority shall not be included unless the social function is held solely to raise funds for a specific charitable purpose; and

(11) the making imperceptible, by or at the direction of a member of a private household, of limited portions of audio or video content of a motion picture, during a performance in or transmitted to that household for private home viewing, from an authorized copy of the motion picture, or the creation or provision of a computer program or other technology that enables such making imperceptible and that is designed and marketed to be used, at the direction of a member of a private household, for such making imperceptible, if no fixed copy of the altered version of the motion picture is created by such computer program or other technology.

The exemptions provided under paragraph (5) shall not be taken into account in any administrative, judicial, or other governmental proceeding to set or adjust the royalties payable to copyright owners for the public performance or display of their works. Royalties payable to copyright owners for any public performance or display of their works other than such performances or displays as are exempted under paragraph (5) shall not be diminished in any respect as a result of such exemption.

In paragraph (2), the term "mediated instructional activities" with respect to the performance or display of a work by digital transmission under this section refers to activities that use such work as an integral part of the class experience, controlled by or under the actual supervision of the instructor and analogous to the type of performance or display that would take place in a live classroom setting. The term does not refer to activities that use, in 1 or more class sessions of a single course, such works as textbooks, course packs, or other material in any media, copies or phonorecords of which are typically purchased or acquired by the students in higher education for their independent use and retention or are typically purchased or acquired for elementary and secondary students for their possession and independent use.

For purposes of paragraph (2), accreditation—

(A) with respect to an institution providing post-secondary education, shall be as determined by a regional or national accrediting agency recognized by the Council on Higher Education Accreditation or the United States Department of Education; and

(B) with respect to an institution providing elementary or secondary education, shall be as recognized by the applicable state certification or licensing procedures.

For purposes of paragraph (2), no governmental body or accredited nonprofit educational institution shall be liable for infringement by reason of the transient or temporary storage of material carried out through the automatic technical process of a digital transmission of the performance or display of that material as authorized under paragraph (2). No such material stored on the system or network controlled or operated by the transmitting body or institution under this paragraph shall be maintained on such system or network in a manner ordinarily accessible to anyone other than anticipated recipients. No such copy shall be maintained on the system or network in a manner ordinarily accessible to such anticipated recipients for a longer period than is reasonably necessary to facilitate the transmissions for which it was made.

For purposes of paragraph (11), the term "making imperceptible" does not include the addition of audio or video content that is performed or displayed over or in place of existing content in a motion picture.

Nothing in paragraph (11) shall be construed to imply further rights under section 106 of this title, or to have any effect on defenses or limitations on rights granted under any other section of this title or under any other paragraph of this section.

§ 117. Limitation on Exclusive Rights: Computer Programs

(a) Making of Additional Copy or Adaptation by Owner of Copy.— Notwithstanding the provisions of section 106, it is not an infringement for the owner of a copy of a computer program to make or authorize the making of another copy or adaptation of that computer program provided:

    (1) that such a new copy or adaptation is created as an essential step in the utilization of the computer program in conjunction with a machine and that it is used in no other manner, or

    (2) that such new copy or adaptation is for archival purposes only and that all archival copies are destroyed in the event that continued possession of the computer program should cease to be rightful.

(b) Lease, Sale, or Other Transfer of Additional Copy or Adaptation.— Any exact copies prepared in accordance with the provisions of this section may be leased, sold, or otherwise transferred, along with the copy from which such copies were prepared, only as part of the lease, sale, or other transfer of all rights in the program. Adaptations so prepared may be transferred only with the authorization of the copyright owner.

(c) Machine Maintenance or Repair.— Notwithstanding the provisions of section 106, it is not an infringement for the owner or lessee of a machine to make or authorize the making of a copy of a computer program if such copy is made solely by virtue of the activation of a machine that lawfully contains an authorized copy of the computer program, for purposes only of maintenance or repair of that machine, if—

    (1) such new copy is used in no other manner and is destroyed immediately after the maintenance or repair is completed; and

    (2) with respect to any computer program or part thereof that is not necessary for that machine to be activated, such program or part thereof is not accessed or used other than to make such new copy by virtue of the activation of the machine.

(d) Definitions.— For purposes of this section—

    (1) the "maintenance" of a machine is the servicing of the machine in order to make it work in accordance with its original specifications and any changes to those specifications authorized for that machine; and

(2) the "repair" of a machine is the restoring of the machine to the state of working in accordance with its original specifications and any changes to those specifications authorized for that machine.

§ 201. Ownership of Copyright

(a) Initial Ownership.— Copyright in a work protected under this title vests initially in the author or authors of the work. The authors of a joint work are co-owners of copyright in the work.

(b) Works Made for Hire.— In the case of a work made for hire, the employer or other person for whom the work was prepared is considered the author for purposes of this title, and, unless the parties have expressly agreed otherwise in a written instrument signed by them, owns all of the rights comprised in the copyright.

(c) Contributions to Collective Works.— Copyright in each separate contribution to a collective work is distinct from copyright in the collective work as a whole, and vests initially in the author of the contribution. In the absence of an express transfer of the copyright or of any rights under it, the owner of copyright in the collective work is presumed to have acquired only the privilege of reproducing and distributing the contribution as part of that particular collective work, any revision of that collective work, and any later collective work in the same series.

(d) Transfer of Ownership.—

(1) The ownership of a copyright may be transferred in whole or in part by any means of conveyance or by operation of law, and may be bequeathed by will or pass as personal property by the applicable laws of intestate succession.

(2) Any of the exclusive rights comprised in a copyright, including any subdivision of any of the rights specified by section 106, may be transferred as provided by clause (1) and owned separately. The owner of any particular exclusive right is entitled, to the extent of that right, to all of the protection and remedies accorded to the copyright owner by this title.

(e) Involuntary Transfer.— When an individual author's ownership of a copyright, or of any of the exclusive rights under a copyright, has not previously been transferred voluntarily by that individual author, no action by any governmental body or other official or organization purporting to seize, expropriate, transfer, or exercise rights of ownership with respect to the copyright, or any of the exclusive rights under a copyright, shall be given effect under this title, except as provided under title 11.

§ 204. Execution of Transfers of Copyright Ownership

(a) A transfer of copyright ownership, other than by operation of law, is not valid unless an instrument of conveyance, or a note or memorandum of the transfer, is in writing and signed by the owner of the rights conveyed or such owner's duly authorized agent.

***

§ 302. Duration of Copyright: Works Created on or after January 1, 1978

(a) In General.— Copyright in a work created on or after January 1, 1978, subsists from its creation and, except as provided by the following subsections, endures for a term consisting of the life of the author and 70 years after the author's death.

(b) Joint Works.— In the case of a joint work prepared by two or more authors who did not work for hire, the copyright endures for a term consisting of the life of the last surviving author and 70 years after such last surviving author's death.

(c) Anonymous Works, Pseudonymous Works, and Works Made for Hire.— In the case of an anonymous work, a pseudonymous work, or a work made for hire, the copyright endures for a term of 95 years from the year of its first publication, or a term of 120 years from the year of its creation, whichever expires first. If, before the end of such term, the identity of one or more of the authors of an anonymous or pseudonymous work is revealed in the records of a registration made for that work under subsections (a) or (d) of section 408, or in the records provided by this subsection, the copyright in the work endures for the term specified by subsection (a) or (b), based on the life of the author or authors whose identity has been revealed. Any person having an interest in the copyright in an anonymous or pseudonymous work may at any time record, in records to be maintained by the Copyright Office for that purpose, a statement identifying one or more authors of the work; the statement shall also identify the person filing it, the nature of that person's interest, the source of the information recorded, and the particular work affected, and shall comply in form and content with requirements that the Register of Copyrights shall prescribe by regulation.

(d) Records Relating to Death of Authors.— Any person having an interest in a copyright may at any time record in the Copyright Office a statement of the date of death of the author of the copyrighted work, or a statement that the author is still living on a particular date. The statement shall identify the person filing it, the nature of that person's interest, and the source of the information recorded, and shall comply in form and content with requirements that the Register of Copyrights shall prescribe by regulation. The Register shall maintain current records of information relating to the death of authors of copyrighted works, based on such recorded statements and, to the extent the Register considers practicable, on data contained in any of the records of the Copyright Office or in other reference sources.

(e) Presumption as to Author's Death.— After a period of 95 years from the year of first publication of a work, or a period of 120 years from the year of its creation, whichever expires first, any person who obtains from the Copyright Office a certified report that the records provided by subsection (d) disclose nothing to indicate that the author of the work is living, or died less than 70 years before, is entitled to the benefits of a presumption that the author has been dead for at least 70 years. Reliance in good faith upon this presumption shall be a complete defense to any action for infringement under this title.

§ 303. Duration of Copyright: Works Created but not Published or Copyrighted Before January 1, 1978

(a) Copyright in a work created before January 1, 1978, but not theretofore in the public domain or copyrighted, subsists from January 1, 1978, and endures for the term provided by section 302. In no case, however, shall the term of copyright in such a work expire before December 31, 2002; and, if the work is published on or before December 31, 2002, the term of copyright shall not expire before December 31, 2047.

(b) The distribution before January 1, 1978, of a phonorecord shall not for any purpose constitute a publication of the musical work embodied therein.

§ 504. Remedies for Infringement: Damages and Profits

(a) In General.— Except as otherwise provided by this title, an infringer of copyright is liable for either—
  (1) the copyright owner's actual damages and any additional profits of the infringer, as provided by subsection (b); or
  (2) statutory damages, as provided by subsection (c).

(b) Actual Damages and Profits.— The copyright owner is entitled to recover the actual damages suffered by him or her as a result of the infringement, and any profits of the infringer that are attributable to the infringement and are not taken into account in computing the actual damages. In establishing the infringer's profits, the copyright owner is required to present proof only of the infringer's gross revenue, and the infringer is required to prove his or her deductible expenses and the elements of profit attributable to factors other than the copyrighted work.

(c) Statutory Damages.—

(1) Except as provided by clause (2) of this subsection, the copyright owner may elect, at any time before final judgment is rendered, to recover, instead of actual damages and profits, an award of statutory damages for all infringements involved in the action, with respect to any one work, for which any one infringer is liable individually, or for which any two or more infringers are liable jointly and severally, in a sum of not less than $750 or more than $30,000 as the court considers just. For the purposes of this subsection, all the parts of a compilation or derivative work constitute one work.

(2) In a case where the copyright owner sustains the burden of proving, and the court finds, that infringement was committed willfully, the court in its discretion may increase the award of statutory damages to a sum of not more than $150,000. In a case where the infringer sustains the burden of proving, and the court finds, that such infringer was not aware and had no reason to believe that his or her acts constituted an infringement of copyright, the court in its discretion may reduce the award of statutory damages to a sum of not less than $200. The court shall remit statutory damages in any case where an infringer believed and had reasonable grounds for believing that his or her use of the copyrighted work was a fair use under section 107, if the infringer was: (i) an employee or agent of a nonprofit educational institution, library, or archives acting within the scope of his or her employment who, or such institution, library, or archives itself, which infringed by reproducing the work in copies or phonorecords; or (ii) a public broadcasting entity which or a person who, as a regular part of the nonprofit activities of a public broadcasting entity (as defined in subsection (g) of section 118) infringed by performing a published nondramatic literary work or by reproducing a transmission program embodying a performance of such a work.

(3) (A) In a case of infringement, it shall be a rebuttable presumption that the infringement was committed willfully for purposes of determining relief if the violator, or a person acting in concert with the violator, knowingly provided or knowingly caused to be provided materially false contact information to a domain name registrar, domain name registry, or other domain name

registration authority in registering, maintaining, or renewing a domain name used in connection with the infringement.

(B) Nothing in this paragraph limits what may be considered willful infringement under this subsection.

(C) For purposes of this paragraph, the term "domain name" has the meaning given that term in section 45 of the Act entitled "An Act to provide for the registration and protection of trademarks used in commerce, to carry out the provisions of certain international conventions, and for other purposes" approved July 5, 1946 (commonly referred to as the "Trademark Act of 1946"; 15 U.S.C. 1127).

(d) Additional Damages in Certain Cases.— In any case in which the court finds that a defendant proprietor of an establishment who claims as a defense that its activities were exempt under section 110 (5) did not have reasonable grounds to believe that its use of a copyrighted work was exempt under such section, the plaintiff shall be entitled to, in addition to any award of damages under this section, an additional award of two times the amount of the license fee that the proprietor of the establishment concerned should have paid the plaintiff for such use during the preceding period of up to 3 years.

§ 507. Limitations on Actions

(a) Criminal Proceedings.— Except as expressly provided otherwise in this title, no criminal proceeding shall be maintained under the provisions of this title unless it is commenced within 5 years after the cause of action arose.

(b) Civil Actions.— No civil action shall be maintained under the provisions of this title unless it is commenced within three years after the claim accrued.

§ 512: Limitations on Liability Relating to Material Online

(a) Transitory Digital Network Communications.— A service provider shall not be liable for monetary relief, or, except as provided in subsection (j), for injunctive or other equitable relief, for infringement of copyright by reason of the provider's transmitting, routing, or providing connections for, material through a system or network controlled or operated by or for the service provider, or by reason of the intermediate and transient storage of that material in the course of such transmitting, routing, or providing connections, if—

(1) the transmission of the material was initiated by or at the direction of a person other than the service provider;

    (2) the transmission, routing, provision of connections, or storage is carried out through an automatic technical process without selection of the material by the service provider;

    (3) the service provider does not select the recipients of the material except as an automatic response to the request of another person;

    (4) no copy of the material made by the service provider in the course of such intermediate or transient storage is maintained on the system or network in a manner ordinarily accessible to anyone other than anticipated recipients, and no such copy is maintained on the system or network in a manner ordinarily accessible to such anticipated recipients for a longer period than is reasonably necessary for the transmission, routing, or provision of connections; and

    (5) the material is transmitted through the system or network without modification of its content.

(b) System Caching.—

    (1) Limitation on liability.— A service provider shall not be liable for monetary relief, or, except as provided in subsection (j), for injunctive or other equitable relief, for infringement of copyright by reason of the intermediate and temporary storage of material on a system or network controlled or operated by or for the service provider in a case in which—

        (A) the material is made available online by a person other than the service provider;

        (B) the material is transmitted from the person described in subparagraph (A) through the system or network to a person other than the person described in subparagraph (A) at the direction of that other person; and

        (C) the storage is carried out through an automatic technical process for the purpose of making the material available to users of the system or network who, after the material is transmitted as described in subparagraph (B), request access to the material from the person described in subparagraph (A), if the conditions set forth in paragraph (2) are met.

    (2) Conditions.— The conditions referred to in paragraph (1) are that—

        (A) the material described in paragraph (1) is transmitted to the subsequent users described in paragraph (1)(C) without modification to its content from the manner in which the material was transmitted from the person described in paragraph (1)(A);

(B) the service provider described in paragraph (1) complies with rules concerning the refreshing, reloading, or other updating of the material when specified by the person making the material available online in accordance with a generally accepted industry standard data communications protocol for the system or network through which that person makes the material available, except that this subparagraph applies only if those rules are not used by the person described in paragraph (1)(A) to prevent or unreasonably impair the intermediate storage to which this subsection applies;

(C) the service provider does not interfere with the ability of technology associated with the material to return to the person described in paragraph (1)(A) the information that would have been available to that person if the material had been obtained by the subsequent users described in paragraph (1)(C) directly from that person, except that this subparagraph applies only if that technology—

    (i) does not significantly interfere with the performance of the provider's system or network or with the intermediate storage of the material;

    (ii) is consistent with generally accepted industry standard communications protocols; and

    (iii) does not extract information from the provider's system or network other than the information that would have been available to the person described in paragraph (1)(A) if the subsequent users had gained access to the material directly from that person;

(D) if the person described in paragraph (1)(A) has in effect a condition that a person must meet prior to having access to the material, such as a condition based on payment of a fee or provision of a password or other information, the service provider permits access to the stored material in significant part only to users of its system or network that have met those conditions and only in accordance with those conditions; and

(E) if the person described in paragraph (1)(A) makes that material available online without the authorization of the copyright owner of the material, the service provider responds expeditiously to remove, or disable access to, the material that is claimed to be infringing upon notification of claimed infringement as described in subsection (c)(3), except that this subparagraph applies only if—

(i) the material has previously been removed from the originating site or access to it has been disabled, or a court has ordered that the material be removed from the originating site or that access to the material on the originating site be disabled; and

(ii) the party giving the notification includes in the notification a statement confirming that the material has been removed from the originating site or access to it has been disabled or that a court has ordered that the material be removed from the originating site or that access to the material on the originating site be disabled.

(c) Information Residing on Systems or Networks At Direction of Users.—

(1) In general.— A service provider shall not be liable for monetary relief, or, except as provided in subsection (j), for injunctive or other equitable relief, for infringement of copyright by reason of the storage at the direction of a user of material that resides on a system or network controlled or operated by or for the service provider, if the service provider—

(A)(i) does not have actual knowledge that the material or an activity using the material on the system or network is infringing;

(ii) in the absence of such actual knowledge, is not aware of facts or circumstances from which infringing activity is apparent; or

(iii) upon obtaining such knowledge or awareness, acts expeditiously to remove, or disable access to, the material;

(B) does not receive a financial benefit directly attributable to the infringing activity, in a case in which the service provider has the right and ability to control such activity; and

(C) upon notification of claimed infringement as described in paragraph (3), responds expeditiously to remove, or disable access to, the material that is claimed to be infringing or to be the subject of infringing activity.

(2) Designated agent.— The limitations on liability established in this subsection apply to a service provider only if the service provider has designated an agent to receive notifications of claimed infringement described in paragraph (3), by making available through its service, including on its website in a location accessible to the public, and by providing to the Copyright Office, substantially the following information:

(A) the name, address, phone number, and electronic mail address of the agent.

(B) other contact information which the Register of Copyrights may deem appropriate.

The Register of Copyrights shall maintain a current directory of agents available to the public for inspection, including through the Internet, in both electronic and hard copy formats, and may require payment of a fee by service providers to cover the costs of maintaining the directory.

(3) Elements of notification.—

(A) To be effective under this subsection, a notification of claimed infringement must be a written communication provided to the designated agent of a service provider that includes substantially the following:

(i) A physical or electronic signature of a person authorized to act on behalf of the owner of an exclusive right that is allegedly infringed.

(ii) Identification of the copyrighted work claimed to have been infringed, or, if multiple copyrighted works at a single online site are covered by a single notification, a representative list of such works at that site.

(iii) Identification of the material that is claimed to be infringing or to be the subject of infringing activity and that is to be removed or access to which is to be disabled, and information reasonably sufficient to permit the service provider to locate the material.

(iv) Information reasonably sufficient to permit the service provider to contact the complaining party, such as an address, telephone number, and, if available, an electronic mail address at which the complaining party may be contacted.

(v) A statement that the complaining party has a good faith belief that use of the material in the manner complained of is not authorized by the copyright owner, its agent, or the law.

(vi) A statement that the information in the notification is accurate, and under penalty of perjury, that the complaining party is authorized to act on behalf of the owner of an exclusive right that is allegedly infringed.

(B) (i) Subject to clause (ii), a notification from a copyright owner or from a person authorized to act on behalf of the copyright owner that fails to comply substantially with the provisions of subparagraph (A) shall not be considered under paragraph (1)(A) in determining whether a service provider has actual knowledge or is aware of facts or circumstances from which infringing activity is apparent.

(ii) In a case in which the notification that is provided to the service provider's designated agent fails to comply substantially with all the provisions of subparagraph (A) but substantially complies with clauses (ii), (iii), and (iv) of subparagraph (A), clause (i) of this subparagraph applies only if the service provider promptly attempts to contact the person making the notification or takes other reasonable steps to assist in the receipt of notification that substantially complies with all the provisions of subparagraph (A).

(d) Information Location Tools.— A service provider shall not be liable for monetary relief, or, except as provided in subsection (j), for injunctive or other equitable relief, for infringement of copyright by reason of the provider referring or linking users to an online location containing infringing material or infringing activity, by using information location tools, including a directory, index, reference, pointer, or hypertext link, if the service provider—

(1) (A) does not have actual knowledge that the material or activity is infringing;

(B) in the absence of such actual knowledge, is not aware of facts or circumstances from which infringing activity is apparent; or

(C) upon obtaining such knowledge or awareness, acts expeditiously to remove, or disable access to, the material;

(2) does not receive a financial benefit directly attributable to the infringing activity, in a case in which the service provider has the right and ability to control such activity; and

(3) upon notification of claimed infringement as described in subsection (c)(3), responds expeditiously to remove, or disable access to, the material that is claimed to be infringing or to be the subject of infringing activity, except that, for purposes of this paragraph, the information described in subsection (c)(3)(A)(iii) shall be identification of the reference or link, to material or activity claimed to be infringing, that is to be removed or access to which is to be disabled, and information reasonably sufficient to permit the service provider to locate that reference or link.

(e) Limitation on Liability of Nonprofit Educational Institutions.—
    (1) When a public or other nonprofit institution of higher education is a service provider, and when a faculty member or graduate student who is an employee of such institution is performing a teaching or research function, for the purposes of subsections (a) and (b) such faculty member or graduate student shall be considered to be a person other than the institution, and for the purposes of subsections (c) and (d) such faculty member's or graduate student's knowledge or awareness of his or her infringing activities shall not be attributed to the institution, if—
      (A) such faculty member's or graduate student's infringing activities do not involve the provision of online access to instructional materials that are or were required or recommended, within the preceding 3-year period, for a course taught at the institution by such faculty member or graduate student;
      (B) the institution has not, within the preceding 3-year period, received more than two notifications described in subsection (c)(3) of claimed infringement by such faculty member or graduate student, and such notifications of claimed infringement were not actionable under subsection (f); and
      (C) the institution provides to all users of its system or network informational materials that accurately describe, and promote compliance with, the laws of the United States relating to copyright.
    (2) For the purposes of this subsection, the limitations on injunctive relief contained in subsections (j)(2) and (j)(3), but not those in (j)(1), shall apply.
(f) Misrepresentations.— Any person who knowingly materially misrepresents under this section—
    (1) that material or activity is infringing, or
    (2) that material or activity was removed or disabled by mistake or misidentification,
shall be liable for any damages, including costs and attorneys' fees, incurred by the alleged infringer, by any copyright owner or copyright owner's authorized licensee, or by a service provider, who is injured by such misrepresentation, as the result of the service provider relying upon such misrepresentation in removing or disabling access to the material or activity claimed to be infringing, or in replacing the removed material or ceasing to disable access to it.

(g) Replacement of Removed or Disabled Material and Limitation on Other Liability.—

   (1) No liability for taking down generally.— Subject to paragraph (2), a service provider shall not be liable to any person for any claim based on the service provider's good faith disabling of access to, or removal of, material or activity claimed to be infringing or based on facts or circumstances from which infringing activity is apparent, regardless of whether the material or activity is ultimately determined to be infringing.

   (2) Exception.— Paragraph (1) shall not apply with respect to material residing at the direction of a subscriber of the service provider on a system or network controlled or operated by or for the service provider that is removed, or to which access is disabled by the service provider, pursuant to a notice provided under subsection (c)(1)(C), unless the service provider—

      (A) takes reasonable steps promptly to notify the subscriber that it has removed or disabled access to the material;

      (B) upon receipt of a counter notification described in paragraph (3), promptly provides the person who provided the notification under subsection (c)(1)(C) with a copy of the counter notification, and informs that person that it will replace the removed material or cease disabling access to it in 10 business days; and

      (C) replaces the removed material and ceases disabling access to it not less than 10, nor more than 14, business days following receipt of the counter notice, unless its designated agent first receives notice from the person who submitted the notification under subsection (c)(1)(C) that such person has filed an action seeking a court order to restrain the subscriber from engaging in infringing activity relating to the material on the service provider's system or network.

   (3) Contents of counter notification.— To be effective under this subsection, a counter notification must be a written communication provided to the service provider's designated agent that includes substantially the following:

      (A) A physical or electronic signature of the subscriber.

      (B) Identification of the material that has been removed or to which access has been disabled and the location at which the material appeared before it was removed or access to it was disabled.

(C) A statement under penalty of perjury that the subscriber has a good faith belief that the material was removed or disabled as a result of mistake or misidentification of the material to be removed or disabled.

(D) The subscriber's name, address, and telephone number, and a statement that the subscriber consents to the jurisdiction of Federal District Court for the judicial district in which the address is located, or if the subscriber's address is outside of the United States, for any judicial district in which the service provider may be found, and that the subscriber will accept service of process from the person who provided notification under subsection (c)(1)(C) or an agent of such person.

(4) Limitation on other liability.— A service provider's compliance with paragraph (2) shall not subject the service provider to liability for copyright infringement with respect to the material identified in the notice provided under subsection (c)(1)(C).

(h) Subpoena To Identify Infringer.—

(1) Request.— A copyright owner or a person authorized to act on the owner's behalf may request the clerk of any United States district court to issue a subpoena to a service provider for identification of an alleged infringer in accordance with this subsection.

(2) Contents of request.— The request may be made by filing with the clerk—

(A) a copy of a notification described in subsection (c)(3)(A);

(B) a proposed subpoena; and

(C) a sworn declaration to the effect that the purpose for which the subpoena is sought is to obtain the identity of an alleged infringer and that such information will only be used for the purpose of protecting rights under this title.

(3) Contents of subpoena.— The subpoena shall authorize and order the service provider receiving the notification and the subpoena to expeditiously disclose to the copyright owner or person authorized by the copyright owner information sufficient to identify the alleged infringer of the material described in the notification to the extent such information is available to the service provider.

(4) Basis for granting subpoena.— If the notification filed satisfies the provisions of subsection (c)(3)(A), the proposed subpoena is in proper form, and the accompanying declaration is properly executed, the clerk shall expeditiously issue and sign the proposed subpoena and return it to the requester for delivery to the service provider.

(5) Actions of service provider receiving subpoena.— Upon receipt of the issued subpoena, either accompanying or subsequent to the receipt of a notification described in subsection (c)(3)(A), the service provider shall expeditiously disclose to the copyright owner or person authorized by the copyright owner the information required by the subpoena, notwithstanding any other provision of law and regardless of whether the service provider responds to the notification.

(6) Rules applicable to subpoena.— Unless otherwise provided by this section or by applicable rules of the court, the procedure for issuance and delivery of the subpoena, and the remedies for non-compliance with the subpoena, shall be governed to the greatest extent practicable by those provisions of the Federal Rules of Civil Procedure governing the issuance, service, and enforcement of a subpoena duces tecum.

(i) Conditions for Eligibility.—

(1) Accommodation of technology.— The limitations on liability established by this section shall apply to a service provider only if the service provider—

(A) has adopted and reasonably implemented, and informs subscribers and account holders of the service provider's system or network of, a policy that provides for the termination in appropriate circumstances of subscribers and account holders of the service provider's system or network who are repeat infringers; and

(B) accommodates and does not interfere with standard technical measures.

(2) Definition.— As used in this subsection, the term "standard technical measures" means technical measures that are used by copyright owners to identify or protect copyrighted works and—

(A) have been developed pursuant to a broad consensus of copyright owners and service providers in an open, fair, voluntary, multi-industry standards process;

(B) are available to any person on reasonable and nondiscriminatory terms; and

(C) do not impose substantial costs on service providers or substantial burdens on their systems or networks.

(j) Injunctions.— The following rules shall apply in the case of any application for an injunction under section 502 against a service provider that is not subject to monetary remedies under this section:

(1) Scope of relief.—

(A) With respect to conduct other than that which qualifies for the limitation on remedies set forth in subsection (a), the court may grant injunctive relief with respect to a service provider only in one or more of the following forms:

    (i) An order restraining the service provider from providing access to infringing material or activity residing at a particular online site on the provider's system or network.

    (ii) An order restraining the service provider from providing access to a subscriber or account holder of the service provider's system or network who is engaging in infringing activity and is identified in the order, by terminating the accounts of the subscriber or account holder that are specified in the order.

    (iii) Such other injunctive relief as the court may consider necessary to prevent or restrain infringement of copyrighted material specified in the order of the court at a particular online location, if such relief is the least burdensome to the service provider among the forms of relief comparably effective for that purpose.

(B) If the service provider qualifies for the limitation on remedies described in subsection (a), the court may only grant injunctive relief in one or both of the following forms:

    (i) An order restraining the service provider from providing access to a subscriber or account holder of the service provider's system or network who is using the provider's service to engage in infringing activity and is identified in the order, by terminating the accounts of the subscriber or account holder that are specified in the order.

    (ii) An order restraining the service provider from providing access, by taking reasonable steps specified in the order to block access, to a specific, identified, online location outside the United States.

(2) Considerations.— The court, in considering the relevant criteria for injunctive relief under applicable law, shall consider—

(A) whether such an injunction, either alone or in combination with other such injunctions issued against the same service provider under this subsection, would significantly burden either the provider or the operation of the provider's system or network;

(B) the magnitude of the harm likely to be suffered by the copyright owner in the digital network environment if steps are not taken to prevent or restrain the infringement;

(C) whether implementation of such an injunction would be technically feasible and effective, and would not interfere with access to noninfringing material at other online locations; and

(D) whether other less burdensome and comparably effective means of preventing or restraining access to the infringing material are available.

(3) Notice and ex parte orders.— Injunctive relief under this subsection shall be available only after notice to the service provider and an opportunity for the service provider to appear are provided, except for orders ensuring the preservation of evidence or other orders having no material adverse effect on the operation of the service provider's communications network.

(k) Definitions.—

(1) Service provider.—

(A) As used in subsection (a), the term "service provider" means an entity offering the transmission, routing, or providing of connections for digital online communications, between or among points specified by a user, of material of the user's choosing, without modification to the content of the material as sent or received.

(B) As used in this section, other than subsection (a), the term "service provider" means a provider of online services or network access, or the operator of facilities therefor, and includes an entity described in subparagraph (A).

(2) Monetary relief.— As used in this section, the term "monetary relief" means damages, costs, attorneys' fees, and any other form of monetary payment.

(l) Other Defenses Not Affected.— The failure of a service provider's conduct to qualify for limitation of liability under this section shall not bear adversely upon the consideration of a defense by the service provider that the service provider's conduct is not infringing under this title or any other defense.

(m) Protection of Privacy.— Nothing in this section shall be construed to condition the applicability of subsections (a) through (d) on—

(1) a service provider monitoring its service or affirmatively seeking facts indicating infringing activity, except to the extent consistent with a standard technical measure complying with the provisions of subsection (i); or

(2) a service provider gaining access to, removing, or disabling access to material in cases in which such conduct is prohibited by law.

(n) Construction.— Subsections (a), (b), (c), and (d) describe separate and distinct functions for purposes of applying this section. Whether a service provider qualifies for the limitation on liability in any one of those subsections shall be based solely on the criteria in that subsection, and shall not affect a determination of whether that service provider qualifies for the limitations on liability under any other such subsection.

§ 602: Infringing Importation or Exportation of Copies or Phonorecords

(a) Infringing Importation or Exportation.—

   (1) Importation.— Importation into the United States, without the authority of the owner of copyright under this title, of copies or phonorecords of a work that have been acquired outside the United States is an infringement of the exclusive right to distribute copies or phonorecords under section 106, actionable under section 501.

   (2) Importation or exportation of infringing items.— Importation into the United States or exportation from the United States, without the authority of the owner of copyright under this title, of copies or phonorecords, the making of which either constituted an infringement of copyright, or which would have constituted an infringement of copyright if this title had been applicable, is an infringement of the exclusive right to distribute copies or phonorecords under section 106, actionable under sections 501 and 506.

   (3) Exceptions.— This subsection does not apply to—

     (A) importation or exportation of copies or phonorecords under the authority or for the use of the Government of the United States or of any State or political subdivision of a State, but not including copies or phonorecords for use in schools, or copies of any audiovisual work imported for purposes other than archival use;

     (B) importation or exportation, for the private use of the importer or exporter and not for distribution, by any person with respect to no more than one copy or phonorecord of any one work at any one time, or by any person arriving from outside the United States or departing from the United States with respect to copies or phonorecords forming part of such person's personal baggage; or

(C) importation by or for an organization operated for scholarly, educational, or religious purposes and not for private gain, with respect to no more than one copy of an audiovisual work solely for its archival purposes, and no more than five copies or phonorecords of any other work for its library lending or archival purposes, unless the importation of such copies or phonorecords is part of an activity consisting of systematic reproduction or distribution, engaged in by such organization in violation of the provisions of section 108 (g)(2).

(b) Import Prohibition.— In a case where the making of the copies or phonorecords would have constituted an infringement of copyright if this title had been applicable, their importation is prohibited. In a case where the copies or phonorecords were lawfully made, United States Customs and Border Protection has no authority to prevent their importation unless the provisions of section 601 are applicable. In either case, the Secretary of the Treasury is authorized to prescribe, by regulation, a procedure under which any person claiming an interest in the copyright in a particular work may, upon payment of a specified fee, be entitled to notification by United States Customs and Border Protection of the importation of articles that appear to be copies or phonorecords of the work.

Appendix P
COPYRIGHT TERM AND THE PUBLIC DOMAIN IN THE UNITED STATES (2012)[*]

ഌൠ

Never Published, Never Registered Works

Type of Work	Copyright Term	What was in the public domain in the U.S. as of 1 January 2012
Unpublished works	Life of the author + 70 years	Works for authors who died before 1942
Unpublished anonymous and pseudonymous works, and works made for hire (corporate authorship)	120 years from date of creation	Works created before 1892
Unpublished works when the death date of the author is not known	120 years from date of creation	Works created before 1892

Works Registered or First Published in the U.S.

Date of Publication	Conditions	Copyright Term
Before 1923	None	None. In the public domain due to copyright expiration.
1923 through 1977	Published without a copyright notice	None. In the public domain due to failure to comply with required formalities.

---

[*] Abridged from Peter Hirtle, "Copyright Term and the Public Domain in the United States," *available at* http://copyright.cornell.edu/resources/publicdomain.cfm. Released under the Creative Commons Attribution 3.0 License. Footnotes and special cases omitted.

1978 to 1 March 1989	Published without notice, and without subsequent registration within 5 years	None. In the public domain due to failure to comply with required formalities.
1978 to 1 March 1989	Published without notice, but with subsequent registration within 5 years	70 years after the death of author. If a work of corporate authorship, 95 years from publication or 120 years from creation, whichever expires first.
1923 through 1963	Published with notice but copyright was not renewed	None. In the public domain due to copyright expiration.
1923 through 1963	Published with notice and the copyright was renewed	95 years after publication date
1964 through 1977	Published with notice	95 years after publication date
1978 to 1 March 1989	Created after 1977 and published with notice	70 years after the death of author. If a work of corporate authorship, 95 years from publication or 120 years from creation, whichever expires first.
1978 to 1 March 1989	Created before 1978 and first published with notice in the specified period	The greater of the term specified in the previous entry or 31 December 2047
From 1 March 1989 through 2002	Created after 1977	70 years after the death of author. If a work of corporate authorship, 95 years from publication or 120 years from creation, whichever expires first
From 1 March 1989 through 2002	Created before 1978 and first published in this period	The greater of the term specified in the previous entry or 31 December 2047
After 2002	None	70 years after the death of author. If a work of corporate authorship, 95 years from publication or 120 years from creation, whichever expires first
Anytime	Works prepared by an officer or employee of the United States Government as part of that person's official duties	None. In the public domain in the United States (17 U.S.C. § 105)

Works First Published Outside the U.S. by
Foreign Nationals or U.S. Citizens Living Abroad

Date of Publication	Conditions	Copyright Term in the United States
Before 1923	None	In the public domain (But see first special case below)
1923 through 1977	Published without compliance with U.S. formalities, and in the public domain in its source country as of 1 January 1996	In the public domain
1923 through 1977	Published in compliance with all U.S. formalities (i.e., notice, renewal)	95 years after publication date
1923 through 1977	Solely published abroad, without compliance with U.S. formalities or republication in the U.S., and not in the public domain in its home country as of 1 January 1996	95 years after publication date
1923 through 1977	Published in the U.S. less than 30 days after publication abroad	Use the U.S. publication chart to determine duration
1923 through 1977	Published in the U.S. more than 30 days after publication abroad, without compliance with U.S. formalities, and not in the public domain in its home country as of 1 January 1996	95 years after publication date
1 January 1978 – 1 March 1989	Published without copyright notice, and in the public domain in its source country as of 1 January 1996	In the public domain
1 January 1978 – 1 March 1989	Published without copyright notice in a country that is a signatory to the Berne Convention is not in the public domain in its source country as of 1 January 1996	70 years after the death of the author, or if work of corporate authorship, 95 years from publication

1 January 1978 – 1 March 1989	Published with copyright notice by a non-U.S. citizen in a country that was party to the Universal Copyright Convention (UCC)	70 years after the death of the author, or if work of corporate authorship, 95 years from publication
After 1 March 1989	Published in a country that is a signatory to the Berne Convention	70 years after the death of the author, or if work of corporate authorship, 95 years from publication
After 1 March 1989	Published in a country with which the United States does not have copyright relations under a treaty	In the public domain

Sound Recordings

(Note: The following information applies only to the sound recording itself, and not to any copyrights in underlying compositions or texts)

Unpublished Sound Recordings, Domestic and Foreign

Date of Fixation/Publication	Conditions	What was in the public domain in the U.S. as of 1 January 2012
Prior to 15 Feb. 1972	Indeterminate	Subject to state common law protection. Enters the public domain on 15 Feb. 2067
After 15 Feb. 1972	Life of the author + 70 years. For unpublished anonymous and pseudonymous works and works made for hire (corporate authorship), 120 years from the date of fixation	Nothing. The soonest anything enters the public domain is 15 Feb. 2067
Unpublished works when the death date of the author is not known	120 years from date of creation	Works created before 1892

Sound Recordings Published in the United States

Fixed prior to 15 Feb. 1972	None	Subject to state statutory and/or common law protection. Fully enters the public domain on 15 Feb. 2067
15 Feb. 1972 to 1978	Published without notice (i.e., phonorecord symbol, year of publication, and name of copyright owner)	In the public domain
15 Feb. 1972 to 1978	Published with notice	95 years from publication. 2068 at the earliest

1978 to 1 March 1989	Published without notice, and without subsequent registration	In the public domain
1978 to 1 March 1989	Published with notice	70 years after death of author, or if work of corporate authorship, the shorter of 95 years from publication, or 120 years from creation. 2049 at the earliest
After 1 March 1989	None	70 years after death of author, or if work of corporate authorship, the shorter of 95 years from publication, or 120 years from creation. 2049 at the earliest

Sound Recordings Published Outside the United States

Prior to 1923	None	Subject to state statutory and/or common law protection. Fully enters the public domain on 15 Feb. 2067
1923 to 1 March 1989	In the public domain in its home country as of 1 Jan. 1996 or there was U.S. publication within 30 days of the foreign publication	Subject to state common law protection. Enters the public domain on 15 Feb. 2067
1923 to 15 Feb. 1972	Not in the public domain in its home country as of 1 Jan. 1996. At least one author of the work was not a U.S. citizen or was living abroad, and there was no U.S. publication within 30 days of the foreign publication	Enters public domain on 15 Feb. 2067
15 Feb. 1972 to 1978	Not in the public domain in its home country as of 1 Jan. 1996. At least one author of the work was not a U.S. citizen or was living abroad, and there was no U.S. publication within 30 days of the foreign publication	95 years from date of publication, 2068 at the earliest

| 1978 to 1 March 1989 | Not in the public domain in its home country as of 1 Jan. 1996. At least one author of the work was not a U.S. citizen or was living abroad, and there was no U.S. publication within 30 days of the foreign publication | 70 years after death of author, or if work of corporate authorship, the shorter of 95 years from publication, or 120 from creation |
| After 1 March 1989 | None | 70 years after death of author, or if work of corporate authorship, the shorter of 95 years from publication, or 120 from creation |

Architectural Works

Date of Design	Date of Construction	Copyright Status
Prior to 1 Dec. 1990	Not constructed by 31 Dec. 2002	Protected only as plans or drawings
Prior to 1 Dec. 1990	Constructed by 1 Dec. 1990	Protected only as plans or drawings
Prior to 1 Dec. 1990	Constructed between 30 Nov. 1990 and 31 Dec. 2002	Building is protected for 70 years after death of author, or if work of corporate authorship, the shorter of 95 after publication, or 120 years from creation
From 1 Dec. 1990	Immaterial	Building is protected for 70 years after death of author, or if work of corporate authorship, the shorter of 95 after publication, or 120 years from creation

TABLE OF CASES

ഔଔଔ

INDEX

❧❧☙☙